To the Beatles
and
in memory of Brian Epstein
for bringing them to us.

To Beatlepeople everywhere.

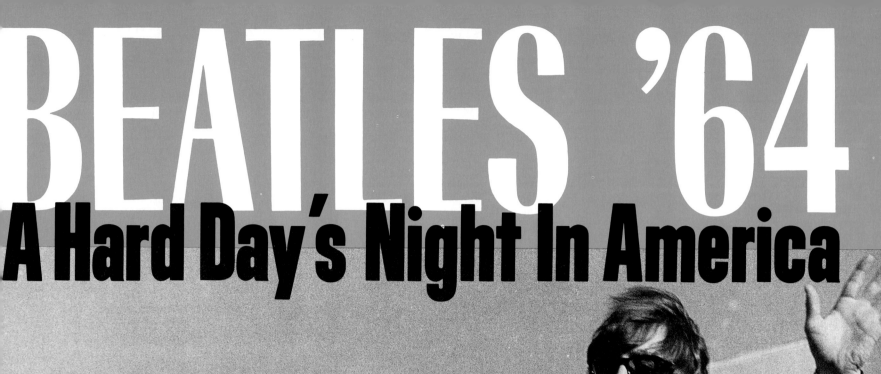

BEATLES '64
A Hard Day's Night In America

PUBLISHED BY DOUBLEDAY
a division of Bantam Doubleday Dell Publishing Group, Inc.
666 Fifth Avenue, New York, New York 10103

DOUBLEDAY and the portrayal of an anchor with a dolphin
are trademarks of Doubleday, a division of
Bantam Doubleday Dell Publishing Group, Inc.

Library of Congress Cataloging-in-Publication Data

Gunther, Curt.
Rayl, A. J. S.
       Beatles '64: a hard day's night in America / photographs by Curt Gunther;
text by A. J. S. Rayl.—1st ed.
          p.   cm.
       ISBN 0-385-24583-1
       1. Beatles.   2. Rock music—United States—1961–1970—History and criticism.   I. Rayl,
A. J. S.   II. Title.
    ML421.B4G85   1989
    782.42166′092′2—dc20   89-32121
                                                                                CIP
Copyright © 1989 by Curt Gunther and A. J. S. Rayl   MN

All Rights Reserved
Printed in the United States of America

September 1989
FIRST EDITION

BOOK MARK

The text of this book was composed
in the typefaces Bodoni Book and Trade Gothic Condensed
by Monotype Composition Co. Inc., Baltimore, Maryland.
The display was set in Radiant Bold Condensed by Graphic Technology Inc.,
New York, New York.

It was printed in 2 colors with the photos printing as duotones
on 70 lb Patina Matte by Kingsport Press, Kingsport, Tennessee.

Designed by Marysarah Quinn and Claire M. Naylon

BEATLES '64
A Hard Day's Night In America

TEXT BY

A.J.S. Rayl

PHOTOGRAPHS BY

Curt Gunther

DOUBLEDAY

NEW YORK LONDON TORONTO SYDNEY AUCKLAND

ITINERARY

Aug. 19 . . . . San Francisco, California—Cow Palace
Aug. 20 . . . . Las Vegas, Nevada—Convention Hall
Aug. 21 . . . . Seattle, Washington—Seattle Center Coliseum
Aug. 22 . . . . Vancouver, British Columbia—Empire Stadium
Aug. 23 . . . . Los Angeles, California—Hollywood Bowl
Aug. 24, 25 . . . . Rest Days—Spent in Los Angeles
Aug. 26 . . . . Denver, Colorado—Red Rocks Stadium
Aug. 27 . . . . Cincinnati, Ohio—Cincinnati Gardens
Aug. 28, 29 . . . . New York City, New York—Forest Hills Tennis Stadium
Aug. 30 . . . . Atlantic City, New Jersey—Convention Hall
Aug. 31, Sept. 1 . . . . Rest Days—Spent in Atlantic City
Sept. 2 . . . . Philadelphia, Pennsylvania—Convention Hall
Sept. 3 . . . . Indianapolis, Indiana—Indiana State Fair Coliseum and Grandstand (2 Shows)
Sept. 4 . . . . Milwaukee, Wisconsin—Milwaukee Auditorium
Sept. 5 . . . . Chicago, Illinois—International Amphitheater
Sept. 6 . . . . Detroit, Michigan—Olympia Stadium
Sept. 7 . . . . Toronto, Ontario—Maple Leaf Gardens
Sept. 8 . . . . Montreal, Quebec—The Forum
Sept. 9, 10 . . . . Rest Days—Spent in Key West, Florida
Sept. 11 . . . . Jacksonville, Florida—Gator Bowl
Sept. 12 . . . . Boston, Massachusetts—Boston Gardens
Sept. 13 . . . . Baltimore, Maryland—Baltimore Civic Center
Sept. 14 . . . . Pittsburgh, Pennsylvania—Pittsburgh Civic Arena
Sept. 15 . . . . Cleveland, Ohio—Public Auditorium
Sept. 16 . . . . New Orleans, Louisiana—City Park Stadium
Sept. 17 . . . . Originally a Rest Day—Kansas City Show Added
Sept. 18 . . . . Dallas, Texas—Memorial Coliseum
Sept. 19 . . . . Rest Day—Spent at Horse Ranch in the Ozarks, Alton, Missouri
Sept. 20 . . . . New York City, New York—Benefit Performance at Paramount Theater
Sept. 21 . . . . Departure to London from Kennedy International Airport

"**L**ADIES, GENTLEMEN—AND BEATLES. The captain has turned on the seat belt sign . . ." the stewardess's voice boomed through the Boeing 707 as it cut through a layer of scattered cirrus clouds, dropping at nearly five hundred miles per hour into the sunny sky over Southern California. John Lennon, Paul McCartney, George Harrison, and Ringo Starr gazed through the first-class cabin windows to survey the metropolis below. Los Angeles sprawled in every direction, shimmering in the heat of the long hot summer of '64. Swimmin' pools. Movie stars. Girls in go-go boots and good times. The Great American Adventure was about to begin.

Anticipation, however, collided with fatigue. For the Beatles, life had become a series of blurred experiences—touring; fleeing from massive crowds of screaming, weeping girls; writing and recording; giving interviews; and starring in their first motion picture. Now, with exhaustion and strain evident in their faces, they were about to launch their first coast-to-coast concert tour of America. Despite his undying belief in the Beatles, manager Brian Epstein was nervous about this venture. America was a very large, very foreign country. And in the next thirty-one days, the Beatles were to perform before more people than any other artists in the history of American pop music—including Elvis Presley—commanding vast venues, most of which had

4

Miami Beach, Florida.

never before even considered hosting a rock 'n' roll group. Even Norman Weiss, the veteran American show business agent who booked the tour, found himself wondering in the still of the night if they really could pull it off. As for John, Paul, George, and Ringo, well . . . they had no idea that this was the most ambitious, potentially largest-grossing tour ever planned in American show business history.

Just five months before, the Beatles had taken America by storm, thundering to the top of the record charts and beaming live into millions of homes on "The Ed Sullivan Show." Their three trial concert appearances had been greeted with a hail of jellybeans and screams of adulation that completely drowned out the music. Everywhere they went, thousands of enthusiastic fans gathered and held vigil. The Beatles' first visit to America had been a triumphant victory, their achievements unprecedented by any previous foreign recording artists. By all accounts, Operation USA was a smashing success. But for British artists, the American record charts had forever been the unobtainable and record executives, journalists, and psychologists held the general assumption that the Beatles were yet another "craze" destined for quick death and a haircut. At this point, neither Epstein nor Weiss were making any bets on when—or if—after this tour, they'd be back.

THE BEATLES' first bid to obtain the unobtainable arrived in a cardboard carton at Capitol Records in Hollywood, California, on a cold, crisp morning in late 1962. The Cuban Missile Crisis had just ended and with America's victorious escape from the brink of nuclear war, the country's already strong sense of nationalism was intensifying. And even though the Civil Rights Movement was igniting a social movement that demanded change, questioning the basic rights and principles upon which the country was founded, America was still viewed, by and large, as the best country in the world. In the music business, a similar America-is-superior mentality had long been prevalent. Record executives maintained the bias that British pop artists were at least ten years behind their American counterparts. So when the monthly carton—which contained some twenty 45-rpm records by British artists—was delivered to the twelfth-floor office of Artists & Repertoire producer Dave Dexter, Jr., it garnered little more than a nod and a sigh, even though it had been shipped from Capitol's London-based parent company.

Founded in the forties by Glenn Wallichs as a maverick, independent label based on the West Coast, Capitol had garnered an impressive enough stable of star artists to become one of the most respected companies in the music business before being purchased in 1955 by the British conglomerate Electric and Musical Industries, better known as EMI. The new owner, however, didn't obligate its American label to release its British or other foreign recordings. Instead, EMI struck an agreement giving Capitol the right of first and second refusal. Since America dominated the entertainment scene throughout the world with its hit records and movies, and since very

little foreign product ever made it in the States, Capitol—home to Nat King Cole, Stan Kenton, Frank Sinatra, the Kingston Trio, and the Beach Boys—reigned autonomously, maintaining creative control over its releases. What, after all, did the British know about the American music scene?

It was Dexter's job to listen to all the records that arrived from EMI companies all over the world and find the ones that stood a chance of being hits in America. Every foreign recording artist wanted to crack America—the largest record market in the world—because beyond the fame, there was a fortune to be made in royalties. Dexter, a jazz producer and former *DownBeat* journalist, heaved a sigh as he looked at the carton of records from England, knowing that even if he did find something appropriately novel or catchy, it probably wouldn't cut the groove at the

Central Park, New York.

7

convinced those guys would mean "absolutely nuthin'" over here. (Ironically, the Beatles' producer, George Martin, had never wanted that particular single to be sent over to the United States.)

It was around this same time that EMI, long frustrated by its lack of inroads into the American market, assigned a new task to one of its subsidiary companies, Transglobal. Based in the Manhattan law office of EMI attorney Paul Marshall, Transglobal's priority was to take all the EMI records rejected by Capitol and, if possible, cut deals with other American labels. When Dexter, and hence Capitol, passed on "Love Me Do," the record ended up at Transglobal.

Within weeks, on January 11, 1963, the Beatles released their second single in England, "Please Please Me" backed with "Ask Me Why." Martin was convinced that it would be their first Number One record in Britain, certainly worthy of the American market. Dexter, his ears still stinging from the harmonica in "Love Me Do," disagreed. "I couldn't count the number of times a British artist was a smash over there and then came over here and died," he says. Cliff Richard, a huge pop star in the British Isles, was the classic example. Though Dexter had thrown his "full support" behind Richard, Capitol's release of his single went nowhere. It had gotten to the point that every time Dexter mentioned a British artist in the weekly A&R meetings, the entire staff moaned, "Oh no, not again." In England, "Please Please Me" started its ascent up the British charts and the Beatles began turning industry heads, particularly at EMI, where executives had initially shown

weekly Thursday morning A&R meeting. Settling himself into his chair next to the turntable, Dexter pried open the carton. The volume of records that passed through his office was overwhelming, numbering in the hundreds every week, so at most he allotted fifteen seconds to any given tune. One of the singles he picked up that morning was "Love Me Do" by a group called the Beatles on the Parlophone label. It had been released in Britain in October and had made it into the British Top 20. "Big deal," Dexter muttered to himself. The needle hit the vinyl. The harmonica moved him immediately, scratching across his jazz-tuned ears. He cringed and then jerked the needle from the turntable,

little faith in this quartet. In America, the single wound up on Marshall's desk at Transglobal next to "Love Me Do."

Marshall made the rounds at several major record labels, all of which turned "Please Please Me" down. Traditionally these companies stayed well within the mainstream, leaving the breaking of new artists and new sounds to the plethora of small independent labels. So, Marshall sent the single out to Vee Jay Records, a basically black label which claimed Jimmy Reed ("Baby What You Want Me to Do?") and Gene Chandler ("Duke of Earl") among those on its roster. In recent months, however, the Chicago-based label had had chart-topping success with a white male vocal group called the Four Seasons, whose "Sherry" climbed to *Billboard*'s Number One position in September 1962. They were interested in repeating that success and the Beatles single afforded a distinct advantage— the tracks were already recorded, produced, and mastered, ready to be pressed on vinyl. No money would be required for production. It was still the era of the single, and on February 23, 1963, Vee Jay released "Please Please Me," the Beatles' first record in America. The group's name was misspelled—Beetles—on the label, but it didn't really matter in the end. The record received only minimal trial airplay, mostly in the major markets, and then quickly disappeared from the airwaves. In Britain, however, true to Martin's prediction, "Please Please Me" became the Beatles' first Number One recording and in April they released their third British single, "From Me to You" backed with "Thank You Girl." At a time when pop singers sang and composers

wrote, and New York's Brill Building was shoo-bopping with competitive song-writing teams, the Beatles were following the paths of rock 'n' roll pioneers like Buddy Holly, Little Richard, and Chuck Berry—writing and recording their own songs, creating a distinct style and sound.

The following month, while the Beatles headlined a British tour for the first time, topping a bill that included America's Roy Orbison and Gerry and the Pacemakers (another British band managed by Epstein and his NEMS Enterprises Ltd.), Vee Jay released "From Me to You." It failed to crack America's Hot 100, fizzling out at 116. In Los Angeles, however, it received enough airplay and audience response to rise briefly to position 31 on KRLA's local Top 40 chart. Within two weeks of the release of the Beatles' recording,

With Shirley Temple Black, daughter Lori. Photo courtesy of Charles Black.

Del Shannon—whose "Runaway" and "Hats Off to Larry" had catapulted him to the top of the charts in 1961—recorded "From Me to You," releasing his version on the Big Top label. It fared better than the original, spending four weeks on the *Billboard* Hot 100 charts, reaching a high position of 77.

Pat Boone, whose hit "Don't Forbid Me" was part of the Beatles' Cavern repertoire, also had designs on recording "From Me to You," after hearing it while on tour in England. But Dot label executives advised against it because of its prior exposure—and failure.

Despite the poor showing of the Beatles' singles in a market where singles reigned supreme, Vee Jay released a full album of Beatles material, titled *Introducing the Beatles*, on July 22. It sold, according to various estimates, somewhere between 600 and 700 copies and never came close to cracking the American album charts. Vee Jay waived its option and the four lads from Liverpool were without an American record label.

In the fall of '63, the Beatles released their fourth single in Britain, "She Loves You," recorded on July 1 in the EMI Studios on Abbey Road. Written on the road between shows, it was, says Neil Aspinall, "the only song they tried to do and record as a premeditated hit." Based on an idea of Paul McCartney's, it was one of the few songs he and John Lennon actually wrote together. From the hook at the beginning, to the more creative third-person lyrical perspective, to the final chord, "She Loves You" certainly had all the earmarks of a smash hit. "That song was really them," recalls George Martin. "They just did it. I thought ending on the major sixth was a bit corny. Glenn Miller had done it years before. But, they all kept telling me, 'No, it's great.' And they were quite right." The song went to Number One on the British charts and became the Beatles' first million-seller. The "yeah, yeah, yeah" in the opening and chorus—adapted from the various versions of "yeahs" and "oh yeahs" in British skiffle and American rock 'n' roll—was on its way to becoming the Beatles' musical signature and the Beatles were on their way to becoming Britain's top pop stars.

Once again the latest effort was shipped to Capitol, and once again Dexter passed on it, and once again the record wound up at Transglobal. Marshall finally secured a one-shot deal for "She Loves You" with Swan Records, a small Philadelphia-based label, and the Beatles' third American single was released on September 16, 1963. It received four-star notice in *Billboard*, meaning that it had sufficient commercial appeal to merit being stocked by the dealers, but "She Loves You" would not be the Beatles' breakthrough record in America. The song received only sparse airplay, most of it in the northeastern part of the country, and sold around a thousand copies.

Despite these defeats, the Beatles' music was slowly beginning to resonate in America: In the northern states bordering Canada, where "Love Me Do" became a hit and crossed the country lines via the airwaves; in the major markets of New York—out of nowhere, according to one story, "She Loves You" placed third in a field of five during disc jockey Murray the K's "Swingin' Soiree" record contest; in Chicago, where Vee Jay was home-

Cow Palace, San Francisco.

based; in Los Angeles, where local listeners had taken a liking to "From Me to You"; and in Philadelphia, where Swan was based.

On October 13, the Beatles performed in Britain before their largest audience to date, headlining "Val Parnell's Sunday Night at the London Palladium." The live show—seen by an estimated 15 million viewers—took the Beatles into living rooms nationwide. The power of television was at once fully realized. Suddenly, even the most staid of taxi drivers recognized John, Paul, George, and Ringo and knew they were—the Beatles. The day after the show, reports of mob scenes outside the theater appeared in all the national papers.

One Fleet Street writer coined the word "Beatlemania" in an attempt to describe fan reaction and it stuck as the undisputed term for this new madness. Subsequently, the Beatles were chosen to appear before Queen Elizabeth at the annual Royal Variety Show in early November. On October 17, the Beatles entered the EMI Studios on Abbey Road and a new era of recording, utilizing for the first time a state-of-the-art four-track system. Among the songs recorded that day was a tune that drew inspiration from the American gospel sound in the form of hand claps, and was called "I Want to Hold Your Hand."

The following week, Brian Epstein was

11

Miami Beach, Florida.

sitting at his desk at the NEMS office in Liverpool, smiling, when his longtime assistant Alistair Taylor reported for work. "This is *it!*" Epstein announced gleefully, holding up the lacquer test disc of "I Want to Hold Your Hand." "Now we go and attack the States!" Taylor, who had accompanied Epstein on the day he descended the narrow stairwell into the dungeonesque Cavern Club to see the Beatles for the first time, knew that Epstein had an incredible gift for knowing what was right at a given time for a given market. Absolutely convinced that this was the record that would crack the American market, Epstein began to devise strategies for Operation USA.

Following a taping for ABC's British show "Thank Your Lucky Stars," the Beatles headed for a short concert tour of Sweden. On October 31, for the first time, several thousand girls gathered at London Airport to await the Beatles' return. With the Queen Mother scheduled to arrived home from a trip to Ireland, and the Prime Minister scheduled to depart for Scotland, airport officials struggled to avert chaos. It was, the Beatles would later assess, the real beginning of Beatlemania. As fate would have it, Ed Sullivan, the host of America's most popular variety program, also passed through London Airport that day. When he asked if the crowd had assembled to greet the Queen Mother, he was promptly informed that this multitude had come together for the Beatles. Sullivan was always on the lookout for rising young talent and he hadn't witnessed this kind of enthusiasm since Elvis Presley. Still, the Beatles were British and in America these young entertainers were virtually unknown.

In the U.K., the Beatles' popularity rose dramatically during the ensuing weeks. Concert halls and television studios where the Beatles appeared were frequently mobbed by fans desperately seeking admittance. The national press and television coverage became so widespread that everyone in England knew of the Beatles. Their British fan club, headquartered in the NEMS office on Mammoth Street, was overflowing with mail, and new clubs were springing up quickly in other countries. United Artists' London office was negotiating for rights to make a movie based on the mania and starring the Beatles.

On Friday, November 1, three weeks before the release of the Beatles' second British album, *With the Beatles*, advance orders for it passed the quarter-million mark. Never before in the history of the British recording industry had there been such demand for an LP. Three days after EMI announced the new Beatle single, "I Want to Hold Your Hand," the advance orders, according to the conglomerate's in-house *EMI-NEWS*, totaled 700,000 and were climbing. All told, sales for the Beatles' singles, EPs,

Liberace at the Las Vegas Convention Hall matinee.

and LPs now exceeded 3 million. In Britain, the Beatles had become nothing less than a national phenomenon. In America, they didn't even have a record deal.

Epstein was determined to change that immediately. His faith in the Beatles was unwavering. In England, he had "shouted from the rooftops," as he put it, functioning as personal manager, press officer, agent, wardrobe consultant, and father-figure until the Beatles finally landed their recording contract with EMI. Now he would do the same in America, employing many of the tactics and calculated moves that had proved successful on their home turf. Operation USA was about to begin.

THE OBVIOUS PLACE for the Beatles was EMI's American label. With their success in Britain securing them a place in British musical history, Epstein launched an attack of direct pressure on EMI's executives. He wanted them to convince Capitol to release "I Want to Hold Your Hand." The Beatles were the biggest thing in British show business and if Capitol executives weren't interested, they must be *made* to be interested. Hardly content to leave the matter to corporate procedure, Epstein picked up the phone and placed a call directly to Capitol Records' president, Alan Livingston. A former A&R man, Livingston frequently became actively involved in the signing of new artists and even though he'd never heard of Brian Epstein, he took the call.

"Mr. Livingston," Epstein started. "We just don't understand it. The Beatles are doing very well in England, why won't you release them over there?" Livingston confessed that he had never actually heard the Beatles, but agreed to listen to the group's latest song and get back to him. Livingston was struck with Epstein's unyielding belief, and after listening to the song—while he wouldn't venture to predict its success Stateside—he liked what he heard well enough to agree to release it and follow it with an album. Epstein's response caught Livingston by surprise: "I'm not going to give them to you unless you agree to spend $40,000 promoting this song." It was an astounding amount of money to spend promoting a single by a group that had previously failed on two other American labels. In fact, the most Capitol had ever laid out promoting a new artist had been $5,000. Livingston wasn't at all convinced the Beatles would hit in America the way they had in England, but the music business was a business of risks and gambles. The Beatles just might be the next big thing. Livingston knew that Capitol, having refused the Beatles three times before, now had no claims to the group under their agreement with EMI, and Epstein could, and would, go elsewhere. "I decided it was a worthwhile gamble," says Livingston.

Meanwhile, other corporate wheels were also turning. L. G. Wood, a senior executive at EMI, had placed a call to his Capitol counterpart, Lloyd Dunn, vice-president in charge of merchandising and sales. "We have this record we really *must* release in the States," said Wood. "It seems your lads in A&R refuse to accept it, which is frightfully embarrassing, because the group is really selling here in a most gratifying fashion." That, Dunn knew, meant they were hot. He agreed to "cooperate fully," if only because he had to occasionally ask for similar favors. Dunn, whose own musical tastes were for Dixieland and what was then termed "pretty music," didn't even bother to listen to the record. "My judgment in that area is so fallible that I felt it would be a mistake," he recalls.

"I told Dexter to put it on the release schedule simply as a favor to a friend and colleague from whom one day I would probably have to ask the same in return."

Dexter, however, says he'd already agreed to push for Capitol's release of "I Want to Hold Your Hand" while at EMI in London during his annual fall trip to visit the label and its European subsidiaries. "Tony Palmer,

Atop the Sahara Hotel, Las Vegas.

who worked in the international department at EMI, had been baiting me with this 'smash' record since before I left Hollywood," Dexter says. On learning that this "smash" record was the latest effort of the Beatles, Dexter agreed "only under protest" to listen to it. This time, he says, it didn't even take fifteen seconds. "The first four bars of the song, that guitar just grabbed me," he says. "A five-year-old kid, an eighty-year-old man would have picked that record." Palmer was pleased, but insisted on some assurance that Capitol would get behind the record. Dexter says that at that point he promised, though it was not within his corporate power, that the company would take out full-page ads in the major music trade magazines, as well as send out a minimum of 2,000 promotional copies (which actually was the standard number of such copies sent on new releases) to radio stations across the country; and he left the office feeling "very, very lucky" to have gotten the group back after waiving on them before.

Since EMI retained foreign rights on the Beatles, there was no actual contract between the group and Capitol Records. The exact date the Beatles were picked up by Capitol has faded in the memories of those involved or been buried with them, but once the corporate wheels began to turn, they spun fast. By mid-November "I Want to Hold Your Hand" was slated for a December 26 release with the album scheduled to follow in January. The Beatles once again had a record label in America, but this time it was one of the most prestigious labels in the industry.

Following the Beatles' Command Perform-

Seattle Center Coliseum.

ance at the Royal Variety Show, which was taped on November 4 for broadcast the following week, Epstein flew to the States with a demo of "I Want to Hold Your Hand." His agenda including a meeting with Brown Meggs, director of Capitol's eastern operations, to discuss marketing plans for the Beatles and to confirm Capitol's sincerity; it also included meetings with executives from other labels, just in case. Epstein's timing was impeccable. After checking into the Regency Hotel, a calculated move to impress the Americans, he soon learned that the Ed Sullivan people had called the NEMS office inquiring about the Beatles. Even before he'd recovered from jet lag, Epstein received a call from a British agent wondering whether or not he wanted the agency to arrange a date with representatives of the Sullivan show. Preferring, as always, to make the arrangements himself, Epstein called Sullivan directly and scheduled a meeting. Beyond being the most popular variety program in the States, "The Ed Sullivan Show" reached a wide cross section of America. There could be no overestimating its importance in introducing America to the Beatles. The show had a reputation for turning virtual unknowns into stars overnight. Epstein was elated.

Despite his always formal demeanor, when he arrived for his appointment with Meggs, his jubilance about the upcoming meeting with Sullivan was readily apparent. "At that moment, the Sullivan meeting was his primary interest in life," recalls Meggs. But Epstein quickly got down to the business of records. Unfamiliar with the company and with the American market, he interrogated Meggs about

Capitol, specific markets, and venues. At Epstein's request, Meggs agreed to supply him—upon release of the Beatles' first Capitol single and album—with "intelligence" on the American market; this would be derived from statistical analyses of where the records were selling and where they weren't.

During the following week, Epstein met several times with Sullivan in the latter's office, Suite 1102 at the Delmonico Hotel, which was also home to Sullivan, who was the master of what he called the "really big shew." The two discussed the Beatles and their phenomenal success in Britain at length, as well as the rise of the Mersey sound and other British artists. Brian insisted that the Beatles would be the biggest thing in the world. Sullivan rejected the thought as a little hype and a lot of managerial enthusiasm. How could any rock group touch Elvis? Still, Sullivan was already suitably impressed with Epstein and interested in booking the Beatles. He called in his producer, Bob Precht, and the three men finalized details. Epstein insisted the Beatles be given top billing for each show in which they performed, but Sullivan never "guaranteed" top billing to anyone. Although Epstein later insisted that Sullivan did acquiesce after two days of dickering, Precht maintains it was impossible. "It was something we just wouldn't have given, particularly to an unknown group," says Precht. "We didn't give—quote—billing to anyone and always reserved the right to promote the show any way we wanted to." By the end of the last meeting, it was decided that the Beatles would appear live on February 9 and 16, the second show to be a remote that would emanate from the Deauville Hotel in Miami, Florida. Precht suggested the possibility of taping a third show for later broadcast. It was agreed that the Beatles would be paid $10,000 for all three shows, $3,500 each for the live shows, $3,000 for the taped performance. (At that point, the fee paid to top performers for one appearance on the show was $7,500.) On that, Sullivan and Epstein shook hands and made a gentlemen's agreement regarding the Beatles' forthcoming American television debut.

Upon returning to his office at the CBS studios, Precht, feeling somewhat uneasy about the amount of money they had agreed to pay this unknown British band, picked up the phone and called Sullivan. "Don't you think we're really extending ourselves here?" he asked. Sullivan's reply was short and to the point: "I think they're worth the investment." That, Precht says, was the end of it. "It was a passing concern, and it was Ed's show. He called the shots."

That weekend, *Time* and *Newsweek* hit the stands. Each devoted its music column to the Beatles. The magazines' London-based reporters had been on hand for the Royal Variety Show. Beyond recounting the Beatlemania that had swept England, they picked up and highlighted an irreverent remark made by Lennon. Epstein had shuddered when Lennon tried out the line backstage. But just before their finale of "Twist and Shout," Lennon used it: "For our last number, I'd like to ask for your help. The people in the cheaper seats clap your hands, and the rest of you, if you'll just rattle your jewelry." It was press coverage no money could have bought.

Seattle.   With assurances from Capitol, a contract in his pocket for the three upcoming Sullivan appearances, copies of *Time* and *Newsweek*, and his own unrelenting belief that "I Want to Hold Your Hand" was destined to become a hit "however moderate" in the States, a victorious Brian Epstein headed back to London and an EMI ceremony at which the Beatles were presented with their first silver disc for sales in excess of 250,000 for "Please Please Me." Three days later, on November 22, while Sir Charles Taylor asked the Home Secretary to withdraw police protection for the Beatles because of the thousands of pounds in overtime pay given to the bobbies, their second album, *With the Beatles*, was released. But the eyes of the world were on Dallas, Texas, that day.

The news of President John F. Kennedy's assassination ricocheted around the world. It was a frame-by-frame death scene, captured on a Brownie 8-mm movie camera, frozen to still life, and emblazoned across the pages of *Life* magazine to be forever locked into the memory. The New Frontier had been blasted apart. The American Dream was shattered. Immediately the rumors began—of the lone Communist assassin, of conspiracies, of an organized crime "hit," of a cover-up; but that day it didn't matter how it had happened, only that it did happen. Television brought it all home, and united a nation in mourning.

While the undercurrents of change were vibrating in many facets of American society before November 22, 1963, the Kennedy assassination shook the beliefs and altered the perceptions of the country's youth forever. It was an act of betrayal and violence that propelled a generation to search for truth and honesty and to challenge the assumptions, both physical and psychological, upon which American society was based. If ever we needed a hand to hold, it was then.

At Capitol Records, 1964 was to be the year of the Beatles, a welcomed, upbeat diversion from America's tragedy. Artistic prejudice against British imports lingered, however, and the Beatles' tapes were sent into Capitol's studios to be reequalized and enhanced so they would sound "brighter" when they were heard on the radio or on American hi-fi systems. The assumption that the recordings would need doctoring came as an insult to producer George Martin. Meanwhile, the marketing and merchandising department came up with a sales promotion theme designed to tie in with the forthcoming Sullivan appearances: "The Beatles Are Coming!" Five million stickers were ordered. Beatle wigs were made in mass quantities for in-store and radio promotion giveaways. A two-page ad announcing the arrival of the Beatles was slated for the December 30 issue of *Billboard*, to be followed by one in *CashBox*.

Traditionally, Capitol would have created and chosen the artwork to be used for single and album jackets, but for the Beatles, photographs were shipped over from England. The black-and-white photograph, taken by Robert Freeman, that was to grace the Beatles' first American album was the same as that on the cover of their second British album, *With the Beatles*. It was a head shot portrait, half shadowed. It was hip and very artsy. The largest quantity of display album jackets ever ordered in Capitol's history was approved and sent to the printer, along with a photograph, taken by Dezo Hoffman, for the "I Want to Hold Your Hand" single jacket.

On December 10, Walter Cronkite introduced a brief film clip of a Beatles' performance during the "CBS Evening News." In Washington, D.C., young Marsha Albert saw the clip and sent a letter to disc jockey Carroll James at WWDC, asking why the Beatles' records weren't being played there. Having seen the news item himself, and ready to "do anything" for listeners, James phoned BOAC airlines and within a couple of days, a stewardess brought him direct from London a copy of the Beatles' latest single. Even before "I Want to Hold Your Hand" had ended, the switchboard lit up. WWDC listeners wanted to hear the song again. James had never before played a song twice, but on this particular night he did. In the weeks that followed, James played the song every night on his

show. Since Capitol had set a release date of December 26, 1963, that meant—even though WWDC had obtained the record from England—that the radio station had broken the air date, and now other radio stations were calling the label wondering what had happened to their promotional copies. Although the post-Christmas release date was the worst, particularly for a new group, and while there had been some debate in Capitol's New York office about postponing the release until January, the company now had no choice but to release the single as planned and get the promotional copies out to other radio stations immediately.

Within the week, Capitol shipped some

21

3,000 promotional copies of "I Want to Hold Your Hand" to radio stations across the country. "There was always the argument—should we wait until the product is in the stores or should we get it to the radio stations and create a demand so that the stores will order it?" Livingston says. In the case of the Beatles, Capitol had, fortunately, decided to go with the latter strategy. It was a good thing. "I Want to Hold Your Hand" exploded over every pop station in the country with a passion and energy unlike any other song on the charts. It evoked a sense of joy that lifted the spirits of a disillusioned generation while offering them escape. The sound was real, straightforward, and happy. The Beatles reminded the youth of America that being young is fun and enjoying it is a birthright.

On December 23, Paul Russell issued a memo from the merchandising department to all offices in the field: "Shortly after the first of the year, you'll have bulk quantities of a unique see-through plastic pin-on button, featuring a shot of the Beatles, with each identified . . . have all of your sales staff wear one . . . offer them to clerks and jocks . . . arrange for radio station giveaways." As for "The Beatles Are Coming!" stickers: "It may sound funny, but we literally want your salesmen to be plastering these stickers on any friendly surface . . . Involve your friends and relatives. Remember the 'Kilroy Was Here' cartoon that appeared everywhere about ten years ago? Well, now it's going to be 'The Beatles Are Coming!' stickers that are everywhere you look." And, "until further notice," all Capitol sales and promotion staff were ordered to wear the Beatle wigs during the

business day. "Get these Beatle wigs around properly, and you'll find you're helping to start the Beatle Hair-Do Craze that should be sweeping the country soon."

Capitol Records was a well-oiled machine, a company readily equipped to promote and handle hits. "When a message went out into the field, it wasn't questioned," recalls Tom Morgan, former Capitol vice-president. "Hollywood was still everything then and Capitol had as good a sales organization as was ever in the record business." Not only did Capitol own and operate its own pressing plants, but, unlike other major record companies, it also owned and operated its own distribution company. "It was like a family in those days," Morgan continues. "When something was happening then everybody got on it and worked." In December 1963 the Beatles were happening. And by Christmastime everybody in the American music industry knew that the Beatles were coming. On December 26, as John, Paul, George, and Ringo performed in the Beatles' Christmas show at the Astoria Cinema in Liverpool, "I Want to Hold Your Hand" was shipped to the American public.

Record store owners and managers of the chain five-and-dimes like Woolworth's, which served as *the* place to buy pop records in many parts of Middle America, were inundated with inquiries about the new record by the British group "with long hair." Capitol was deluged with orders the likes of which the company had never before experienced, the likes of which *no* record company had ever before experienced. An unprecedented 250,000 copies had been made, but wouldn't come close to meeting the demand. The record was literally selling out of the box. In England, the single had been backed with the ballady "This Boy." The American flip-side, however, was "I Saw Her Standing There"—pure, unadulterated rock 'n' roll.

By this point, Capitol had invested around $10,000 in promotion, Livingston estimates, and although the company continued their "The Beatles Are Coming!" campaign, even Livingston admits it wasn't really necessary. Within two weeks of the record's release, Capitol had orders for more than one million copies. Pressing plant workers were put on overtime, and then on three separate shifts working around the clock. Capitol still could not meet the demand, and finally resorted to hiring the competition—RCA—to press additional copies on a custom basis to meet the demand. "I Want to Hold Your Hand" quickly eclipsed Elvis' "Hound Dog" (released, coincidentally, on RCA) as the fastest-selling single in the history of recorded music. And, it kept on selling. It was the biggest record that Capitol—or any record company, for that matter—had ever released.

Disc jockeys quickly realized that the Beatles had been this way before, and copies of the Vee Jay and Swan releases were rediscovered and put into rotation. Early in January, Capitol shipped out a promotional EP— "Highlights from *Meet the Beatles*"—to radio stations. It featured three songs and an open-ended interview, which allowed disc jockeys in each city to fill in the questions, making it seem as if they had the Beatles with them. Suddenly, this British group which three months before couldn't get arrested in America was now permeating the airwaves.

Jack Paar, who attended the Royal Command Performance in November had not only seen the Beatles, but like his arch rival Sullivan, witnessed Beatlemania up close. Paar brought back—courtesy of the BBC— filmed footage of the quartet singing "She Loves You" and broadcast it during his prime-time Jack Paar program on NBC on January 3, 1964. It was the Beatles' first appearance on American television.

Exactly one week later, "I Want to Hold Your Hand" entered the *Billboard* Hot 100 chart at 92 with a star, signifying upward movement. Suddenly, things began moving so fast, in so many different areas, that at least one facet of Beatle business soon skidded out of NEMS control. By mid-January, some sixty lawsuits over merchandising rights filed against the Beatles created a massive legal wrangle. EMI's Paul Marshall was brought on board to resolve the matter. While Walt Disney had pioneered the concept of entertainment merchandising throughout the world with Mickey Mouse, in the arena of rock 'n' roll it was an unrealized money-maker. As NEMS grew, Brian Epstein had been taking on more responsibilities and more clients; he wound up delegating the business of Beatles merchandising to his London attorney David Jacobs, who, according to Marshall, delegated the task to his secretary. By the end of 1963, some 150 licenses—many of them conflicting—had been issued. On top of that, a principal license—which in effect superceded the other licenses—was granted to a company that took the name Stramsact and was headed by Nicky Byrne. It was a mess. Recalls Marshall: "Jacobs' secretary was the one who actually handled the licensing and she handled it with a one-page form, filling in the blanks with the name of the company and product it would produce and filling it out for just about anybody who asked." Marshall spent three days in a New York hotel conference room with the various litigants before finally resolving the conflicts and heading to London. By the time he arrived, Jacobs' secretary had issued four more licenses. Marshall issued his resignation. "It was amateur night."

On January 16, the Beatles began a three-week stand at the Olympia Theater in Paris. Epstein had booked the engagement as part of the Beatles' world tour, and as a sort of prelude to America. The Beatles had conquered England, Germany, and Sweden. Now it was on to Paris and then—America.

With typical Epstein flair, the Beatles were checked into Paris' posh George V Hotel. Their fee for the Olympia stand would not even cover the expenses, but Epstein knew the Beatles' image was worth the investment. There were dozens of meetings to be held in Paris and many people to impress. Producer Walter Shenson and screenwriter Alun Owen would be arriving to discuss the forthcoming as-yet-untitled movie. London show business tailor D. A. Millings would be flying in to fit them with new suits for the movie and for their trip to America. The Beatles were also slated to go into Pathe-Marconi Studios with George Martin to record a German version of "She Loves You," along with one of their new songs, "Can't Buy Me Love." But most important in terms of making an impression was the fact that several members of the American media, including representatives of such pres-

tigious powerhouses as *Life*, the New York *Times*, the Washington *Post*, AP, and CBS, had all requested interviews with the Beatles and Epstein prior to their departure for America and in time to meet deadlines.

Norman Weiss, a vice-president of General Artists Corporation (GAC), a major entertainment booking agency based in New York, arrived backstage at the Olympia on opening night. Weiss, there representing Trini Lopez, actually had another mission. On behalf of agent-turned-promoter Sid Bernstein he wanted to secure the Beatles for a date at Carnegie Hall. He walked up to Epstein and introduced himself. They hit it off. Weiss made his pitch. "It really flipped Brian," Weiss recalls. Brian immediately went to the Beatles' dressing room to relay the news and Weiss was promptly escorted in to meet, as Brian always referred to them, "the boys." For $7,000 against 60 percent of the gross receipts, the Beatles would perform two concerts—back to back—on February 12, Lincoln's birthday and a national holiday in America. The timing seemed perfect. These Carnegie performances would come three days after the group's first appearance on the Sullivan show. The Carnegie Hall officials didn't know it yet, but they had just opened their doors to rock 'n' roll for the first time. Weiss, who was at once taken with the group, suggested they do another concert before Carnegie to get a feel for American audiences. It would, he noted, also help offset the cost of the trip, which neither the Sullivan show nor Capitol would pick up. They decided on Washington, D.C., "simply because of the logistics," Weiss says. The two shook hands, sealing the deals. It

was for the Beatles, Epstein, and Weiss the beginning of a long and profitable relationship. "We did more deals on handshakes, without signing anything up front," recalls Weiss. "In all my years in show business, I never dealt with anyone more honest or legitimate than Brian Epstein." But with good news, came bad. Three times during the Beatles' opening night performance in Paris their equipment broke down. It was hardly a good omen, and it was even worse for the image, particularly when coupled with the negative reviews that greeted them the next morning. But nothing

that happened in Paris mattered once "the news" arrived from America. It came by telegram late that opening night and Brian assembled John, Paul, George, and Ringo to tell them about it. "I Want to Hold Your Hand" was Number One in America. It was true—there for the world to see in the January 17 issue of *CashBox*. The Beatles had accomplished what no other British pop artist had ever done. They had obtained the unobtainable. They toasted with champagne, ordered up sandwiches, and "didn't sleep much that night," as George Martin puts it. "None of us

25

the same kind of cap Lennon had worn for the cover photograph of his recently released first book, *In His Own Write.* "John felt—we all felt—it was an indication that something else—other than what we had heard about—was going on musically and otherwise in America," recalls Neil Aspinall. "It was a link."

On January 20, Capitol released *Meet the Beatles,* which, on advance orders alone, had shipped gold. For a pop group, this was astounding. Albums, which list priced at $2.99, had always been considered more of an afterthought, another way to re-sell singles. In the meantime, Vee Jay and Swan jumped on the bandwagon, shipping out the stock of Beatles records that had been gathering dust in storerooms, as well as promptly pressing more copies. Since Swan's one-shot deal with "She Loves You" had yet to expire, Capitol was without legal recourse. The company did, however, file a lawsuit against Vee Jay, demanding that they cease and desist manufacturing Beatles records. Vee Jay appealed, claiming they retained rights to the Beatles material they'd already released. In the interim, the Chicago Circuit Court judge ruled that Vee Jay could continue manufacturing Beatles records until a final decision was rendered. Vee Jay hired the Southern Plastics plant in Illinois to stamp the vinyl on a twenty-four-hour basis. For Capitol, it was an infuriating, embarrassing legal mess that would take several months to resolve.

realized the impact it would come to have on the rest of our lives."

"There are moments you never forget and the first Number One in America, well . . . that only happens once, doesn't it?" McCartney says.

That this success occurred just weeks before their scheduled appearance on the Sullivan show could never have been planned or promoted into reality. Something was going on in America. "You just can't buy things like that," Mal Evans reflected years later. "A Number One in America as we arrived to do a major TV show? It just blew us away." During a shopping trip for new records in Paris, one of the Beatles picked up a copy of *Freewheelin'* by a new American artist named Bob Dylan. It seemed, by its very cover, to bode goods things for the Beatles in America. This new American singer was wearing

For the Beatles, it was a remarkable stroke of fate. In England, their success had followed a year-long buildup, with singles and albums released at the usual planned intervals to maximize sales potential. In America, the Beatles were the exception to the rule. Within weeks of Capitol's release of "I Want to Hold Your Hand," a flood of Beatle records on five different labels competed for position on the charts. In addition to "I Want to Hold Your Hand"/"I Saw Her Standing There" and *Meet the Beatles* on Capitol, from which dee-jays were beginning to rotate the other nine songs, and "She Loves You"/"I'll Get You" on Swan, Vee Jay rereleased "Please Please Me"/"From Me to You" and "Do You Want to Know a Secret?"/"Thank You Girl" as well as the album *Introducing the Beatles.* Furthermore, Vee Jay created the Tollie label to release two more singles, "Twist and Shout"/"There's a Place" and "Love Me Do"/"P.S. I Love You." (Vee Jay would later repackage the same collection of songs, releasing a four-song EP titled "The Beatles," an album titled *Jolly What! The Beatles and Frank Ifield on Stage*, and a two-record set titled *The Beatles vs. the Four Seasons*.) MGM—which had secured rights to early, actually pre-Beatles material—released "My Bonnie"/"The Saints" by Tony Sheridan and the Beatles.

Musically, the Beatles hit America like a tidal wave, virtually turning the music industry upside down. The pop music scene in America had been cruising along the middle-of-the-road mainstream with such Number One hits as Nino Tempo and April Stevens' "Deep Purple," Bobby Vinton's "Blue Velvet"/"There! I Said It Again," Dale and Grace's "I'm Leaving It Up to You," and the Singing Nun's "Dominique." While the Kingsmen's "Louie Louie" and the Ronettes' "Be My Baby," neither of which made it to the top of the charts, veered off the homogenized path, the Beatles songs crashed against the mainstream. The sound of Top 40 radio changed almost overnight. The course of pop music was changed forever.

Numerous observers defined the Beatles' music as American fifties rock 'n' roll bouncing back across the Atlantic. The Beatles certainly owed much to America's rock pioneers. "We were in fact taking your product and reshaping it and sending it back to you, taking a lot of influences from black music and making them palatable for whites in America," says Martin. The Beatles were actually teaching young Americans what rock 'n' roll was all about, introducing them to Chuck Berry and Little Richard in the process. Their English influence, however, created a sound distinctive enough to be labeled; it was called Mersey Beat. "To me, it was just music," reflects McCartney. "Mersey Beat—I mean what the hell's that one? We didn't call it that, nobody else said it, except this fellow who turned up one day and said, 'It's Mersey Beat,' and everyone else went, 'Well, that's what it's called, man.' It was really just some bit of music—some fellows on guitars, bass, and drums, with a little bit of a show and we got out there and did it."

In 1964, seventeen-year-olds became the single largest age demographic in the country and American youth, in this era of affluence, had buying power never before experienced. Preteens and teenagers hit the record stores in droves. By the end of January, "I Want to Hold Your Hand" had sold more than two million copies, "She Loves You" one million, and *Meet the Beatles* more than 750,000.

"Sure, there was a lot of hype," said Capitol vice-president Voyle Gilmour. "But all the hype in the world isn't going to sell a bad product." He was right. For young Beatle fans, all the wigs in the world couldn't do what the music could.

In late January, Nicky Byrne and his partners flew to New York to set up Seltaeb (Beatles spelled backwards), the American arm of Stramsact, Byrne's British merchandising business. Byrne and the Stramsact/ Seltaeb partners stood to gain a fortune with the contract they had signed with NEMS— their take was 90 percent compared to NEMS'

10 percent. According to Byrne, he simply filled in the blanks and attorney David Jacobs signed the agreement, no questions asked. Plenty of questions would be asked in forthcoming weeks. Seltaeb leased office space on Fifth Avenue, and within hours of opening for business it had businessmen and would-be Beatle entrepreneurs waiting in the lobby. In exchange for either a cash advance and/or a percentage of the royalties, Byrne as principal licensee issued the merchandising rights for Beatles memorabilia, from T-shirts to tennis shoes, and egg cups to pennants. The Baskin-Robbins ice cream chain even created Bea-

tlenut ice cream. The Reliant Shirt Corporation, which distributed its Beatles' products through Sears and other chain department stores, paid $25,000 up front for the right to manufacture three-button T-shirts and sweatshirts featuring the Beatles' faces and names. Within the first week of sales they had orders for more than one million. Byrne, in an effort to chase the fast and furious merchandising deals, arranged for a radio station promotional giveaway with New York's pop radio stations— free T-shirts for every girl who went to meet the Beatles at the airport.

While curiosity abounded about this new group and a sense of excitement permeated record stores, the mania had yet to fully hit America. The Kennedy assassination and all the unanswered questions it raised were still very much on the minds of most Americans and it was a story that continued to dominate the news. More than ever, there was a need for something upbeat, and *Life* magazine rolled out the red carpet for the Beatles' arrival with a feature titled "Here Come Those Beatles" in the January 31 issue. *Newsweek*'s February 3 issue featured the group in its music column to them, announcing "The Beatles Is Coming!" The general-interest, oversized magazines—

Los Angeles.

Los Angeles.

Life, Look, The Saturday Evening Post—and the news weeklies, *Time* and *Newsweek*—ruled the newsstands and obtaining coverage in these journalistic powerhouses was a media coup. In the early sixties, there was no rock press. There were, however, a number of teen magazines which seemed to sense the Beatles impending popularity. *TeenScreen*, followed by *Dig!* and *Datebook* were all risking the odds, readying special one-shot issues devoted to the Beatles.

Capitol's Brown Meggs meanwhile made reservations for the Beatles at the Plaza Hotel. "Brian heard that it was *the* place to stay in New York," says Meggs. Contrary to the myth that the Plaza management had no idea who John Lennon, Paul McCartney, George Harrison, and Ringo Starr were, Meggs, for one, fully briefed hotel executives from the moment the reservations were made. "They became immediately concerned about the need for extra security and wanted to know if Capitol would participate in the additional cost," Meggs continues. Capitol declined, noting that the publicity the Plaza would reap from having the Beatles as guests would more than cover the cost for additional security. Norman Weiss also spoke with Plaza officials. "There was just no way we couldn't let them know," he explains.

Upon his return from Paris, Weiss also phoned the New York Police Department to advise them of what—most likely—was to come with the arrival of the Beatles in February, and to secure extra police units around the hotel and venues. This was "not for the Beatles so much as for the fans themselves, to keep them from killing themselves," he explains. "They didn't want to believe me." Meggs met with the same resistance when he phoned the NYPD for the same reasons. "The response was basically 'It won't be a problem, we move famous people in and out of places every day.'" But Meggs, "seriously concerned" about the potential for disaster, sent the captain copies of European magazines that carried articles on Beatles riots and mobs overseas. Within a couple of days the captain was on the phone requesting a meeting, the first of many meetings between the NYPD and the Beatles' various representatives to discuss strategies. A special squad of twenty horse-mounted patrolmen was assigned to keep twenty-four-hour watch around the Plaza Hotel where the Beatles would be staying, with an underground garage converted to resting quarters for both the patrolmen and their mounts.

In the weeks preceding the Beatles' arrival in America, it was business-as-usual at the Sullivan show. "For several weeks there had been a knowledge and an awareness of who the Beatles were, and for those of us on the staff there was *almost* the feeling that this was important, but nobody knew how important," recalls Sullivan's producer, Bob Precht. The show's production assistant, Vince Calandra, was the first to review the Capitol promotional kit. "We thought, 'Who are these guys and what makes them so different?'" says Calandra. "We really thought they'd be just like any other group—just another flash in the pan. Nobody had any idea what was going to happen. And then the ticket requests started coming in." Every preteen and teenage girl had already laid claim to her favorite Beatle and knew the vital statistics of all of them. They knew also that John was the intelligent Beatle; Paul, the cute one; George, the quiet one; Ringo, the sad one.

On February 3 the Beatles visited the American Embassy in Paris, to obtain visas and work permits. Two days later, with the Olympia engagement finally fulfilled, the Beatles left Paris and returned to London with only forty-eight hours to rest and prepare for their trip. Their press agent, Brian Sommerville, headed out to New York that day to make press conference arrangements and to field the growing list of interview requests.

An estimated 2,000 fans assembled at London Airport to see the Beatles off on February 7. The schoolgirls cheered, screamed, and waved banners as the Fab Four, along with Epstein, road managers Neil Aspinall and Mal Evans, Cynthia Lennon, American record producer Phil Spector, and a small contingent of British journalists and photographers, boarded Pan Am's Flight 101. By 2:30 P.M. London time, the Beatles were airborne and on their way to America for the first time.

31

During the flight, the business never stopped. Neil and Mal, sitting in the economy section of the plane, forged signatures on promotional glossy photos. Meanwhile, numerous businessmen who had been unable to reach Epstein by telephone spent most of the flight trying to get him to respond to handwritten messages which they passed via the stewardesses.

George was the only Beatle who had been to America; he had visited his sister Louise the summer before. She had married and moved to Illinois. Initially, George had planned to spend a week with Louise in the Midwest, but the Beatles' sudden rise to fame in the States changed those plans. They decided she would fly into New York. In a moment of reflection, George turned to the Liverpool *Echo* reporter who shared his name and wondered out loud: "America has everything. What do they want us for?" It was a thought that crossed every Beatle's mind again and again. And a question that, while speaking to Spector, Paul McCartney asked too.

Meanwhile, in New York everybody seemed to know of their forthcoming arrival. Disc jockeys, who peppered their frantic banterings with Beatle slang words like "fab," "gear," and "cheeky," used the word "Beatle" as often as possible. Any crumb of Beatle news was trumpeted like it was a five-bell bulletin. Disc jockeys from every pop station urged listeners to go out to the airport and "welcome the Beatles to America." Their arrival was supposed to have been secret, but when it came to the Beatles such secrets were never kept for long. Several days before, WINS' Murray the K had announced to all of New York the

Beatles' airline, flight number, and estimated time of arrival, something that caused much concern among Capitol's executives. Their flight and arrival time were repeatedly announced as WINS, WMCA, and WABC battled for listeners.

At 1:20 P.M., the Beatles' plane touched down at the recently renamed Kennedy International Airport. They emerged several minutes later to a scene that took their breaths away. Neither Sullivan nor Capitol had spent a dollar promoting the Beatles' actual arrival, but no amount of promotion could have guaranteed such a turnout, and 110 of New York's finest were hard-pressed to control it. An estimated 3,000 young people, mostly girls, who were packed four-deep in the upper arcade, wailed and screamed and shouted the names of their favorite Beatles, creating a roar that drowned out the jet engines. They waved homemade banners and signs that read "Welcome" and "We Love You Beatles," and they chanted *"We want the Beatles! We want the Beatles!"* Another thousand or so waited downstairs just outside the roped-off lobby. An airport official stood shaking his head when reporters asked for a comment: "We've never seen anything like this before. Never."

"Is the President's plane about to land?" The Beatles looked at one another, wondering, Aspinall recalls. But they quickly realized that the crowd had amassed solely for them. Then they were ushered, smiling and waving, into Customs and then on to the first floor of the main terminal to face some one hundred journalists and photographers, all of whom seemed to be shouting questions or flashing strobes. The room was packed. Several photographers were pulling on and verbally harassing press officer Sommerville. "We bought an exclusive story and can't even get a picture of them looking at us?" shouted one New York *Journal-American* photographer. A frantic Sommerville threw up his arms and shouted what the press already knew: "This has gotten *completely* out of control!"

At first, the Beatles were somewhat taken aback by the mass of media before them, but they handled it the way they did just about everything—with a sense of irreverent honesty and intelligent humor. "So this is America," mused Ringo. "They all seem out of their minds."

"Are you in favor of lunacy?" came the first question heard by the Beatles.

"Yeah," said Paul. "It's healthy."

"Will you be getting a haircut?"

"*No*," they all answered.

"We had one yesterday," said George.

"Will you sing something?"

"No, we need money first," snapped Lennon, raising a round of laughter and breaking the ice.

"Which one of you is really bald?"

"I'm bald," said Paul.

"We're *all* bald," corrected John.

"Is there any truth to the rumor that you're really just four Elvis Presleys?"

"No, nah, we're not," said Ringo, shaking in imitation of the King. The media roared.

"What is the secret of your success?"

"We have a press agent," cracked Ringo.

"What do you think of the campaign in Detroit to 'Stamp out the Beatles'?"

"We have a campaign to stamp out Detroit!" John shot back.

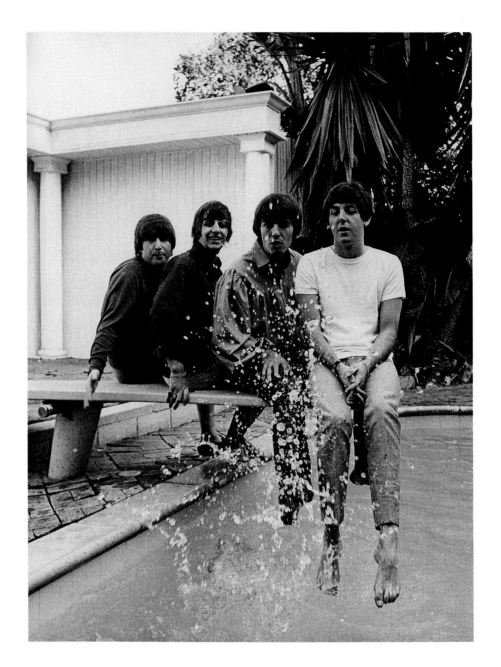

Los Angeles.

Denver.

"Are you part of a social rebellion against the older generation?"

"No, it's a dirty lie," said Paul. "Yeah, a dirty lie," the others chimed in.

The Beatles wowed the American media by making them smile.

Amidst much chaos, the Beatles were steered out the rear entrance to where four Cadillac limousines—one for each Beatle—waited to drive them to the Plaza Hotel. Ultimately, police could not restrain the youthful masses and in the ensuing crush Brian Epstein was left behind to hail a cab. John, Paul, George, Ringo, and Meggs jumped into one limousine and took off, leaving the other

three limousines empty. "That was the best reception ever," said Lennon, as the Beatles got their first look at New York from the limousine windows and heard their music in America for the first time.

As the cars pulled up to the Plaza, hundreds of fans, known among themselves as Beatlepeople, crowded West Fifty-eighth street, but were effectively restrained by police as the Beatles sprinted inside. They were rushed up to the twelfth floor and sequestered in the Presidential Suite, a ten-room suite overlooking Fifty-eighth Street. Two guards were on duty around the clock. Every few seconds the elevator door would open and a group of determined young people would make a hopeless mad dash for the corridor, only to be scooped up by the attending guards and hustled back into the elevator. George, who was suffering from a sore throat, was ensconced in one of the bedrooms, while Ringo sat in the living room watching television, as Paul and John spun the radio dial to different stations, listening to their own songs as the disc jockeys heralded their arrival.

A report circulated within press circles that the Plaza management would not have accepted the reservations had they known who the Beatles were. Plaza officials, however, refused comment. Despite the advance warning and preparation, employees were showing obvious signs of strain and fatigue. Nobody—least of all the Beatles—had anticipated this kind of reaction. "They would have paid us anything—*anything*—to get out," says Weiss.

Upstairs, the Beatles drank it in. All of New York seemed to be at their feet. It was intoxicating. It was all, as Paul said, too much. The persistent chanting of *"We want the Beatles! We want the Beatles!"* collided with the voices of fans who sang what would become the unofficial Beatles fan song. It was adapted from a song in the movie loosely based on Elvis' rise to fame, *Bye Bye Birdie*—"We love you, Bea-tles, oh yes we dooo, we love you Bea-tles and we'll be truu-oo." The din shot upward. "I think everybody has gone daft," John said, loving it. Room service arrived, trays ladened with rum, Scotch and Coca-Cola and buckets of ice. Telegrams came in by the handful and fan letters were delivered in bulging sacks. "We get twelve thousand letters a day," Ringo beamed to one reporter. "Yeah," John smiled wryly, "and we're going

to answer *every* one." As the networks broadcast the news, John, Paul, and Ringo watched their arrival with the television sound turned completely down and the radio blaring. CBS and ABC, along with some local stations, all covered the Beatles' arrival at the airport and hotel. Only NBC's Chet Huntley declined to air the footage.

Neil and Mal returned to the task of forging the Beatles' signatures onto photographs, while Cynthia remained discreetly in the background. Visitors and business associates came and went with difficulty that night, including Capitol Records executives, WINS' Murray the K and other dee-jays, and the Ronettes, as well as George's personal guests—his sister Louise Harrison Caldwell and the hotel doctor. After checking in herself, Louise headed upstairs to the twelfth floor. A security guard intercepted her and asked: "Where do you think you're going?" When she told him she was going to meet her brother, the guard snorted: "Do you know how many times *that* one's been tried today?" A reporter assumed the task of announcing her. Within minutes George steered her back down the hall and into the inner sanctum. Later George's condition was diagnosed as strep throat and the doctor asked Louise to attend to her brother, telling her, "You're the only female left in this city who is sane."

Brian headed out to the Four Seasons for dinner with Geoffrey Ellis, an old friend from Liverpool, leaving the boys and Neil and Mal behind, listening to music and the crowd below. "There was so much commotion, and the music from the radio combined with their images on the TV, it was very surreal," recalls Ellis. An inspired John went to the window, waved to the crowd: "Cheers!" he yelled. Just then a cop walked in and shouted to Neil, "Tell him to *stop* going to the window!" Neil turned to John and yelled, "*Stop* going to the window!" The cop left. They all laughed.

"When I finally managed to get upstairs to their suite, I realized that they hadn't realized what was happening over here," reflects Capitol president Livingston. "They knew they were selling records, but they didn't comprehend the impact of that. They were impressed and even a bit awestruck by it all."

The following morning, John, Paul, Ringo, and George, who was wearing a turtleneck to keep his throat warm, munched on chicken sandwiches and gave another press conference in the Plaza's Baroque Room. When a lady reporter chastised Ringo for smoking and setting a bad example for teenagers, Ringo responded, "Who's a teenager? I'm twenty-three." Snapped John, "We're not here to set examples for teenagers."

"What's the greatest threat to your career—dandruff or nuclear warfare?" asked another reporter. "Nuclear warfare," replied Ringo, adding, "we've already got dandruff." Afterward George headed back to his room, and John, Paul, and Ringo took a walk through Central Park, so photojournalists, Curt Gunther among them, could photograph them on American soil. "Who are these kids with long hair? What's the big deal?" Gunther wondered, checking out the contingent around him. That day "I Saw Her Standing There" entered *Billboard*'s Hot 100 chart at 68 and Vee Jay's rerelease of the album *Introducing the Beatles* jumped up to 59 on the album chart.

In the afternoon, the Beatles—minus George—went to the CBS studios on West Fifty-third and Broadway for a sound check and camera-blocking for Sunday night's Sullivan show. Fifty-two police officers and ten mounted patrolmen kept order outside the theater as the limousine pulled up and deposited John, Paul, Ringo, Brian, Neil, and Mal. Sullivan, nervous about George's absence, turned to Epstein and said, "He'd better be here tomorrow or I'm gonna put on a wig and I'll be a Beatle!" Epstein assured Sullivan that George would be there, then asked for "the exact words" to Sullivan's introduction. "I would like you to get out of here," Sullivan said, half smiling. For the rehearsal, the Beatles sang at half-voice, but played at full volume. Paul and John insisted, much to the surprise of the Sullivan staffers, on going into the control booth and listening to the playback of their rehearsal. No other musical act had ever made such a request. But they were adamant—and very concerned about the sound.

As they entered the control booth, John, Paul, and Ringo beheld racks of khaki-painted components. "This place looks like it's been pinched from a Messerschmitt," laughed Lennon. Since professional television recording equipment was still somewhat primitive, Art Shine, the show's audio director, had taken surplus military equipment—all of which had been painted khaki—and jerry-rigged a more refined component system. As they listened to the playback, John and Paul made verbal notes and suggestions regarding the balance. The Beatles wanted their sound to be mixed

with the music just as loud as the lyrics. Shine looked at Precht, who looked at Sullivan. It was customary for the lyric to be brought out—that's what the Sullivan audience was used to; that's the way they wanted to hear the music. The Beatles stood their ground. "We had to adjust our thinking," says Precht.

Back at the hotel, the Beatles gave interviews to disc jockeys, and willingly consented to recording customized I.D.'s or station plugs. Later, they escaped for a night on the town. Stops included the Playboy Club—"The bunnies are even more adorable than we are," offered Paul—and the Peppermint Lounge,

where Ringo twisted to Beatle tunes played by a local band.

On Sunday afternoon, February 9, much to their delight, the Beatles performed in a dress rehearsal with an audience because of the incredible demand for tickets and because the segment for the show to be aired on February 28 was being taped. The Beatles' success in America had surprised everybody. Even Sullivan, who had recently been the topic of scuttlebutt around CBS. The show had been on for sixteen years and predictions were it would soon see its final hour. But Sullivan's instincts regarding talent, once again,

Denver.

37

were right on track and booking the Beatles was proving to be one of his grandest coups. Sullivan may not have *guaranteed* the Beatles top billing, but top billing is exactly what they got.

He opened the show as he always did, with a monologue—during which he read a welcoming telegram sent to the Beatles from Elvis and his manager, Colonel Tom Parker. Screams of excitement forced him to pause and ask the overexcited kids to give their "respectful attention" to the show's other performers. "And if you don't," he threatened, "I'll call in a barber!" Then, following the first commercial break, the cameras cut back to Sullivan, who had to raise his voice to be heard: "Our city—indeed the country—has never seen anything like these four young men from Liverpool. Ladies and gentlemen, the Beatles!"

The young girls in the studio that afternoon, and later that evening, screamed or stared catatonically, mirroring the response in living rooms across America. "And these are the people who are going to be running the country twenty years from now?" asked one orchestra member to another. "I think they're more enthusiastic here than at home," assessed Cynthia Lennon, who stood in the back of the studio to watch the show.

The stage was decorated with six white arrows pointing inward, to symbolize, set designer Bill Bohnert told reporters, "the fact that the Beatles are here." And so they were. From New York to California, from Texas to Minnesota, and all points in between, America watched as the Beatles broke into the opening strains of "All My Loving," breaking televi-

Denver.

sion audience ratings in the process. Then they launched into their version of Meredith Willson's "'Till There Was You" from *The Music Man*, picking up the pace with the segment's finale of "She Loves You." Yeah, yeah, yeah! As they performed, it become clear that the Beatles had captured the heart and soul of a generation.

As the cameramen cut back and forth from long shots to close-ups to, atypically, shots of the girls in the balcony, it was as if there were some kind of mass kinetic transference. Something magical was happening. Nobody watching even noticed that one of their mikes went temporarily dead. Following the Sullivan

show's other performers, the Beatles returned and ripped into "I Saw Her Standing There," segueing right into a finale of their first Number One hit in America, "I Want to Hold Your Hand." In countless homes across the country, parents stared unbelievingly at the screen, disgusted by the mops of hair, completely baffled by the music, and concerned about its obvious effect on their children. Adults, and especially psychologists and psychiatrists, would spend the rest of the year trying to figure it all out. American kids, however, simply reacted to the music, and felt new hope. Generational battle lines were drawn that night, as life and the prospects for the future shifted like colored pebbles in a kaleidoscope. It was a moment seized, never to be forgotten.

The Beatles spent a grand total of thirteen and a half minutes onstage, more than any of the other performers, and Sullivan staffers were relieved when the show was over. "It was really kind of scary," remembers Precht. "With live television anything can happen and with the reaction of that audience, well . . . we were well aware that the potential for disaster was there and were more than a little nervous."

The following morning, reviews of the Beatles' performance were mixed. "Televised Beatlemania appeared to be a fine mass placebo, wrote the New York *Times'* Jack Gould. And as the Washington *Post's* Lawrecen Laurent saw it: "They are, apparently, part of some kind of malicious, bi-lateral entertainment trade agreement."

No one managed to capture the essence of the Beatles or even begin to describe what it was that made them so appealing. Either you felt the music or you didn't. While the American media jumped on the story, coverage focused on the phenomenon, not the group's musical potential. Although some critics briefly commented on the songwriting of Lennon and McCartney, nobody cited their consistency or

Arrival in Cincinnati.

their prolific abilities, perhaps because rock 'n' roll was still viewed as the bastard child of American contemporary music. Furthermore, no one seemed to notice that beyond the music, the Beatles' wit and irreverence were reflecting a new attitude, a different way of thinking that was being quickly adopted by American youth.

When the Nielsen ratings came in on Monday morning, Sullivan, Precht, and other Sullivan staffers gathered to review them. The numbers had to be big. They knew that. But they didn't expect them to go through the roof. An astonishing 73,700,000 viewers had tuned in, making it not only the largest audience for any Sullivan show, but the largest audience in television history. Even evangelist Billy Graham had broken down and watched television on the Sabbath: "I don't dig them. I hope they get a haircut when they get older." Most American parents agreed. For Sullivan, the show reaffirmed his ability to recognize talent at an early stage and present it to his audience. For the Beatles, it was one of the single most important bookings Epstein ever arranged—even though the audience numbers were just too big for them to grasp. "There were so many things happening in so many different directions, it was like total euphoria, but the numbers just, well . . . didn't really register," recalls Aspinall.

On Tuesday, February 11, a snowstorm raged across the East Coast. The Beatles were scheduled to fly to Washington, D.C., for their first concert in the States—but, shaken by memories of Buddy Holly, who had died in an airplane crash on February 2, 1959, the Beatles refused to fly. Arrangements were

Ringo shows off his Saint Christopher medal, Delmonico Hotel, New York.

43

hastily made for them to take the train into Washington. Just after 1 P.M., the Beatles and their entourage, which included TV crews, journalists, and photographers, boarded the *King George*, an old Richmond, Fredericksburg, and Potomac Railroad sleeper car, at Penn Station for the trip to their first concert on American soil. On the train, John and Paul and George strummed acoustical guitars and answered reporters' questions. Despite their secret switch in plans, and eight inches of snow, Washington's Union Square was jammed with some 2,000 fans as the train, twenty minutes late, finally pulled into Union Station. A mass shriek and utter pandemonium turned the smiles of police officers into grimaces. Newsmen, many wearing the Russian fur caps that were currently in vogue, stood on the platform awaiting the emergence of their assignment. Metropolitan Police Inspector John Hughes boarded the train and a few minutes later emerged. "*Eeeeeekkkkkk!*" he chortled, imitating the Beatlepeople's cry, drawing guffaws from the media. As the Beatles stepped from the train, they stepped into laughter and the clicking of shutters. Behind a flying wedge of Washington police officers, they walked the length of the platform and headed into the eye of the storm. The crowd moved in, and the police strained, sweat dripping from their faces, to hold their line as the Beatles and their entourage disappeared safely into limousines bound for the Coliseum. There they conducted a sound check and gave a press conference:

"How do the Beatles react to criticism that they're not very good?"

New York.

"We're not," replied George.

"Did the Beatles come to America to get revenge, perhaps for the Revolution?"

"No, no. We just came for the money," quipped Ringo.

The American media was amused and bewildered by the Beatles.

Following the press conference the Beatles went to the WWDC studio for an interview with disc jockey Carroll James. He asked them about their influences. "Small Blind Johnny" came the response.

"Small Blind Johnny?" asked Carroll.

"Oh yes, he played with Big Deaf Arthur."

"John, they call you the chief Beatle . . ."

"Carroll," John replied, "I don't call you names!"

"Excluding America and England, what are your favorite countries you've visited?"

"Excluding America and England, what's left?" asked John.

"Does anyone in the group speak a foreign language?"

"We all speak fluent shoe," said Paul.

After checking into the Shoreham Hotel, the Beatles headed for the Coliseum. Cynthia stayed behind, alone, in the hotel room. That night 8,092 fans, mostly girls, witnessed the Beatles' first American concert, while 362 police officers stood guard. The din rose to decibel-shattering levels as the Beatles were lead onstage at 8:31 P.M. by a phalanx of policemen. Flashes from cameras lit the entire Coliseum. Then, suddenly ten thousand tiny missiles were launched from every direction. The Beatles were pelted with jellybeans, the harder American counterpart to England's soft and chewy jelly babies. "My God, they hurt," said Ringo. The screaming never let up during the entire thirty minutes of the Beatles' performance: "Roll Over Beethoven," "From Me to You," "I Saw Her Standing There," "This Boy," "All My Loving," "I Wanna Be Your Man," "Please Please Me," "Till There Was You," "She Loves You," "I Want to Hold Your Hand," "Twist and Shout," and ending with "Long Tall Sally." The old boxing ring had been set up so that the audience surrounded the Beatles. A mechanical malfunction required Mal to come onstage after every three songs or so, to turn Ringo's drums around to face another section of the shrieking crowd. During the show, when Lennon leaned

into the microphone to tell the audience to "shut up," the screams only increased. There was no doubting it: The Beatles had arrived in America. And they were well on their way to becoming the biggest thing in the world, just as Epstein had envisioned. They received a total of $12,184.76 for their performance, which was captured on film by CBS for later showing as a closed-circuit special in theaters across America.

Since they could hear little, if any, of the four musicians on stage, reporters reviewed the audience. "An 8,000-voice choir performed last night at Washington Coliseum . . . accompanied incidentally by four young British artists who call themselves the Beatles," reported Leroy Aarons in the Washington *Post*. "The effect . . . is like being downwind from a jet during take-off. Interesting possibilities, what with the trend toward electronic music and all. One was impressed by the versatility of the choral group. . . . Their range invites comparison with Yma Sumac, their intensity of emotion with the victim in a Hitchcock film, and Caruso would envy their volume."

Later that night, the Beatles attended a reception at the British Embassy. Word of their impending arrival was leaked and as police encircled the Embassy, fans encircled them. While the Beatles were onstage at the Coliseum, a quiet, formal staff dance to benefit the National Association for the Prevention of Cruelty to Children, had been held at the Embassy. The Beatles had been "chosen" for the dubious honor of giving out the raffle prizes at the end of the gala affaire. It was the kind of appearance that was completely

New York.

Lennon added, pointing to George. When Sir David began to address George as John, George interrupted and pointed to Ringo, who said, "No, I'm Charlie. He's John." Cheeky Liverpool humor. The game continued for several minutes until the completely confused ambassador realized what was going on. The Beatles remained—undauntingly—the Beatles.

"Attention! Beatles are now approaching the area." Lady Ormsby-Gore, looking quite royal, entered the rotunda surrounded by the four guests of honor. "Please don't throw jellybeans," Paul called down to the guests. "Throw peppermint creams, instead. They're softer when they hit." Diplomats and invited guests didn't throw jellybeans, but they did shriek and squeal. Some even pushed, and a few actually kicked those blocking them in order to get a good look at what one diplomatic wife called "those darling little baby boys." Of course, by the time those darling boys arrived, most everyone had had more than their fair share of spiked punch and spirits. The Beatles—all too cognizant of the class difference and the bittersweet irony of this Beatlemania-afflicted social elite—descended the staircase. The guests surged forward, moving in on them. The four were pulled in different directions and separated from each other.

A small mob surrounded each Beatle. Pens and paper in hand, the members demanded autographs and answers to their questions. One noble woman threw her arms around Paul and stared adoringly into his eyes. "Which one are you?" she asked. "Roger," he replied. "Roger what?" she asked. "Roger

against the grain of the Beatles' apolitical stance, and completely against their own personal desires; but it was something to which Epstein had committed them and once a commitment was made, it was honored.

While John, Paul, George, Ringo, and Brian met privately with Sir David Ormsby-Gore and his lady, the dance guests and press crowded around the stairway which led up to the ambassador's residence in the Embassy rotunda. Sir Ormsby-Gore, who had been a close political ally of John F. Kennedy, was a liberal and well liked on his home turf, and the meeting with him was amiable, if somewhat unsettling to the ambassador. At the outset, confused about their identities, Sir David asked John if he was, in fact, John. "No, I'm Fred," replied Lennon. "He's John,"

McCluskey the Fifth," he said, slipping out from under her grasp. At one point, John pushed away the pens being shoved at him and headed for the bar. "These people have no bloody manners," he said, scowling. An Embassy official approached him: "Come on, now, go do your stuff." John turned. "I'm getting out of here." Calmly, Ringo appeared and took hold of John's arm. "Come on, let's go do our stuff and get it over with."

The behavior of England's social elite on this occasion was appalling. One stately-looking woman approached Ringo with a pair of scissors, determined to clip a lock of his hair. Cursing her, Ringo ducked and saved his hair. The Beatles couldn't wait to leave. One of the raffle prizes, not too surprisingly, was a signed Beatles album. "We can get you a Frank Sinatra for the same price," Ringo offered as he handed it over to the lucky winner.

News of the less-than-noble conduct circulated back to Britain and the question of whether or not the Beatles were in fact mistreated was raised. Despite the display of rudeness, Epstein was not interested in making an issue of it. Instead, he sent a thank-you note to Lady Ormsby-Gore, but the Beatles would never again make such an appearance.

On the following day, February 12—a

New York.

national holiday celebrating Abraham Lincoln's birthday—the Beatles returned to New York by train, entertaining the press for much of the two-hour ride. Ringo began slipping and sliding down, over and around seats. John and George then traded coats—for no obvious reason. Then, Ringo grabbed every camera he could loosen from the grasp of photographers and draped them around his neck and arms, shoving his way through the crowd.

"Excuse me! *Life* magazine!" he shouted. "Exclusive! *Life* magazine!" Paul went to the back of the car to take "artistic pictures" out the window. "Ahh," he shouted, "Railway lines. Got it! A barn. Got it!" George then climbed up into one of the luggage racks and pretended to fall asleep. Ringo, having deposited the cameras, hunkered down and scurried back through the crowd, this time wearing a woman's fur coat and hat. George jumped down from the luggage rack and reappeared several minutes later, wearing a porter's coat and hat, serving soft drinks on a tray. John surveyed the scene, nodding with occasional approval: "That's foony."

Weiss and Epstein had decided to fly back and meet the boys, with limousines, at Penn Station. Though the time of the Beatles' arrival was, once again, supposed to have been secret, the word, once again, got out and thousands of fans jammed into the Station. A group of young fans, seeing the limo, approached the window and looked inside. "It's not them" the leader announced to her two young friends. "It's just two dirty old men!" Weiss and Epstein looked at each other—and then laughed. But on this particular day, the last laugh was on them. Although they had arrived well ahead of schedule, they couldn't get through the crowds to reach the Beatles. Meanwhile, the Beatles faced the dangerous proposition of riding to the hotel in New York taxi cabs. There wasn't any choice this time. Without a second to spare they were hustled into a couple of cabs, and arrived at the Plaza none the worse for wear. They had enough time for a quick shower, shave, and change of clothes before their Carnegie Hall concerts.

That night as the Beatles performed their two shows—each lasting approximately thirty-five minutes—Brian was beside himself with happiness. As he watched his boys perform on the famous stage, tears streamed down his face. Since tickets had quickly sold out and since there were no guest passes to be had, and additional two hundred seats were placed on the stage to accommodate VIPs and special guests, among them Lauren Bacall and Mrs.

Happy Rockefeller. Jellybeans splatted onto the stage. Flashes from cameras lit the music hall. Youthful, shrill screams drowned out the music. The Beatles grossed $9,335.78 for both shows. Like the Washington *Post*, the New York *Times* reported: "Three thousand screaming girls held a concert at Carnegie Hall with the Beatles serving as inaudible accompanists."

After the performance, Epstein was guided out into the cold night air of Manhattan by Sid Bernstein, who hailed a cab to take them over to Madison Square Garden. There Bernstein gave his pitch: $25,000 plus a $5,000 donation to the British Cancer Fund if the Beatles would agree to play Madison Square Garden. Tickets, Bernstein assured, could be printed and would sell out immediately. Epstein scanned the arena, then turned to Bernstein and said: "Let's leave this for next time."

On their last night in New York, the Beatles left their hotel around 1:30 A.M. and visited the Headliner Club, then went to the Improvisation, a coffee house, before returning at dawn. One reporter who patiently awaited them at the Plaza, inquired if it had been a quiet night. "No," said Paul. "We met Stella Stevens, Tuesday Weld, and Jill Haworth—and they're not exactly quiet girls."

Meanwhile, the impact of the Beatles' Sullivan appearance was being felt in cities all across the United States. Local record stores became *the* place to be. From tiny towns to big cities, the scene was the same. Dozens of girls waited anxiously as an overwrought clerk lifted a huge cardboard box and dropped it onto the counter. Thud! Rip! One flap. Rip! The other flap. The box, finally opened, revealed in glorious black and white John, Paul, George, and Ringo. In a matter of seconds, the cardboard shell was all that remained.

Later that day, Feb. 13, the Beatles boarded National Airlines Flight 11—greeted by the flight crew, a few of whom had purchased Beatle wigs to celebrate the occasion—and took off for Miami and their next live performance on "The Ed Sullivan Show," to be broadcast from the Deauville Hotel. During the two-hour flight, the other eighty passengers alternately hovered around them, asking for autographs. Ringo slept while Paul, George, and John, who sat quietly in the last row with Cynthia, spent most of the flight signing stacks of photographs. As the plane began its initial descent, Ringo awoke and asked for a life-preserver while peering out the window "looking for sharks." Despite their overwhelming success in New York and Washington, Paul asked stewardess Carol Gallagher, "Do you think anybody will be in Miami to meet us?"

In Miami, radio stations WFUN and WQAM had announced the flight's arrival time. Since the Sullivan show, it seemed as if the Beatles were all anybody wanted to hear on the radio, and despite the number of Beatle records on the market, disc jockeys found it impossible to satiate their listeners' appetite. The mania had swept the country. An estimated crowd of seven thousand tanned Florida teenagers, nearly twice as many people as had met the Beatles in New York, packed the observation decks at Miami International Airport and Concourse 3 where the plane was scheduled to arrive. When Flight 11 touched down just before 4 P.M., the screams of welcome once

again drowned out the jet engines, but this time the scene turned into mayhem. Fans climbed on top of airline counters, smashed a plate glass door, shattered twenty-three louvered glass windows, and tore up twelve fiberglass chairs; the riot caused an estimated $2,000 worth of damage. As the crowd began forcing open a door leading to the concrete apron outside, it took the strength of seven men—police officers and National Airlines employees—to keep it closed. Miraculously, only seven casualties, mostly minor cuts and bruises, were reported.

A circuslike atmosphere was beginning to surround the Beatles' appearances. In Miami, they were greeted not only by the crowd but by three bug-extermination trucks, which had, no doubt, turned out in hopes of getting some free publicity; and by a chimpanzee, four girls in swimsuits, and eight fraudulent Beatles, four of whom were staffers on the Miami *Herald*. Donning Beatle wigs, toting guitar cases, and riding along corridors in a borrowed National Airlines power wagon, the four newsmen attracted, according to the story they filed, "no more attention than an old Elvis Presley movie. They saw us for what we were: squares in Beatles' clothing, trying to con 7,000 savvy teenagers. It wasn't a fair match." In the end, they all fled, concluding: "A Beatle just can't be imitated."

When it came to the Real Things, however, the crowd got little more than a glimpse. Two limousines pulled up to the ramp and within seconds the Beatles and their entourage were off to Miami Beach and the Deauville, complete with a motorcycle escort. They roared onto the highway only to get lodged in a four-

mile traffic jam which, ironically, their arrival had created. Miami's chief of police, angry about how the radio stations "stirred up those kids," threatened to write the FCC. "It's a total lack of public service," he said. Furthermore, the "unauthorized Beatling" spelled detention for most and the Dade County school superintendent ordered school principals to enforce makeup time after class, the usual school policy for hooky players.

At the Deauville, quickly dubbed "Beatle Central," it took the Beatles only twelve seconds to get from their limousines into the hotel elevator. They shared a three-bedroom suite, guarded twenty-four hours a day by Pinkerton detectives. John bunked, of course,

with Cynthia, Paul shared a room with Ringo, and George with dee-jay Murray the K, who'd already dubbed himself the "Fifth Beatle." Police surrounded the resort hotel from the rooftop to the basement. Special passes were issued to guests and hotel employees, but, as in New York and Washington, it didn't stop the fans from trying to gain entrance.

The switchboard at the Deauville was overloaded with calls requesting tickets for the Sullivan show, until secretaries were finally given the order to shut off the calls. Companies from all over the United States sent products for the Beatles to try—probably praying that the Beatles would be photographed with the product in view. The Deau-

51

ville storerooms were loaded with crates of Coca-Cola and Pepsi, among countless other items.

That night, the Beatles—John accompanied by Cynthia, the others with local girls on their arms—hit the local bistros, including the Mau Mau Lounge, where they listened to the Coasters and danced the "Mashed Potato." At 11 P.M., Police Sgt. Buddy Dresner was assigned to take charge of the Beatle Patrol at the Deauville, with two dozen officers under his command. Dresner would become the Beatles' personal bodyguard during their stay in Miami, and, thereafter, conducted nightly bed checks. "There were no women in their rooms," says Dresner. "And no drugs—only Scotch and Coke."

On February 15, the day before their second Sullivan show appearance, *Meet the Beatles* hit Number One on *Billboard*'s album charts, and would remain there for eleven weeks. The Tony Sheridan/Beatles song "My Bonnie" entered at 67. The Beatles rehearsed—in swimming trunks—in the hotel's Napoleon Room.

On February 16, the Beatles, trapped by the crowd, nearly missed their cue. But with only seconds to spare, they bounded onto the stage and ripped into "She Loves You," followed by "This Boy," and "All My Loving."

52

They closed the show with "I Saw Her Standing There," "From Me to You," and "I Want to Hold Your Hand." Boxing champs Sonny Liston and Joe Louis were among the 3,200 in the audience.

Following their performance, Harold Conrad, who was promoting the upcoming Cassius Clay–Sonny Liston bout for the heavyweight boxing championship, went backstage and asked Sullivan if he could meet the Beatles. Sullivan took Conrad up to their suite and introduced him. "I think Clay is going to win," Paul said. Conrad asked them if they'd like to see Clay work out. Epstein had already quashed the idea when Conrad approached him the day before, but John said, "Don't worry about Brian, we'll handle him." The next morning, the Beatles went to Clay's training camp and posed for pictures with the "Beautiful One." John, Paul, George, and Ringo lay down on their backs and told Clay— who was about to change his name to Muhammad Ali—to stand over them with his gloved hands in a victory pose. "I thought it was real nice—the gimmick being," Ali says, "'Clay stomps the Beatles.'" "They were regular, friendly, everyday fellows," Ali remembers. "Success hadn't gone to their heads."

That night, following a barbecue dinner, Dresner took them to their first drive-in movie, where they saw Elvis Presley's *Fun in Acapulco*.

During their stay at the Deauville, the Beatles also took in Don Rickles' floor show and went cruising on a yacht. The Florida sunshine proved such a respite from the cold winter weather that awaited them back home that they decided to stay for a few more days and Dresner made arrangements for them on Star Island. Their arrival was heralded by sirens. John, Paul, George, and Ringo waded into the Atlantic waters, followed by photographers and dozens of local girls. For the next four days, the Beatles lounged in the sun and tried to relax.

At 5:18 P.M. on February 21, four suntanned Beatles headed back, tourist class, to New York, where they would catch another flight on to London. Pressure from the Miami Police Department had ensured that disc jockeys would not mention the departure time, but five hundred teenagers managed to find out and were on hand to say farewell. As they boarded the Eastern jet, Ringo turned for one last look and sighed, "It's snowing in London right now."

Important lessons had been learned during this first trip to America, including how not to be taken. The value of the Beatles' name(s), images, voices—in other words, merchandising—was realized. A New York *Times* article on February 17 highlighted Stramsact/Seltaeb chief Nicky Byrne's projection that Beatles' merchandise in America would garner some $50 million before the year had ended. Epstein was furious. He, and hence the boys, had been burned by the deal with Stramsact and Seltaeb. (Upon their return to England, Epstein filed suit against the corporation for excessive business expenses and failure to report all earnings. When the legal smoke cleared, NEMS' share of the merchandising was increased from 10 to 45 percent and Byrne was on his way out of the picture.)

In New York, several thousand teenagers gathered to send off the Beatles. Despite the massive police force on hand, some one hundred Pan Am mechanics were drafted into guard duty. Loaded down with American records, clothes, and a $253,000 check from Capitol—their share of the 2.5 million records sold to date in the States—the Beatles headed for home. There was no doubt from any quarter: The Beatles had conquered America.

The impact of the Beatles' visit was enormous. Their success opened the provincially guilded gates of America to numerous other British pop bands. Once considered the scourge, British bands were now in hot demand; and American record executives, promoters, and entrepreneurs were traveling to England in search of the next Beatles. Although the Beatles and the Mersey sound were considered a fad, nearly every American record label jumped on the bandwagon. The British Invasion had begun. English rock bands were quickly signed up: the Dave Clark Five. The Rolling Stones. Manfred Mann. Freddie and the Dreamers. Herman's Hermits. Wayne Fontana and the Mindbenders, and many others. Because of the Beatles, the British were about to assume leadership in American pop music.

More important to the Beatles was the fact that the overwhelming success of the trip meant the time was right for a full, coast-to-coast concert tour of America. Following their first appearance on "The Ed Sullivan Show," Epstein had been besieged with other offers from booking agents, all eager to arrange an American tour. However he had already enlisted Norman Weiss, someone he respected

and knew he could trust. Even before the Beatles departed for London, the two men had started to map out plans.

Meanwhile, the Beatles' "strange celebrity," as *Time* magazine defined it, continued to intrigue the American media. The established powerhouse publications like *Life*, *Look*, *The Saturday Evening Post*, *Esquire*, *Time*, and *Newsweek* continued to produce an almost steady stream of articles trying to make sense of it all; while a few articles delved into the Beatles' individual personalities and, through Epstein, the business aspects of their success, the focus, for most part, remained primarily on the phenomenon, not the music. Those publications which did tackle critical analyses of the music usually condemned it. *Newsweek*, in its February 24 issue, offered this appraisal:

Musically, they are a near-disaster; guitars slamming out a merciless beat that does away with secondary rhythms, harmony and melody. Their lyrics (punctuated by nutty shouts of "yeah, yeah, yeah!") are a catastrophe, a preposterous farrago of Valentine-card romantic sentiments.

In March, *The Saturday Evening Post* likened the "Beatle Craze" to Davy Crockett, and predicted impending doom:

Crazes tend to die a horribly abrupt death. It was not so long ago, after all, that a good many unwary businessmen got caught with warehouses full of coonskin caps when the Crockett craze stopped almost without warning.

Beatlepeople scoffed at such predictions. How, they wondered, could so many experienced journalists not hear the music?

"The kids were onto us," remembers Ringo. "Nobody thought we were musicians until the [London] *Sunday Times* wrote about it. We were the ones on the records and we didn't understand what all this aeolian cadence stuff was about. We just played music and the kids were onto us. You can't fool the children—at least not all of the time."

There was, however, at least one bad omen which indicated that, perhaps, those predictions of doom were already coming true. On March 14 and 15, the closed-circuit film of the Beatles' Washington, D.C., Coliseum concert played in theaters across America. While closed-circuit had been utilized successfully with boxing events, the concept didn't catch on with the Beatles' show, and the venture flopped. Weiss was perplexed and disappointed with the closed-circuit venture.

The Beatles continued to dominate American record charts, however, and the bids for Beatle concerts were pouring into the GAC offices from promoters all across the country. "It was ludicrous," recalls Weiss. "We had fifty times as many offers as we could handle." It would be the largest-grossing tour in show business history—with a minimum of $20,000 per show required up front against 40 to 80 percent of the gate. It was an unheard-of amount of money to be asking—even Bob Hope was only getting $15,000 a performance, and he was at the top of the show biz heap—nevertheless promoters were confident that the Beatles would still draw huge crowds in five months. Weiss, along with Dan Cleary, based in GAC's Beverly Hills office, screened the offers based on the reputations of the promoters, the verification of venues—most of

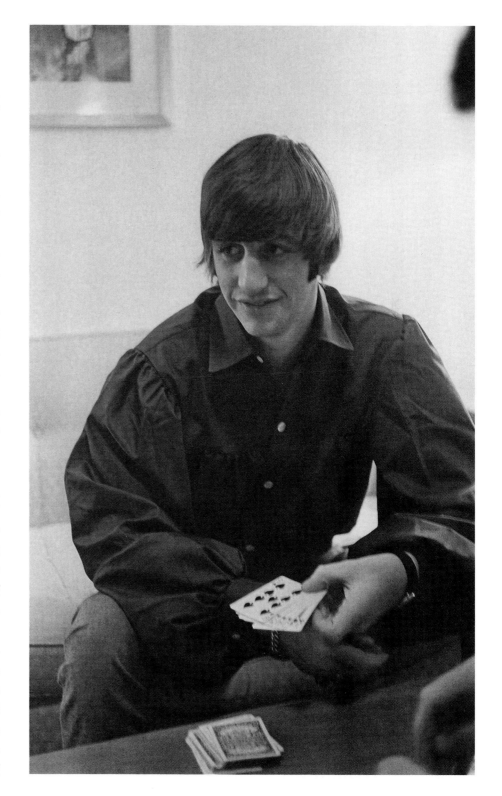

which ranged from seven to twenty thousand seats and had never hosted a rock show before—and the likelihood of ticket sellouts.

For some promoters, making the deal to present the Beatles was no small feat. "I had never done a concert before in my life," recalls then-KRLA disc jockey Bob Eubanks. "But when the Beatles came along and wanted $25,000 up front, plus 60 percent of the gross receipts over $40,000, the other concert promoters in town refused to pay that amount of money. Because I was on the radio, I could feel what was happening. But it was a catch-22, because the Hollywood Bowl said, 'You can't book the Bowl unless you have the Beatles,' and the Beatles' agents said, 'You can't book the Beatles if you don't have the Bowl.'" Eubanks finally pulled the two parties together by telephone and sealed the deal. To raise the $25,000 up front money, Eubanks went to the Security Pacific Bank in Woodland Hills, California, and asked for a loan using a house that he co-owned as collateral. "They literally asked us to leave," Eubanks says. "They told us we were crazy to ask for money for something like that." He finally ended up at a little storefront bank, Trans World, in the San Fernando Valley. "I walked up to this

George and Jackie DeShannon play Monopoly at the Lafayette Motor Inn, Atlantic City.

woman named Liz Miller and told her I wanted to present the Beatles at the Hollywood Bowl. She said, 'My son is a big Beatles fan.'" So Eubanks made the pitch and got the loan. The Beatles' show at the Hollywood Bowl was just a piece of paper away.

Meanwhile, in New York, "the logistics were a nightmare," says Weiss. The cities had to be chosen in a logical order so that the group could make the jumps between shows and with so many offers, a normally routine task for Weiss turned chaotic. Within a couple of weeks, however, he managed to coordinate offers and prepare a list of potential cities and venues, and cabled it to Brian Epstein in London. There, in the new NEMS offices on Argyll Street, just a few prestigious doors down from the London Palladium, Brian began sifting through the offers, as he poured over the recent market reports received from Capitol Records. "Brian wanted to go to the cities where the Beatles were selling the most records," says Weiss. "He was very concerned about this tour, because we just didn't know what was going to happen."

Contracts were drawn up by NEMS (which had been contracted to serve as producer for The Beatles, LTD., the corporation formed by Lennon, McCartney, Harrison, and Starr); and through GAC, which was contracted at 5 percent of the earnings to serve as the American booking agents, they were forwarded to the promoters. The contracts were essentially standardized—only the dollar amount required up front and the percentage guaranteed against the gate varied from city to city, depending on the capacity of the venue.

The contracts placed a ceiling of $5.50 on ticket prices. "Brian simply refused to allow the promoters to charge more," says Weiss. "He and the boys felt strongly about that age group of kids not being ripped off, and that was no small amount for that age group anyway. Everybody was looking to make a killing and they all assumed Brian wanted to make one too, but his main concern was always the number of records sold."

The contracts further stipulated that the promoters were to supply at least one hundred uniformed police officers at the show; furnish "a hi-fidelity sound system with an adequate number of speakers, four floor-stand Hi-Fi microphones with detachable heads and forty feet of cord for each microphone" as well as "a first-class sound engineer." The dimensions of the stage were required to be not less than twenty-five feet square and at least five feet high.

The promoters were also to provide the Beatles and the "entire cast" with "clean and adequate dressing room facilities." And, for the first time in a rock 'n' roll performance contract, Weiss and Epstein decided to add a rider that also required the promoter to provide "four cots, mirrors, an ice cooler, portable TV set and clean towels." It was done "out of necessity, not ego," says Weiss. "We were pretty sure that once we got them in, there wouldn't be any way for them to come and go as they pleased. They would have to stay put, maybe for some long hours." Additionally, the promoters were to provide two seven-passenger Cadillac limousines "air conditioned if possible" with chauffeurs for the Beatles. Aware of the racial segregation that existed in the American South, the Beatles requested the following clause: "Artists will not be required to perform before a segregated audience."

In exchange, NEMS would provide "the services of the Beatles plus complete supporting show."

By the end of March, as the Beatles finished filming and recording the soundtrack for their first movie, now titled *A Hard Day's Night*, the itinerary for the American tour was set. The itinerary, however, was only the beginning. Opening acts had to be hired and arrangements for transportation, accommodations, and police protection had to be secured. Since GAC was one of, if not *the*, leading booking agency for the music business, Weiss drew up a list of pop music acts he knew were available and thought would be appropriate. Brian and the Beatles settled on the chosen lineup: the Righteous Brothers, who had achieved notable success on the West Coast with a hit called "Little Latin Lupe Lu"; Jackie DeShannon, an up-and-coming young singer whose version of "When You Walk in the Room" had recently cracked the Hot 100; the Exciters, a three-woman, one-man group from Jamaica, New York, whose "Tell Him" had been a smash hit a couple of years back; and the Bill Black Combo, which had hit in the late fifties—Black used to back Elvis Presley—with six songs in the Top 20, among them "White Silver Sands." The Bill Black Combo would open the show with a couple of songs, then back the rest of the opening acts. (Black, however, would not be part of the touring lineup.) They were contracted on a weekly basis and paid accordingly. The Bill Black Combo received $1,500 a week; Jackie DeShannon, $1,250; the Exciters, $1,000; and the Righteous Brothers, $750.

With thirty-one performances in twenty-four cities, the only way to make the jumps would be by air. At first, commercial airlines were considered, but in light of the potential crowds and pandemonium, nobody really believed they could meet an airline's departure schedule. Instead they would have to charter an aircraft, something that had never been done on this scale before. American Flyers Airlines, a Dallas-based company that frequently transported armed forces personnel, was hired and a ninety-two-passenger Lockheed Electra II was reserved at a cost of around $75,000. American Flyers would meet the Beatles' entourage in San Francisco, carry them through the tour, and then drop them off in New York City. They would average 650 miles a day and fly as many as 1,670 in a single hop. Known as the "pilot's dream ship," the Electra II would cruise at 400 mph at altitudes high above turbulence, and with its jet-prop engines it could land at even small airports. "Again we did it out of necessity," recalls Weiss.

As for accommodations, Epstein and Weiss drew up a list of preferred first-class lodgings in the various cities for the Beatles, and for Brian, who usually stayed at a separate hotel. New York City-based Red Carpet Travel Service was enlisted to make the arrangements, along with hiring caterers where needed, and securing reasonably priced accommodations for the opening acts. When the desired hotels rejected the reservations, unwilling or unable

to deal with what came along with the Beatles—as happened several times—the entourage often ended up with whatever they could
get, which sometimes meant roadway-like
motels. "It's the most stimulating task I've
ever tackled," said a spokesman for Red
Carpet. "We have had some difficulty per-
suading the caterers from coast to coast that
we must have fresh supplies of corn flakes or
the tour will collapse."

The issue of police protection to and from
airports, hotels, and concert halls was crucial.
Weiss enlisted his aide, Ed Leffler, who had
served in the Army's counterintelligence corps,

as the tour's advance man and police liaison.
In nearly every city Leffler initially encountered a stock reaction: "Don't tell us how to
do our job. We've protected *presidents* before."
Leffler offered a stock retaliation: "How many
records has the President of the United States
sold?" It usually proved to be a point well
made.

Since the Beatles would be spending four
days in Los Angeles, Weiss turned to his old
colleague and friend, GAC agent Roy Gerber,
to find ways in which to entertain the Beatles
on the West Coast. Gerber, dubbed the tour's
social director, turned his immediate attention

to planning a post–Hollywood Bowl concert party. Not only would it celebrate the Beatles' show, but rock 'n' roll's entrance to a once sedate, sophisticated music arena.

By April, arrangements for the Beatles' tour of America had been finalized. The positions of tour managers, however, had yet to be filled and Weiss was working on that one.

Indianapolis.

From the British front, Neil Aspinall and Mal Evans, as always, would accompany the Beatles and Brian as road managers. Derek Taylor, a journalist who Epstein had hired to ghost-write his autobiography, *A Cellarful of Noise*, was brought on board as press officer, replacing Brian Sommerville. Additionally, Epstein hired Bess Coleman in New York to coordinate press details with Derek. Coleman,

who was British, had worked for EMI's press office in London and on the initial Beatles' campaign before moving to New York. During meetings about the American phase of the Beatles' upcoming world tour, Epstein established some inflexible rules: Absolutely no photographs with famous people and Taylor was not to "go mad" and have press conferences in every city. If, Epstein asserted, a press conference was "absolutely necessary," the promoters were to arrange and pay for it.

Over on Great Pulteney Street in Soho, the Beatles' tailor D. A. Millings, who made suits for Cliff Richard, the Everly Brothers, Bill Haley, the Four Tops, and the Temptations, among others, went to work on the wardrobe for the tour, with the assistance of his son Gordon. This time a classical Chesterfield design in dark gray and dark blue, with velvet collars, was chosen. The trousers, however, were designed to fit not classically but snugly. The suits—which earned their own notice from American journalists—were constructed from a lightweight wool and mohair, which effected a high sheen under stage lights. A half-dozen were ordered for each Beatle. "We'd always have to make extra trousers, though, because they quite often never came back from the cleaners," recalls Gordon Millings. Having a pair of Beatle pants was, most certainly, a priceless treasure. Their boots remained the same—Cuban heel, with an elastic side from Annello and David on Charing Cross Road.

The Beatles could have done a lot wrong following their overwhelmingly successful first trip to America. It would have been easy for them to ride the coattails of fame and churn out like-sounding hits, but John, Paul, George, and Ringo believed in their ability to progress and create as musicians. Despite their sudden worldwide acceptance, they seemed to have a sustaining respect for who they were. They were relatively unfazed by the storm that surrounded them. Success, as so many noted, did not go to their heads. Instead they concentrated on their work, and the end result was a continuous string of hits on record charts around the world. Their talent was becoming undeniable. In America, the Beatles had dominated the charts through the winter and well into spring. On April 4, "Can't Buy Me Love," the new single from the *A Hard Day's Night* soundtrack, moved into the Number One position on *Billboard*'s Hot 100 chart. The song established five chart records: (1) the largest advance sales—2,100,000 worldwide; (2) the greatest monopoly of the Hot 100, on March 28, with ten singles, surpassing the record number of nine set by Elvis Presley in December 1956; and fourteen as of April 11, surpassing their own record; (3) the greatest monopoly of the Top 5, with "Can't Buy Me Love," "Twist and Shout," "She Loves You," "I Want to Hold Your Hand," and "Please Please Me"; (4) the biggest leap to Number One, "Can't Buy Me Love," which jumped from 27 to 1 in a single week; and (5) most consecutive Number One singles, with "I Want to Hold Your Hand," "She Loves You," and "Can't Buy Me Love."

"The Beatles were selling *all* the records, so the rest of us in the record business were twiddling our thumbs, saying, 'What's goin' on here?' " says pop crooner Pat Boone. "It hardly made sense to go into the studio and record, since even *if* you got airplay, you were going to have to settle for lower sales. *None* of us were selling records for a while and that was a big liability." If he couldn't beat them, Boone decided he would join them. He secured a merchandising license to manufacture lithographs of oil paintings of the Beatles, and tied it into a promotional campaign. Each set was numbered, giving some thirty young fans across the country a chance to win a ticket to see the Beatles in Las Vegas. Sales numbered in the hundreds of thousands, and Boone cut his musical losses.

When tickets for the Beatles' show went on sale at the chosen venues across the country in mid-April, Beatlemania struck again. In most cities fans lined up the night before and many ticket offices were mobbed. Officials at the Hollywood Bowl, for example, had informed promoter Eubanks that it was "physically impossible" to sell out a show in one day. But just three hours after the Bowl's box office opened, in one of the most frantic rushes ticket sellers had ever witnessed, every last ticket was gone. Bowl officials were stunned. Eubanks hustled to make arrangements for a second show, but Epstein declined, uncertain if a second performance would sell out.

On June 4, as the Beatles began their world tour in Copenhagen, Denmark, the British Invasion was in full swing. The Dave Clark Five and the Rolling Stones were touring the States and Weiss wound up enlisting the tour managers of both—Ira Sidelle and Bob Bonis—for the Beatles' tour. Sidelle would be responsible for all box office and money matters. Bonis would oversee the physical details for the Beatles and their opening acts,

in essence making sure everyone was where they were supposed to be when they were supposed to be there.

The Beatles returned to London briefly on July 6, to attend the world premiere of *A Hard Day's Night* at the London Pavilion. Princess Margaret and Lord Snowdon were also in attendance and the crowd outside, estimated at twelve thousand, finally forced the closure of Piccadilly Circus. The following week, United Artists announced that the first pressing for the film's soundtrack would be two million in the United States alone. On August

1, *A Hard Day's Night* opened simultaneously in five hundred American theaters to full houses and, deservedly, to reviews that ranged from warm to radiant. Several film reviewers likened the Beatles to the Marx Brothers. No greater compliment could have been paid.

In the five months since the Beatles' first visit, conflict and a sense of imminent change had pervaded America, and the season had come to be known as the Long Hot Summer. On July 2, President Lyndon B. Johnson signed the most comprehensive civil rights act in U.S. history. It decreed, among other

Indianapolis.

things, that public accommodations were to be integrated and job discrimination based on sex, religion, or race was prohibited. Dr. Martin Luther King, Jr.'s work for civil rights had made racial equality a part of the American vocabulary and earned him a nomination (and ultimately the award) for the Nobel Peace Prize. Although the movement enlisted many young white as well as black Americans, things weren't moving fast enough for some blacks and race riots had recently erupted in New York City and Rochester. And the anger was spreading.

Then there was that "problem" in Southeast Asia. Intermittent filmed news reports of Vietnam began to creep into American living rooms via television. On August 2, Walter Cronkite on the "CBS Evening News" announced that a U.S. destroyer had been attacked by North Vietnamese PT boats in the Gulf of Tonkin. Two days later, the United States retaliated with "reprisal raids" that sent sixty-four bombers to North Vietnam; and, on August 7, Congress passed the Gulf of Tonkin Resolution, empowering the president to take military action in response to aggression against

63

U.S. forces and to support our allies, upon request, in Southeast Asia. Later reports would reveal that the United States had provoked the "attack" by accompanying South Vietnamese boats shelling North Vietnam to within ten miles offshore, and still later Americans would learn that the sunken North Vietnamese PT boats probably hadn't even fired a single shot while chasing the destroyer out to sea. Despite the gloss with which government propaganda hid the truth, the first real cries of the anti-war movement began. On the weekend following the Gulf of Tonkin reso-

lution, demonstrators, termed "young leftists" by the establishment and the media, marched in Times Square. Police arrested 38 people. Several demonstrators were knocked to the ground and dragged bleeding to police vans, while a crowd of about 250 spectators cheered.

On the other coast, the first "puff-in" to protest anti-marijuana laws occurred in San Francisco on August 16 when a lone demonstrator walked up to the information desk at the Hall of Justice, pulled out a "reefer," and lit up. Twenty-seven-year-old Lowell Eggemeier, who earlier had announced his in-

Indianapolis.

tentions of "turning on" within those hallowed marbled walls, was promptly led away to the prison upstairs.

In the meantime, Americans waited for the report on Kennedy's assassination from the specially formed Warren Commission. Had Lee Harvey Oswald acted alone? Inside word was already leaking out that the commission would conclude that he had. But New York *Journal-American* columnist Dorothy Kilgallen had obtained and printed a copy of the transcript of Jack Ruby's testimony, which lent credence to the conspiracy theory. Her

article would be picked up and printed by newspapers throughout America.

Violence. Misplaced values. Hidden truths. Hypocrisy. It just didn't feel like the land of the free and home of the brave anymore. An undercurrent of restlessness was flowing through American society. The kind of innocence that had blinded middle-class American childhood with bliss was on the run. Things were beginning to get weird.

Among American youth, a sociological revolution—or, perhaps, evolution—was underway and the Beatles, however unintention-

65

ally, had already contributed significantly to it. Since February, their "long hair" had become what was hip for the new generation, as well as a symbol of individual freedom and choice and of their rebellion against conservative American morality. For the vast majority of American adults, this hair business, British or not, wasn't cute anymore. And now it was perceived to be threatening the very fabric of American society. It was a sign of degeneration. And it was intolerable. Furthermore the Beatles had an irreverent attitude, part wit and part cheeky disrespect, that questioned rigid, uptight American values *and* questioned authority. The Beatles, through their music, their attitude, and their looks, were influencing as well as mirroring the restlessness of American youth. Shades of McCarthyism emanated from the religious right when the Christian Crusade warned American parents of what was termed the "Communist Beatle pact." As the Crusade's Dean Noebel put it: "The Communists have contrived an elaborate, calculating and scientific technique directed at rendering a generation of American youth useless through nerve-jarring mental deterioration and retardation." The generation gap was turning into an abyss and the predictions of the Beatles' impending demise loomed large for all kinds of reasons in both the British and American press.

Everyone but the fans wondered when the bubble would burst. The press was clamoring to write about it and most observers were betting that it would all come to a crashing halt very soon. In England, newspapers and magazines had been sizzling with headlines that breathed life into death-of-the-Beatles rumors. On Fleet Street, "Beatles Break Up" stories were a dime a dozen, as were articles on the "secret wedding" of Paul and British actress Jane Asher, because marriage was considered career suicide for a teen idol.

While America's established magazines and newspapers steered well clear of rumors or any innuendo that could not be confirmed, their articles were saturated with a sense of gloom and doom and adopted a moral stance that questioned the impact the Beatles were having on teenagers. Janey Milstead, then *TeenScreen* editor, says, "Contrary to popular belief, the Beatles were not a product of publicity. We were never lavished with material about the Beatles. It was scarce as hen's teeth, so the teen press relied on what we called 'creative talk.' " When *TeenScreen* published an article that claimed Paul was married, mail poured in—all of it negative. Milstead put her job on the line and wrote an apology. The response was overwhelmingly positive. "They were the most literate, intelligent letters I got from any kids in my life," says Milstead. "They seemed to be a special breed, different from the other kids. Those kinds of 'creative' stories didn't stop anywhere else, but they *did* stop in *TeenScreen*. It was truth and justice for the Beatles."

In August, with the release of *A Hard Day's Night* and the coming of the tour, the Beatles became Big News again in the American media as a whole. The powerhouse publications sought more intimate personal angles and every publication was seeking Beatle scoops. The competition was, in a word—vicious. "It got to the point with the media where it was, 'Okay, well now, what can we do? We've said everything there is to say about it, the only thing to do is knock it,' and so they knocked it," George Harrison says. "While everybody now talks about the Beatles being loved—we were loved one minute, then they hated our guts. One minute they were pattin' us on the back, the next minute they were stabbing us in the back."

As for the Top 40 radio, the Beatles were *the* story. In Los Angeles, KRLA dee-jay Dave Hull endeared himself to Beatle fans by being the first in the market to get a live interview with John and George during a stopover at LAX while they were en route to a Hawaiian vacation. But he was getting desperate for new Beatle news. "I decided that in order to answer the questions before anyone else, I would have to make up the rumors," he recalls. So Hull went on the air night after night with the latest inside Beatlenews: "There's no truth to the rumor that Ringo has cancer. . . ." And the same thing was happening up and down the radio dial in city after city after city.

It was the oldest journalistic trick in the book and columnists Walter Winchell and Louella Parsons were forever hearing from a source that Paul was secretly married or that Ringo was "deathly ill" or that John was "definitely" leaving the group. Truth just didn't seem to matter at all. In one column, Winchell told his readers that he had spoken with the promoter of the Beatles' Hollywood Bowl concert and indeed there would be a second show. When promoter Eubanks read

the column he picked up the phone and called Winchell at the Hotel Ambassador. "Mr. Winchell," Eubanks began, "I'm a great admirer of yours. In fact, I used to listen to you on the radio when I was a kid and I read your column today. You see, I'm the promoter of the Beatles' show, and the truth is there *isn't* going to be a second show. I just thought you

should know. . . ." The response he got blew him away: "Go to hell, *kid!*" Winchell yelled. The next thing he heard was a dial tone. "It was journalistic whoring and everybody," says Eubanks, "was doing it."

It seemed ironic that one of the most insightful and entertaining articles written since the Beatles' arrival on the American scene would launch them into a full-blown

Indianapolis.

Indianapolis.

religious controversy. In an August edition of *The Saturday Evening Post*, there was a piece called "Summer Madness: The Beatles Are Back" written by Alfred G. Aronowitz, the first American journalist to establish a relationship with the band. In the article their press officer, Derek Taylor, provided a quote that offended religious leaders across the country, and had them on their knees, praying for the salvation of America's youth. "It's as if they've founded a new religion. They're completely anti-Christ . . . so anti-Christ they shock me. . . ." It seared straight to the moral heart of American culture.

If things weren't tenuous enough, the Beatles were now being challenged on the American record charts by some of the groups that had followed in their wake. The Rolling Stones had already garnered a strong base of fans and were being touted by many as England's new favorite band. Gerry and the Pacemakers and Billy J. Kramer and the Dakotas, both also part of the Epstein stable, and the Animals and Herman's Hermits and the Dave Clark Five and Freddie and the Dreamers all had hit records, some of which were faring better than some of the Beatles' vinyl offerings.

When would the bubble burst?

AS THE STORM of speculation, impending doom, competition, and religious controversy thundered around them, the Boeing 707 banked into its final descent to Los Angeles International Airport, and the Beatles, along with Brian Epstein and Neil Aspinall, began gathering up newspapers, magazines, notebooks, "ciggies," and playing cards and stuffing them into pockets and flight bags. This was it. The Great American Adventure was about to begin. They would clear U.S. Customs in Los Angeles, then reboard and head north to San Francisco, where the tour would officially begin tomorrow night at the Cow Palace.

The potential for disaster was lurking around every corner. But things had been moving way too fast for any of the Beatles to dwell on the negative or even to stand back and objectively consider what it all meant, or could mean. Their style was not to take anything—particularly their fame—too seriously. Although they were always apprehen-sive about crowds, they harbored no fears about America. It was the musical promised land, the birthplace of rock 'n' roll, home to nearly all of their major influences.

And they certainly didn't suffer from any delusions. The Beatles had never really expected their success to last very long anyway. "Maybe five years," Lennon had optimistically predicted during an interview back home. They knew full well that the music business held no guarantees. Anything could happen anytime. What they didn't know was that something already had. The tour hadn't even begun, but, in the City of Angels anyway, their "plans," as the Los Angeles *Times* so aptly reported on this particular morning, "were coming apart at the seams . . ."

LOS ANGELES, CALIFORNIA

AUGUST 18, 1964:

Just five days before the Beatles' scheduled arrival in Los Angeles to perform at the Hollywood Bowl, the prestigious Hotel Ambassador had canceled their August 22–26 reservations. "After exploring all possible measures that might be taken, it would be impossible to ensure protection for the Beatles, the hotel guests or the teenage Beatle fans," hotel manager Fred J. Hayman said in a statement issued to the press. If that wasn't enough, Lockheed Airport, a private facility where the Beatles' chartered jet had been scheduled to land on Sunday, was now denying them clearance because officials didn't want "teenagers ruining the airport." And this was L.A., home and host to celebrities and news-makers of every status.

The article in the *Times* gave no hint of the Beatles' scheduled arrival to clear U.S. Customs, but Beatlepeople never relied on newspapers for information. AM Radio. That was the lifeline. In Los Angeles, there were two pop stations—KFWB and KRLA—and the competition was bitter. KFWB had long been ranked Number One in the market, but now with KRLA's Bob Eubanks promoting the concert, KRLA was moving in for the kill, proclaiming itself the official Beatles station. Just before noon, the Big News of the day broke—on KRLA.

"Hey! All you Beatlepeople listenin' out there— Today is B-Day! That's right! And you heard it here first—on your official Beatles station. The Beatles are wingin' in from London on Pan Am Airlines and they'll be landin' out at International Airport at about four o'clock . . . they have to clear customs here first. . . ." The word was out. Within minutes, KFWB was on the air with its own version of the announcement, and within the hour it was picked up as news by other stations. A Beatles secret could not be kept—especially if a radio station stood to gain the highest audience share.

The infiltration of International Airport began around noon. Beatlepeople arrived, decked out in flowered shifts, stretch pants, shorts, madras blouses, T-shirts, and cut-offs, and claimed territory cluster by cluster near the boarding counter or against the windows that overlooked the docking bay where the Boeing 707 would be towed to rest. Music blasted from transistor radios that formed the nucleus of every cluster. Knobs spun up and down the dials. Tinny, crackling sounds of Top 40 melodies, mostly the Beatles' new songs from *A Hard Day's Night*, interspersed with such songs as the Supremes' "Baby Love," the Searchers' "Needles and Pins,"

Elvis' "Viva Las Vegas," and the Beach Boys' latest, "I Get Around," battled for command of the airspace with the speedy patter of the dee-jays. The sounds careened off the rotunda walls, producing a chaotic audio bounce that echoed throughout the terminal. It was the last place any adult wanted to enter, but newsmen and photographers braved heat and humanity, waiting for their story to drop out of the sky. As the crowd grew, the temperature inside rose into the nineties and airport officials placed emergency calls for extra security. The smell of sweat hung in the air. Surges of adrenaline shot through the crowd.

By 3 P.M., Pan Am's waiting areas had swelled to capacity. Beatlepeople and newspeople had assumed command of the entire rotunda, causing delays and confusion. Through the crowd blocking the counter, Hollywood's reigning couple, Richard Burton and Elizabeth Taylor, emerged all but unnoticed. The couple surveyed the scene with wide-eyed bemusement. They were accustomed to crowds, but this, well . . . this was something else. Newsmen, with about a dozen fans falling in line behind them, approached the newlyweds tossing out the obligatory questions. The Burtons were on their way to Puerto Vallarta for a vacation. Their marriage? It would last "for a while," said Burton. "For fifty years," Taylor corrected, smiling. Standing up on her tiptoes, Taylor looked beyond the immediate group that had gathered around them, and saw the still-growing multitude in the rotunda. "The Beatles," one of the reporters confessed. Taylor looked at the newsman: "Oh?" As the Burtons headed toward their departure gate,

Elizabeth squeezed her husband's arm. "Gosh," she whispered, "they make us look like Mickey Mouse."

At 4:15 P.M., Pan Am's Boeing 707, dubbed "The Beatles Clipper," touched down. Inside the first class cabin, the Beatles applauded, as they usually did—flying made them all, George in particular, nervous and memories of Buddy Holly's fate always lingered.

In the terminal, the Beatlepeople, numbering near one thousand, screamed and cried and shouted with glee, blowing away all predictions that the Beatles' popularity was diminishing. They jumped and strained to better their view as the plane taxied toward the docking bay. Though this was a smaller crowd than the ones that had greeted the Beatles in February in New York and Miami, these kids had gathered on short notice and their enthusiasm more than made up for any lack of numbers. "We want the Beatles! We want the Beatles!" The chant was always the same, always roared in loud and fevered pitches. Beatlepeople scrambled and pushed for a better vantage point. "Adults were driven out of the rotunda in search of asylum," the *Times*' Jack Smith would later report. A line of LAPD officers formed to further block access to the windows after the weight against the panes became dangerous. "It scares you," puffed the lieutenant in charge of security detail. "It's just beyond me. I've *never* seen anything like this."

One by one, Ringo, George, Paul, and John disembarked from the plane. Looking up, almost in unison, they saw the fans pressed

Indianapolis.

against the windows. They smiled and waved. Then they were gone. Airport security had arranged for the Beatles to go from their plane, through an outside doorway, into customs and then into another room hastily set up for the press, without ever passing within reach of the fans.

Inside the rotunda, reporters and photographers were hurriedly assembled and escorted through a side door in a cordoned-off area. Fans began pushing forward into the police line, some sobbing, others shouting or screaming hysterically. To be this close and not get any more than a glimpse seemed inconceivable. Their wails and pleadings resounded on the other side of the wall where the Beatles casually talked with members of the local press.

The temperature inside the waiting room

rose to an oppressive 110 degrees with the camera lights. The Beatles sat behind two folding tables facing thirteen microphones and some thirty—mostly uncomprehending—newsmen. The impromptu press conference proved awkwardly amiable.

"Where will you stay now that the Ambassador has canceled your reservations?"

"I—I don't know," said John hoarsely, caught off-guard as he tried to peel off his sport coat and loosen his tie. "We only just found out about that ourselves. So, what's the weather been like 'ere?"

"Hot," several reporters answered.

"And San Francisco?"

"Hot. But cooler than here."

"What about being denied landing clearance at Lockheed Airport, did you know about that?" another newsman asked.

"Not until *now*," said Paul.

"Are you guys going to Disneyland?"

"I don't know," replied George. "But if we do, we'll do it secretly."

"John, is there any truth to the rumor that you're quitting the band?"

John heaved a sigh. "No, there's not. We keep sayin' it. We keep denying it. It's all just lies. Do you think you could straighten them out?"

As they spoke, GAC's Roy Gerber was already looking for a place for the Beatles to stay when they returned in five days, and American Flyers' personnel were negotiating with LAX for landing clearance. It would all, they knew, be taken care of, and right now the Beatles were too beat to be concerned. They'd been on the plane for fifteen hours. At 5:20 P.M., they boarded the Boeing 707 once again for the last short hop into San Francisco.

Indianapolis.

SAN FRANCISCO

The crowd of five thousand awaiting the Beatles' arrival at San Francisco International Airport wiped the sweat from their faces and the dust from their eyes, and jockied for position. A few of the younger Beatlepeople were mashed against the steel mesh walls that enclosed them.

Some had begun assembling twenty-eight hours earlier, as San Mateo County sheriffs and San Francisco County lawmen were huddled in strategy meetings with Derek Taylor and Mal Evans, who had just arrived. Moments after the Beatles landed, a San Mateo sheriff's deputy was standing before Mal and Derek, shouting something about getting the Beatles out of the airport area as quickly as possible, and declaring that in *no* way were they going to foul up the safety regulations and law and order of San Mateo County. They couldn't believe anyone could shout so loud and both Derek and Mal were intimidated. "There will be a great many people waiting here for them," Derek began in his ever calm, diplomatic style, "and if we don't do something, there *will* be trouble." The deputy snarled. "*Don't* tell *me* what my job is or there *will* be *trouble!*" Derek and Mal looked at each other, then back at the deputy. This wasn't going to be easy.

At the new Hilton Hotel, employees prepared for the Invasion. (The plush Fairmont Hotel, though initially accepting the Beatles' reservations, had just backed out and Hilton officials, knowing that the Beatles spelled publicity, had warmly accepted them.) As part of the Beatle briefing, thirteen department heads were sent to the New Royal Theater to see *A Hard Day's Night.* The Hilton security staff was increased, and SFPD officers were also assigned hotel duty. A special "Beatles Headquarters" was set up in the hotel, including a command post for Beatles Fan Club brass. In celebration of the occasion, the Hilton Hotel Gazebo Room chefs had even created Beatle Burgers—four open-faced little hamburgers (the size of silver dollars) topped, mop-like, with shredded lettuce. Priced at eighty cents an order, they were "already selling like hotcakes."

Meanwhile, back at the airport, the steam had dissipated, and the San Mateo sheriff's deputies agreed to a compromise. They would cordon off a twenty-five-foot square area on a little used grassy field, about a mile northwest of the main airport terminal, and construct a sort of corral around it with four-foot-high steel mesh fencing. They would build a corridor in the middle of it, through which the Beatles would pass, supposedly out of reach of the fans. And they dubbed it "Beatleville."

In the hours before the Beatles' arrival in San Francisco, a squealing skirmish broke out between the local Beatles Fan Club and the combined forces of the Oakland and peninsula clubs. Deputy Mike Dow tried to keep the peace for a couple of hours by playing Beatles records on the public address system, but tensions were mounting. As sheriff's deputies ordered the waiting fans to move back from the walls of Beatleville, the local girls—who had organized themselves as "Beatle Bobbies"—decided to issue their own orders. That triggered a loud and negative response. When the pushing and shoving turned rowdy, Dow threatened to play Elvis Presley records, and tempers finally cooled. An evangelical group arrived, in direct response to the recent *Saturday Evening Post* article, and began to picket the fans with signs that read: "Beatle Worship Is Idolatry," and "Beatles Make Fools of the Children Because of the Delinquent, Ungodly Parents." They feared for the future of America. Deputies, however, feared for their safety and escorted them away.

The Hilton, meanwhile, had been surrounded by some four thousand fans since midafternoon and the lobby was teeming with young girls, and cops. Two dozen police, private detectives, and hotel security guards were roaming through the lobby and upper corridors. Hotel maid Augustine Lewis heard screams coming from one room on the sixth floor as she was tending to her duties and thought nothing much about it. It had been happening all day. Everywhere, on every floor the sound of shrieking was heard. But when she returned to the room at three-thirty to conduct one of two daily inspections of the room, she found Gertrude Goodman, fifty, a former Army nurse, sprawled unconscious on the floor. Goodman had been slugged with a pistol, knocked unconscious and robbed of $80, credit cards, and the keys to her tan '63 Ford station wagon. She had come into town to visit her husband—in the hospital. Goodman regained consciousness and was rushed to the hospital, where she was listed in stable condition.

At 6:25 P.M., the Beatles stepped out of the Boeing 707 and into a waiting black limousine. Several hundred yards away, the Beatlepeople rocked Beatleville with, as the San Francisco *Chronicle* put it, "the sort of demonstration that used to win Academy Awards for Bette Davis." As the limousine neared the pen, Derek, concerned about the flimsy corridor through Beatleville, asked, "Do you really want to do this?" They looked out the windows. "Come on, fellas," Ringo shouted, flinging open the door, "Let's give it a go."

The Beatles bounded into the pen. The walls of Beatleville began to shake, rattle, and sway. A deputy sheriff grunted as he leaned against one side of the fence. "If this gives way, we're all dead!" he shouted. The crowd surged again, and again, kicking up dust. Several young kids were literally smashed up against the fence, unable to move, paralyzed by the crush of bodies against them. More deputies than had manned the recent Republican Convention were on hand, but they were losing ground fast. Less than twenty seconds later, the Beatles narrowly escaped. "It was a disaster," Derek recalls. "They boxed the Beatles in and they boxed the kids in and then the pen got so surrounded that rather than being a channel in—a way in and

Indianapolis.

way out—they got locked into a boxing ring and the crowd was coming in around them. But I never saw anything so skilled as John, Paul, George, and Ringo. From the first time I saw them, they knew how to move through crowds and were always very good, very coordinated. They never lingered or loitered. They had a very fast loping stride and if the police didn't get in their way, they always got through. It was—heads down and whoosh, gone!"

On the freeway leading into San Francisco, hundreds of fans, perched atop nearly every overpass, waving signs of welcome and "luv." At 7:08 P.M., the Beatles' limousine approached the Hilton from a side entrance on O'Farrell Street, where only a dozen or so lucky fans were on guard. As it slowed to a stop, the doors swung open. The Beatles sprinted into the hotel and to a service elevator that took them up to the fifteenth floor. They headed into their suite, tired and hungry. In most hotels on the tour, the Beatles would share a two-bedroom suite. In the better hotels, such as the San Francisco Hilton, their suite would usually feature a central living room with a bedroom flanking each side. Paul and George, both of whom tended to value their sleep more, shared one bedroom, with Ringo and John in the other. The living room could be used as a hospitality room for members of the press and invited guests, but the Beatles

75

Indianapolis.

would always have the freedom to leave, even if the guests didn't. Brian Epstein always took separate quarters, often in a different hotel. The opening acts were, for the most part, booked into different, less expensive hotels. For a couple of stops, however, Brian had decided to book an entire floor, to accommodate the entire cast and crew of the Beatles Show.

Downstairs in the lobby, fans refused to believe they'd missed the Beatles' entrance. At 7:20 P.M., a police officer announced that they were in their rooms and would not be making a public appearance. Pandemonium ensued, culminating in a mad dash for the elevators.

Later, after a shower and something to eat, the Beatles snuck down the service elevator and into another room for a press conference. They lined up behind a cluster of microphones, and began to pantomime a dance to music that only they heard. "Do we go to the barber?" Ringo repeated the first question. "Why certainly we do. We go every three weeks regularly."

"Is your hair wind-blown or not?"

"I took a shower, that's all," said John.

"Why is John the only married Beatle?"

"We all get married in the end," replied Ringo.

"How long do you expect Beatlemania to keep up?"

"That's a hard question to answer. We all feel fit," said Ringo.

"I have just written *Snow White and the Seventy Warts*," interjected Lennon. The Beatles began dancing again. Suddenly there was a rumbling. Everyone stared at the sliding panel doors behind the Beatles. They opened. A group of young girls stood staring, momentarily dumbstruck. Then—they screamed. The Beatles ran out another door, into the nearest service elevator, and back to their rooms, where they lounged on their beds and listened to the radio.

Back in the press room, photographer Curt Gunther cornered Derek Taylor. "Joe Louis is out to get me," he said. Gunther inhaled long and hard on his menthol cigarette, then snickered. Derek was amused, and impressed. It worked. Curt had commandeered his attention, and conversation began. Before it was over, the proposition was laid out: Gunther wanted to join the tour, but what with all the crowds and insanity, he wanted to ride along on the Beatles' plane. How else could he be assured of getting to each place on time to cover the story? "So what'll it take?" Curt stared Derek in the eye, bolstering it with a long, long look. He had a way of convincing people to do things they really didn't want to do. Derek agreed to talk with Epstein and let him know later.

Brian had a special, and very exclusive, relationship with the Beatles. "He often told me that his ideal state was to be alone with the four of them backstage," recalls Derek. "Just the five of them. And no one else. He was always terribly nervous that the boys might not approve of people he'd chosen for whatever tasks and sometimes that was the case. They would get on him, get very cheeky and all that, you know, 'Get rid of that cock, Brian. We can't *stand* him!'"

Still, this was the American tour and several British newsmen were already part of the traveling entourage—Ivor Davis of the *Daily Express*, who would also wind up ghosting George's special column on the American tour for the paper, and his photographer Bill Lovelace; Ian Smith of the London *Observer*; George Harrison, Sr., of the Liverpool *Echo*;

Indianapolis.

Tony Delano of the *Daily Mirror*; and Chris Hutchins from *Melody Maker*. In addition, Americans Larry Kane, news director for Miami's big Top 40 station WFUN, and disc jockey Jim Stagg from Cleveland's KYW, who was temporarily filling in for the news director,

Art Schreiber, while Schreiber wrapped up coverage of the Democratic National Convention in Atlantic City, and Hollywood freelancer Ron Joy had also secured passage on the tour. Derek pressed Gunther's case as important press coverage. By the end of the evening, Gunther had his berth on the plane—for a cost of $2,500, to cover transportation and hotels.

By midnight, all but a few scattered bundles of fans had gone home. Those that remained spent the night riding the elevators up to the fifteenth floor only to be blocked from exiting, and sent back down to the lobby.

SAN FRANCISCO

AUGUST 19, 1964:

Just before 2 A.M., Norman Weiss, John, Ringo, and Derek snuck out of the hotel and headed for a secluded bar in Chinatown for a late Chinese meal and drinks. All but Norman tossed a few back rather quickly, trying to relax. "I was not sober, but not entirely drunk either," recalls Taylor. "None of us remembered much about it, but we had a wonderful time." At the bar was Dale Robertson, the star of the hit TV series "Wells Fargo." The show was enormously successful in England, so there at the bar sat someone who had long been, as Taylor put it, "a remote and wonderful star, a cowboy actor." The Beatles had become household names, but deep down inside they were still, in Taylor's words, "as provincial as could be." The bar was all but empty, so John, Ringo, and Derek sat there for a couple of hours, drinking and talking with Robertson, indulged by Weiss. Meeting the star of "Wells Fargo" seemed an appropriate beginning to the Great American Adventure. There was, as there always seemed to be, a girl in the picture. "She really wanted to be with us," remembers Derek. "And I didn't want any trouble like that." At 4:30 A.M. they slipped back into the hotel, followed some paces behind by the girl, who had somehow lost her shoes and insisted they were in the limousine. While Weiss attended to the matter, Derek, John, and Ringo headed up to their rooms and collapsed.

By mid-morning, some two thousand fans had congregated around the Hilton Hotel. Hundreds stood on the concrete plaza just off Taylor Street and stared steadfastly at the windows above, some chanting, others calling the Beatles' names. The Beatles' suite, however, was on the other side of the hotel. The local newspapers carried stories on the Beatles' arrival on the front page, along with the announcement that American military strength in Vietnam had reached 17,200 men in a buildup expected to reach 21,000.

Inside the Hilton, at least two fans got through the human barricades and up to the Beatles' central hospitality room. The two were Joby Gordon and Cris Harris, who managed to convince "an old lady" to forge a note from Cow Palace promoter Paul Catalana; she then accompanied them through hotel officials and police security to be received by Paul McCartney himself. On their way out, Paul let Cris hold his hand. And, she bubbled, "One of the girls got to touch his hair."

At 6:45 P.M., the Beatles took the elevator to the garage and got into a limousine. The driver squealed out onto the streets, and raced past the crowd. "One of our biggest worries was that somewhere along the line someone might get hit by the car," says Ed Leffler. "Most of the time, the driver had an obstructed view at best. Kids literally hurled themselves on top of the car."

Outside the Cow Palace scalpers hung in the shadows, asking $25 to $45 each for $6.50 tickets. The $5.50 ceiling price had already begun to be altered by the promoters on an individual basis. At the entrances, ticket-takers wore Beatle wigs. Many looked more like Moe than like Ringo, George, John, or Paul. The crowd had begun to file into the area as early as 5 A.M. By 7 P.M. the Palace was filled, with the show scheduled to start at 8 P.M.

The Bill Black Combo played a couple of songs first, then backed the Exciters, the Righteous Brothers, and Jackie DeShannon through their sets. Nobody at the Cow Palace wanted to see any group or singer but the Beatles, and their restlessness was not only evident—it was blatant. Several times, chanting broke out: *"We want the Beatles! We want the Beatles!"* It served, acknowledged or not, as an omen for the opening acts. For those in the audience, including the parents who had accompanied their children and were hoping this would all be over soon, waiting for the Beatles to come onstage was pure agony. The intermission was almost welcomed.

In their trailer backstage, the Beatles were introduced to folksinger Joan Baez and they talked, about music mostly. Later they gave a press conference, and Derek Taylor was confronted by numerous "young girls with braces" brandishing press cards and seeking admittance. This would happen throughout the tour, as he soon would learn. One of the teen magazines, *Datebook*, offered its readers, for the price of a stamp, press cards, and the status of being a *"Datebook* reporter." "My training was really—from the cradle to the grave—to be polite to people and here were these nice kids who undoubtedly bought Beatle records and they did, indeed, have press cards and they were, really, much more valid than a lot of these nasty journalists who didn't know or care about the music or the Beatles," recalls Taylor. He liked the *Datebook* kids, but they were, he admits, "a nuisance." Not only did they irritate the professional working journalists by taking up space and time, but they asked "baby" questions. Taylor solved the problem by allowing the *Datebook* kids in on a standing-room-only basis.

It was their third meeting with the press since arriving in the States twenty-four hours before, and their characteristic zip and wit remained somewhat elusive, in the throes of jet lag.

"Please don't throw jellybeans—they're dangerous," Ringo said.

"Do the Beatles have pillow fights?" asked another press card-carrying teenager.

"No, we don't," said Ringo.

"Do you plan to stay together?" asked a *Datebook* reporter.

"I don't know. We might get fed up," responded John.

During the intermission, a sheriff's deputy spotted Shirley Temple in the audience, and escorted her party backstage to meet the Beatles. "I had not asked to go back, because I *really* didn't think there was a chance for such a thing," recalls Hollywood's most famous child star. Backstage, Temple and eight-year-old daughter Lori broke Epstein's inflexible rule about celebrity photographs. The uproar among the photographers as to who would document this historic occasion resulted in Temple's husband, Charles Black, being chosen for the honor.

As the Beatles took the stage, at 9:29 P.M., dressed in their dark blue suits, it seemed as though a summer lightning storm had hit the Palace: Thousands of flashbulbs popped, lighting up the entire arena. The high-frequency sound of young girls shrieking and screaming drowned out the music and jellybeans dropped like hailstones on the stage. Since the stage was surrounded by seats, and fans were on all sides, Ringo was pelted regularly from behind. Recalls McCartney: "We'd step in them and they'd stick to our guitar leads and our shoes. The kids must've thought I was trying out new dance

steps, but I was always just trying to get unstuck. And—we didn't even eat them!" The show was momentarily stopped twice when an announcer ran onstage and pleaded, "You're hurting the Beatles!" The jellybeans then fell to an occasional drizzle and the Beatles ripped through ten songs in thirty-one minutes. The girls, outnumbering boys ten to one, stood on their chairs, waved their arms, screamed, stamped their feet, burst into tears, and a few even fainted. Fainting was a sort of fad in some parts of the country, though some genuinely did pass out from truly being overwhelmed by it all. While the Beatles were onstage, at least one deputy sheriff was still smiling: "You can figure it this way—that's sixteen thousand kids who aren't out stealing hubcaps." A dozen or so required attention at the first-aid stations that had been set up inside the Palace. One boy dislocated his shoulder, but most of the other patients suffered from bruises or hyperventilation.

At 10:02, it was all over. The Cow Palace had been filled to capacity—17,130 tickets sold. The Beatles' show grossed $91,670, beating by $40,000 the previous palace record set by Chubby Checker in January 1962. The net take came to $49,800.00.

Following the show, two limousines raced from the back of the arena, with hundreds of girls chasing behind them. The Beatles, however, were still in their dressing rooms. They had decided to go on to Las Vegas that night, rather than waiting for daylight. Paul, for one, was all for moving on, preferring to wake up in the city in which they were to play that day. They left one hour later—in an ambulance—and went directly to the airport. After

Indianapolis.

waving good-bye to several thousand fans, they boarded the American Flyers Electra II, which would carry them throughout the tour.

Local caterers had been hired in each city, and as they boarded the plane that night, they were greeted by stewardesses dressed in white, topped with pillbox hats, and a spread of food and plenty of Scotch, Coke, and bourbon. Something of a ritual began that night. They headed for the rear of the plane, which was reserved for them, and ordered food and drinks. Then, since this was their first flight on the aircraft, they started to check it out. "What's this for, then?" George asked a stewardess pointing to a rope ladder in one of the overhead racks. Just in case of an emergency landing, she replied. George looked at the rope. It couldn't have been more than a couple of meters long. "I guess this means we'll be flying comfortably at ten feet then?"

It would take an hour or so for their equipment and the opening acts to arrive, and meanwhile they would have dinner. Most evenings they would drink, talk, read, play music, poker or blackjack, depending on the night and the mood. The traveling press were told not to intrude on the Beatles' privacy. The plane was their sanctuary, even if it didn't feel too safe at times. That's not to say that there wouldn't be some rock 'n' roll nights. Tonight was one. It was the beginning of the tour, something to be toasted, and everyone was overindulging. With all the new faces on board there were further introductions and unfinished conversations that would keep everyone up for the next few flights.

LAS VEGAS, NEVADA

AUGUST 20, 1964:

At 1:45 A.M., twelve hours ahead of schedule, the Beatles' jet touched down at a remote section of the airfield, out by the old terminal at McCarran Field. "Mum" was the word at the airport, and the Beatles' arrival was a smoothly maneuvered one. Only a handful of girls were waiting at the new terminal and they missed the Beatles completely. Even Las Vegas *Sun* reporters found "an iron curtain of silence," and "secrecy worthy of a visit by Khrushchev," and couldn't get airport officials to break their silence. But one guard had accidentally dropped a hint and as the Beatles emerged from the plane, local photographers were there to greet them. The Beatles were quickly hustled into waiting limousines and under the cover of darkness pulled up to the Sahara Hotel.

But they would not escape so easily that night. Word of their early arrival had gotten out and a crowd that grew to an estimated two thousand was waiting for them at the Sahara. At 2:30 A.M., the Beatles were quickly ushered in through a back door, taken to a waiting freight elevator, and deposited in Suite 4722. Ringo went immediately to the TV set. Paul flopped down on one of the beds. John and George went into another of the suite's rooms to look for something to eat. On every floor there were small groups of running, screaming girls, searching for the Liverpudlians. Elevator doors popped open, and, just as in San Francisco, security guards closed them back up the way they'd arrived, filled with grinning teenage ingenues. Epstein quickly cleared the suite of outsiders. Exhausted, drained from the Nevada heat and still feeling the effects of jet lag, the Beatles settled in for the night and tried to sleep through the screams rising from the war being waged in the lobby below.

"If the Viet Cong had laid siege to the hotel, it might have been more welcome," reported the *Sun*'s City Editor Dave Bradley. Bands of young people charged at doors blocked by policemen and tried to break through. Others tried to bribe reporters for their press cards. Fans shouted for their favorite Beatle as if he just might magically appear: "Ringo-*o-o*." "Johnee-*e-e*." "Paaa-ull-ul." "George-*e-e*." The names echoed throughout the casino and up and down the elevator shafts as someone kept paging them over the hotel's intercom system. Through all this, the constant chant of *"We want the Beatles! We want the Beatles!"* acted as a sort of "white noise."

Throughout the day, reinforcements armed with binoculars and transistors arrived to wait in the scorching 100-plus-degree desert heat for a glimpse, a nod, a wave, or a wink from a Beatle. Hundreds of sheriff's deputies and city police formed human barricades or patrolled the Sahara grounds to prevent the Beatlepeople from infiltrating the tower where the Beatles' suite was located. Capitol's Dave Dexter arrived with his daughter. He had planned on taking her to the Convention Center show and hoped to introduce her. It was a mission unaccomplished. "I was so stupid," says Dexter. "There were so many thousands of people. There were dogs running around barking. It was a wild, hot, hot day. And there was just no chance of getting in through that crowd."

After a brunch of tea and corn flakes, the Beatles risked the odds on two slot machines, which had been brought up to them since it was virtually impossible for them to go to the casino. They took turns putting in dimes and pulling the lever. None of them, however, won anything, and they quickly tired of the game.

Surrounded by police escorts, the Beatles left the Sahara for the Las Vegas Convention Center around 3 P.M., successfully eluding the crowd as they were hustled into the hall. Since two shows were scheduled—at 4 P.M. and 8 P.M.—the normal two-hour length of each show was shortened by twenty minutes, although the line-up remained the same. Both shows had sold out, each drawing a capacity

85

crowd of about seven thousand. Both shows induced the screams, hails of jellybeans, and flashbulb lightning that were now trademarks of American Beatlemania. More than one hundred security guards, some from as far away as Phoenix, served to keep the crowds more or less orderly.

Liberace, who was opening at the Riviera, showed up for the matinee, dressed in a light gray Eaton-style suit, similar to the ones popularized by the Beatles. After the show, he went backstage to meet them. Since the "no celebrities backstage" rule seemed destined to be broken, as it had been in San Francisco, Taylor made a decision: "If I could slip it to the boys and they accepted, fine. We wouldn't keep them out. And Liberace was really very, very nice. He came up and simply said, 'I want to meet these young artists who are doing such amazing things.' " While introductions and meetings continued to annoy Brian, they were becoming, for Taylor, unavoidable. No matter where they went there would always be some celebrity or VIP who had special wants or needs or rights of entry.

Pat Boone also showed up backstage, with copies of his Beatles lithographs in hand. During his conversation with the boys, he showed them the prints. "What's all this?" Paul asked, pointing to his fingers which, when the original group photograph had been taken, had been holding a cigarette, but now were hanging idly in the air. "I think the artist Leo Janssen, took it upon himself to make the change, anticipating that I wouldn't have wanted to merchandise a picture of anybody smoking," says Boone. Paul wrinkled

his eyebrows. "Well, Pat, you know if we smoke, we smoke."

"WE BROUGHT WITH our records an overall image," recalls Ringo. "We were the first ones in rock 'n' roll that didn't kid the kids about drinking milk and America was shocked. 'A Scotch and Coke?' they'd ask. 'On TV and radio?' And we'd go, 'Yeah, a Scotch and Coke.' Or smoking: 'You can't *smoke!*' We came along and I think that our public understood that we were just honest lads and it got us into trouble sometimes, but we didn't give in to the hypocrisy."

Trouble on this particular night came in the form of a bomb threat during their second performance of the day. A search by the Clark County sheriff's office, however, failed to turn up anything. It was the first of numerous threats the Beatles would receive in forthcoming weeks. Following the performance they didn't waste any time getting back to the Sahara Hotel, where gifts and fan mail from all across the country had been pouring in. Ringo, who early on had professed his love for science fiction, had received so many books he was, as he put it, "in danger of reading myself to death."

VIPs, record executives, and girls who'd managed to break through the barricades or finagle an invitation, packed the Beatles' central living room. "There were always people around, always, whether it was policemen or girls or journalists or whoever," says Taylor. On this night, the guests weren't leaving.

LAS VEGAS

AUGUST 21, 1964:

As night turned to day, the inner circle, one by one, departed the main suite. Lennon had been sitting on one of the beds in his room, guitar in hands, working on a new song, while a mingling of guests, including a couple of young girls, hung around. Aspinall and Taylor, unable to rid the room of guests, finally gave up and left to go downstairs to gamble and find some breakfast. When they arrived back in the room they found the two girls sleeping, fully clothed, on one of the still-made beds. Lennon, still working on the song, was in

Indiana State Fair Coliseum.

pretty much the same position he was in when they'd left him, on the other bed. It was obvious that no one had been violated, not John and not the girls. But it didn't look good. Even before Aspinall and Taylor could decide how to get the girls out, a sergeant from the Las Vegas Police Department was pounding on the door, demanding entrance. He stormed in, rustled the young girls awake, and escorted them out, shouting into a walkie-talkie as he did. They were, it turned out, underage. But one of them was a cousin of Patti Boyd—George's girlfriend—or that's what she said anyway, and she certainly looked the part. That afternoon the Beatles boarded their chartered airplane and headed for Seattle. For Lennon, the whole incident was a shrug, but it wouldn't be the last he heard of it.

During the three-hour-and-forty-five-minute flight to Seattle, the Beatles listened to rhythm & blues records—Little Anthony and the Imperials, James Brown, and others—on a portable record player that belonged to the Exciters.

SEATTLE, WASHINGTON

Beatlepeople began converging at dawn at the Beatle arrival points—Seattle-Tacoma Airport, the Edgewater Inn, and the Seattle Center Coliseum—claiming the most strategic spots they could find. Girls tried anything and everything to penetrate the barricades—hiding in delivery trucks, attempting to bribe reporters for press cards, and even, when all else failed, stampeding the doors and entrances. Despite the intense security, a few always seemed to get through, at least temporarily. Early in the morning, four young stowaways were discovered in a restroom at the Edgewater and were promptly ejected. Hotel manager Don Wright ordered the staff to check every room and closet again before noon, and the check turned up three girls under a bed in one room and two more under a bed in another room. Meanwhile, the hotel desk was being buried beneath cakes, cookies, telegrams, and fan mail for the Beatles.

Edgewater staff members equipped with new walkie-talkies linked the front gate with the office and roof of the Edgewater, which had been fully booked for weeks. By 6 A.M. a temporary wall, constructed of plywood and barbed wire, was erected around the hotel, and Coast Guard and Marine patrols guarded Elliott Bay which bordered one side of the Edgewater. As the day wore on, the crowd intermittently broke out in choruses of "We love you, Bea-tles, oh yes we dooo . . ." while constantly training binoculars on the windows of the Edgewater.

By late afternoon, the street in front of the hotel was jammed and an estimated crowd of one thousand broiled in the late afternoon sun. As the Beatles' limousine came into view, the crowd surged forward. Some of the more adventurous flung themselves onto the black limousine as it sped toward the entrance. Breaking loose from the patrolmen holding them back, hundreds of fans moved in on and surrounded the car. It slowed to a crawl. Finally, the limousine driver managed to ease through the mass of shrieking fans and maneuver up to the lobby entrance. The Beatles were hustled up a seldom-used flight of stairs to their suite on the second floor, which looked out over Elliott Bay.

Later the Beatles met members of the local media, and fished out the window in their main suite. They didn't catch anything, but the Coast Guard, who were fishing for aquatically inclined fans, did reel in a catch or two. By now it was clear that the Beatles would see very little of America. They would see, instead—much as Wilfred Brambell, in the role of Paul's grandfather in *A Hard Day's Night*, put it—"a plane and a room, a car and a room, and a room and a room." But they were here to work and all of this came with the territory. "Believe me, we're having a good time," Ringo confessed. "The press says we're fed up, but we're not fed up—it's part of our job," added George. "Oh, we'll never get used to it," sighed Paul. The idle hours in the hotels, backstage, and on the plane were usually filled playing cards, poker and blackjack in particular, reading everything from newspapers to fan mail, writing music, doing interviews, and occasionally meeting local girls. When Miss Teenage

America, Charmaine Smith, showed up for her "scheduled appointment" with the Beatles, guards refused her entrance. Smith, who was on assignment from the Miss Teenage America Pageant to hold a private promotional audience with the Beatles, was peeved. "What a way to spend a birthday," she huffed. In desperation she turned to comedian Allan Sherman, who was also staying at the hotel. Sherman made arrangements for Smith at the Coliseum, and gave her a note he guaranteed would gain her admittance: "Get this girl in to see the Beatles, or else," it read. Sherman signed it with a skull and crossbones.

By 7:30 P.M., the Coliseum was jammed with 14,045 spectators, a security force of fifty Seattle police officers, four sheriff's deputies, the fire chief and fourteen firemen, and one hundred Navy volunteers who dubbed themselves "Beatle guards for a night." Preparation at the Coliseum included, oddly, the removal of some 112 aluminum door handles from the inside of the doors "to keep the doors shut during the performance and to prevent thefts," officials said. Outside, scalpers were selling five-dollar tickets for fifteen dollars.

While the opening acts went through their paces, the weary Beatles gave a press conference backstage. During their first visit to the States, it was Ringo who had earned the honor of being America's favorite Beatle, and his popularity as such continued on this first concert tour.

"Why do you get more fan mail in Seattle than the other Beatles?" asked one reporter.

"I dunno. I suppose it's because more

Indiana State Fair Coliseum.

people write to me," said Ringo matter-of-factly.

"Your new film has gotten very good reviews, some even compared you to the Marx Brothers. Are you pleased?"

"Oh yes, Ringo's sort of Groucho," said John.

"How long do you think you'll last, how many more years?"

" 'Til death do us part," chimed John.

"How much money do you make?"

"A lot," snapped George.

The press conferences were quickly becoming a bore. The same questions were asked over and over again and the one subject the Beatles were eager to talk about—their music—was the one topic that was forever being overlooked. On the way back to their dressing room, a young girl suddenly plummeted twenty-five feet down an air shaft, landing on the cement floor right in front of Ringo. When she came to, she looked up to see the sad-eyed drummer with Norman Weiss and several others looking her over. She must have thought she was dreaming when Ringo offered her his Coke. They helped her up and asked her to wait until the ambulance attendants got there. Obviously startled, the young girl remained speechless. "Are you sure you're all right, luv?" asked Ringo. Demurely, she nodded, then suddenly bolted back into the throngs.

Ringo and Norman joined the others in the dressing room for an autograph session and, among other obligations, the meeting with Charmaine Smith, Miss Teenage America. "They're really very nice," Smith said.

But she added: "As soon as the kids find something new, the Beatles will be on their way out."

At 9:30 P.M. the Beatles dashed through a backstage aisle of security guards and up onto the stage. Flashbulbs again lit the arena, jellybeans pelted the stage, and the screams were thunderous. The Seattle *Daily Times* likened the show to being "in a crazed capsule pitching through the chasms of space. There was no escape. Scenes beyond the worst horror movies unreeled without let-up." Again, nobody could hear much, if any, of the music. Girls bounced, wept, tore at their hair, screamed, clutched their throats, pulled at their faces, swooned, and gestured pleadingly. One girl leapt out of the audience and managed to make it up onto the stage, but officers quickly seized her. Outside, groups of ticketless teens crashed the gates, storming the ramps. A few made it in. Most were apprehended by police and dragged back out.

At 10 P.M., the Beatles sprinted off the stage, surrounded, as usual, by a convoy of guards. Fans refused to leave, many rushing the stage to retrieve squashed jellybeans, cigarette butts, anything *they* might have touched or stepped on. Casualties numbered around thirty-five, mostly young girls treated at the Coliseum's first-aid room for fainting spells or hysterics that had left them helpless. The few thousand people waiting outside the Coliseum quickly reassembled at the Edgewater.

As part of the Beatles' escape ruse, a Cadillac limousine drove out from behind the

Coliseum. It was attacked by twenty teenagers. The roof caved in, the trunk was smashed, and the door handles were ripped off. The Beatles were not inside, but they weren't where they were supposed to be either. A crowd of fans had broken through police lines and was blocking the backstage door, trapping them inside. It took nearly an hour for security guards to drag the fans away from the exit. The Beatles finally escaped in a darkened ambulance, which took them back to the Edgewater for the night.

SEATTLE

AUGUST 22, 1964:

The next morning, George slept while Paul and Ringo watched TV and John gave an interview about his first book, *In His Own Write*, which had, to the surprise of many, become a best-seller. It was a collection of short stories and sketches that highlighted "puns on words." As Lennon told the interviewer, "Basically, these things were just for me. I didn't think people would accept the book as they did. I really didn't think the book would get reviewed by the book reviewers."

Meanwhile Seattle adults were still reeling from the spectacle of the night before. In an article syndicated nationwide, Dr. Bernard Saibel, the supervisor of the Washington State Division of Community Services, which operated twenty-three child guidance clinics, reviewed the Beatles' Seattle performance to analyze the behavior of teenage fans. He found the concert to be "an orgy for teenagers," the experience "unbelievable and frightening." Wrote Saibel: "The hysteria and loss of control go far beyond the impact of the music. This is not simply a release . . . but a very destructive process . . . defying in emotional ecstasy the restraints which authorities try to place on them." Seattle had never witnessed anything to compare with the reaction to the Beatles.

At noon the Beatles left their rooms and headed back to the Seattle-Tacoma Airport, bound for Vancouver, Canada. The Edgewater, however, remained under siege from souvenir hunters. "We've had so many people down here looking for souvenirs, we're still having to maintain our security," said hotel manager Wright. The orange rug that carpeted the Beatles' suite was purchased by a company named MacDougall-Southwick. Plans were to cut it up and sell pieces as mementos. The Edgewater was all too happy to get rid of the rug, since word had traveled through the hotel grapevine that the room was destined to be torn up by fans anyway.

As the Beatles' jet neared the border, it was refused entry to Canada. In the rush to get out of Seattle one small detail had been forgotten—U.S. Customs. The pilot turned the craft around and headed back to the Seattle-Tacoma Airport, where the Beatles and their entourage completed the inspection in about twenty minutes. At 4:50 P.M., they were Vancouver-bound once again. **Milwaukee.**

VANCOUVER, BRITISH COLUMBIA, CANADA

AUGUST 22, 1964:

She was eleven years old, almost twelve, the young Seattle girl said between sobs. And she had come to Vancouver in hopes of seeing the Beatles perform. She hadn't been able to get a ticket to the show in Seattle, so . . . The policeman handed her another Kleenex, and she blew her nose. She was one of countless young girls who would leave home by any means available to them in order to see the Beatles. That would not be this young girl's good fortune, not this year anyway. The Vancouver police had already called her parents and she was going home.

The Beatles' show at Vancouver's Empire Stadium was scheduled as part of the Pacific National Exhibition, a fourteen-day fair, which opened that morning with a parade of forty floats. The street in front of the Hotel Georgia, where the Beatles were scheduled to check in prior to their stadium performance, was jammed with parade-going fans, and the management had to call twice for police assistance as fans, packed six deep, blocked all movement from the curb to the hotel's front doors. Nobody could, or really wanted to, move. A

boarded-up side entrance on Howe Street was quickly decorated with a lipstick message: "We Love the Beatles."

One unfortunate soul, dressed in a dark shirt and wearing shades and a dark golf cap was driven past the hotel, sitting in the back seat of a red car. Someone shouted: "There's Ringo!" It was a case of mistaken identity, but the crowd, numbering around three thousand, mobbed the car. "The car seems to have been squashed to the ground under the sheer weight of the youngsters," said Police Inspector F. C. Bud Errington. In the melee, two youths snatched revolvers from police officers and while the officers managed to safely retrieve their weapons, Errington ordered all of his men to disarm to prevent any further pranks or accidents.

The Beatles' plane touched down at Vancouver Airport around 6 P.M. Upon hearing about the crowd awaiting their arrival at the Hotel Georgia, Weiss and Epstein huddled and decided to skip the hotel entirely. Instead, the Beatles and various members of their entourage were taken on a brisk driving tour

94

of Vancouver, finally arriving at the stadium around 7 P.M. to the screams of thousands of fans waiting to enter.

Inside, four crush barriers—constructed from four-foot-high fencing—had been set up on the field in front of the stage to keep the 20,261 ticket holders at a safe distance; one hundred police officers were on duty to make sure the crush barriers held. During the performances of the Bill Black Combo, the Exciters, Jackie DeShannon, and the Righteous Brothers, the audience clapped and chanted for the Beatles. Tensions mounted and the kids moved forward, pushing up against the barriers. Among the opening acts, a camaraderie was developing. "We had to face the *war* together," says Righteous Brother Bill Medley. "As opening acts, we didn't stand a chance. I remember watching the kids in front being squashed, while we were singing. The nurses came and went and it would happen just the same at every outdoor show."

When the Beatles ran onstage at 9:23 P.M., nearly one third of the audience rushed the stage, jamming up against the barriers. In the stampede, some fell and were trampled. Police moved in again and again to retrieve the fallen fans from almost certain death. Police and stadium employees managed, barely, to hold the barriers up. "There's no comparison with any other crowd I've seen," said Police Inspector Errington. "These people have lost all ability to think."

Meanwhile, outside, policemen were trying to restrain thousands of ticketless young fans surrounding the stadium. Seconds after the Beatles began playing, the west gate buckled under the strain of the bodies ramming against it and at least a dozen fans made it inside before police could raise the gate back up, bracing it up with the weight of their own bodies. Moments later fans stormed the south gate, the one closest to the stage, and several more made it inside. Further attacks kept coming until Errington called in police dogs to help secure the gate.

Flashbulbs popped, jellybeans dropped, and the screams produced the anticipated decibel-shattering din. Twice the crowd was asked to move back. Twice they refused. The two first-aid stations resembled an adolescent war zone: Young girls, many of them wearing new—now torn—clothes, sobbed uncontrollably, melting from the heat and hysteria, while others vomited from overexcitement. The fire warden took one look at the aid posts and immediately ordered oxygen-inhalator units. Through it all the Beatles never missed a beat, or not one that anybody noticed. When they hit the last chord of "Long Tall Sally," their usual finale, the Beatles took their now-famous deep bow, guitars slung to the side, Ringo over his drums; then they pulled themselves upright and ran for the southeast exit, where police had already cleared a path to three waiting limousines. Police escort motorcycles roared, guiding the limousines to the exit gate. In an effort to stop the procession, a young boy threw his bicycle in front of the lead escort motorcycle, but all the entourage vehicles managed to swerve around it. In less than thirty seconds the Beatles were gone. The final body count: one hundred casualties—mostly cases of hysteria. Nine people were taken to the local-area hospital for treatment of broken ribs, sprained ribs, one broken leg, bruises, abrasions, and cuts. "One hundred policemen—that's all that stood between the way it wound up and a national tragedy," said Errington.

By 10:20, the field and stadium stands had been cleared and the Pacific National Exhibition's nightly fireworks were launched. Under the cover of exploding, sparkling pyrotechnics, dozens of fans descended upon the stage, ripping out the decorations for souvenirs, but police moved in and chased them away. Protecting the Beatles was one of the most difficult tasks the Vancouver Police Department had ever been given, according to Deputy Chief Constable John Fisk. "This was because of the lack of information given to us," he said. "At no time were we more than fifteen minutes ahead of the Beatles." From here on out, if the tour was to continue without disaster to either the fans or the Beatles, a cloak-and-dagger secrecy about their arrivals and departures was going to have to be instituted.

The Beatles headed straight for the airport with their crew, and while they hadn't gone anywhere near their Hotel Georgia suite, they agreed to pay the $350 bill anyway.

LOS ANGELES

SUNDAY, AUGUST 23, 1964:

The Beatles' jet arrived in Los Angeles at 3:55 A.M. From the plane, the boys made a hasty departure through a series of back doors and into waiting limousines, successfully eluding one hundred teenagers who had waited all night on the chance the Beatles would arrive early. "I hate you! I hate you, you swine!" shouted one hysterically distraught girl.

After the Hotel Ambassador had canceled their reservations, the self-described social director Roy Gerber wound up renting the Bel Air mansion of British actor Reginald Owens at 356 St. Pierre Road. For $1,000, plus a $200 deposit for "breakage," the Beatles had a two-acre retreat complete with swimming pool for four days. Brian Epstein had taken a bungalow at the Beverly Hills Hotel and the rest of the cast and crew checked into the Beverly Hillcrest. The Beatles, with Neil, Mal, and Derek, pulled into the estate at about 4:30 A.M. and found two maids, a houseboy, and a cook—Lance Stevens of the Casserole Catering Service—as well as security guards at their service. The Owens mansion was an old-Hollywood-style home, with large spacious rooms and ornate decorations. They roamed through the house, peeking around walls and opening doors. John and Derek, who had made a pact earlier to jump into the first swimming pool they saw in L.A., headed out the back door and despite the early morning clouds dove into the cool blue water. Weakened by the strain of the tour, as well as the stimulants and alcohol that kept their eyes open and the stress at bay, they both nearly succumbed to their own weight in the water. Neil and Mal dragged them out.

While the Beatles finally settled in for some breakfast and rest, the U.S. Guards, a private security firm, moved into the Hollywood Bowl around 7 A.M., joining members of the Los Angeles Police Department, who had been on duty since Mitch Miller left the stage the night before. The Bowl, normally reserved for summer symphonies under the sky, would open its doors to rock 'n' roll for the first time tonight, and with the line already forming at the main gate, everyone involved was concerned. Cyril Lloyd Preece, ex-superintendent of Scotland Yard, had been hired by U.S. Guards to supervise the Beatles' security. He set up a command post at the Furniture Mart down the street and began briefing his men. "Patience and tolerance—that's what's needed to handle this situation," he told them. "But we must never let a boy or girl come in physical contact with a Beatle," warned Ernest A. Padilla, president of the security organization. "If that ever happens, a riot could ensue. It just takes one kid to start a stampede." Preece nodded, adding: "Fans love to touch the performers, especially

their heads. They will want to be able to say later, 'I touched a Beatle.' "

Hollywood Bowl officials decided to open the gates at 5:20 P.M., forty minutes early, because thousands of restless ticket holders kept surging toward the gates. As they were admitted entrance, a cry from countless shrill

young voices rippled through the crowd. "Oh my god! We're going to see the Beatles!" Savvy ticket takers wore army helmets, while vendors hawked programs and rented binoculars in record numbers. "Put yourself in Ringo's lap!" shouted one binocular pitchman. "I Love Ringo" buttons were selling twice as fast as the others. One Ringo look-alike wandered about the grounds, playing the role to the hilt all afternoon, signing "autographs,"

Backstage at the Olympic Stadium, Detroit.

97

arousing envy from other males nearby. More than fifteen hundred ticketless fans roamed the hills behind the Bowl just beyond the ring of security guards and considered their options for sneaking into the arena after nightfall.

This afternoon, Weiss and Epstein, along with Epstein's attorney Walter Hofer, ap-

Detroit.

proached John, Derek, and Neil about the "incident" in Las Vegas. The mother of one of the girls was threatening to sue. The charge: exposing minors to ridicule. "It was a fright," recalls Taylor. "The mother was most certainly in the hotel, down at the tables, and knew where the girls were. Suddenly John and Neil and I were accused of exposing these girls to ridicule. I didn't know then and I don't know

now what it means, but it looked bloody awful for us." It would have to be taken care of. Meaning *what*? Lennon wanted to know. "They said, 'We've got to give these women $10,000 to get them off our backs,' " recalls Aspinall. "It was right over my head. And John was going, 'For what?' He was one of those guys who felt strongly that if he hadn't done anything wrong, then why should he give in to blackmail threats? And *nobody* had done anything wrong." The Beatles, and more specifically John, had been set up. The payoff was made. The Beatles had been burned, but saved from scandal.

About 6:30 P.M., they left their Bel Air retreat and were driven over the hills of the Santa Monica Mountains and into Studio City, down Ventura Boulevard to the Cinnamon Cinder, a teenage nightclub owned in part by Eubanks, for what was billed as "a serious press conference." It was certainly one of the largest, attended by some two hundred working journalists and photographers from the newspapers, fanzines, wire services, and teen magazines as well as TV stations, and an undetermined number of press-card-carrying teenagers—including, of course, the *Datebook* kids and local fan club brass. As the press conference got under way, hundreds of teenagers converged on the Cinnamon Cinder. "Everybody was really pretty nervous and there were long pauses between questions," says then *TeenScreen* editor Janey Milstead.

"What do you think about the recent comments made by a Seattle psychiatrist, saying the Beatles are a menace?"

"Psychiatrists are a menace, too," responded George drily.

98

George, everybody knew they were there. The place had not been secured and chaos set in. George and Ringo had to be lifted over the crowd and placed in their seats. "I always saw the Beatles in certain circumstances as a bit like Tom Thumb, who in Victorian times was wheeled around like a freak, a cute freak, but a freak nonetheless," says Taylor. "And in certain circumstances, the Beatles were seen as novelties or freaks, like a panda with five legs—'how very interesting.'"

When a photographer came over, Harrison asked him not to take pictures but he began snapping anyway and then left. He returned several minutes later and began shooting again, despite George's repeated requests to stop. Infuriated, George hurled a drink at him, which sloshed onto actress Mamie Van Doren, who was maneuvering over to the table,

and things started to get wild. Derek went to the stage to plead for quiet. The crowd shouted back, "Get lost!" He did. And so did John, George, Ringo, and the rest of the entourage. "It had been their one attempt to live normally for a couple of hours and even that couldn't happen," recalls Bess Coleman. "It was a flop," says Taylor. A photograph of George throwing the drink was run on the front page of the Los Angeles *Herald-Examiner* the following day, much to the chagrin of Epstein. "Not only did we have a bad time, but we'd broken the rules—we'd gone out of the house, got into difficulties and a bad photograph appeared and it was a mess," says Taylor. "It was nobody's fault, except our own inexperience in taking the guarantee of someone else that everything would be all right. We should've known better."

LOS ANGELES

WEDNESDAY, AUGUST 26, 1964:

The Beatles were up by 9 A.M. to pack and head for the airport. As they drove away from Beatle Manor, a caravan of cars pulled in behind them. On the freeway, one car, packed with seven girls, managed to pull in close enough to throw a scroll containing the signatures of thirty thousand California Beatle boosters into the Beatles' limousine. The

driver, however, was quickly pulled over by the California Highway Patrol for following a car too closely.

At the airport, the Beatles moved fast, as they usually did, eluding an estimated five thousand fans who'd come to say good-bye. They were guided through back doors and hallways to their American Flyers Electra,

which was hidden at the extreme western end of the field. KRLA's Dave Hull and Jim Steck were on hand to record the farewell. As they waved good-bye to Paul, the last Beatle to disappear into the aircraft, Steck turned to Hull. "We really oughta get on that plane," he said. Responded Hull: "All we have to do is walk up that ramp." They looked at each other, then back at the plane. Hull called to their young assistant, handed her his tapes with instructions to get them back to the station immediately, and they walked up the plane's ramp and followed the stewardess' directions, the press forward, the crew aft. They passed Neil and Mal, who smiled, obviously thinking nothing of their presence. Many disc jockeys would pick up the tour much like a political campaign, riding it for a few cities and then jumping off. One of the invited guests for this flight was Joan Baez. By 11:15 A.M. the Beatles were airborne and on their way to Denver. The original itinerary had actually called for a later departure, but the plan now called for them not to arrive anywhere on schedule, in hopes of avoiding the overwhelming crush of fans.

John relaxes in a suite previously occupied by Elizabeth Taylor and Richard Burton, Toronto.

DENVER, COLORADO

WEDNESDAY, AUGUST 26, 1964:

"I can't control 'em!" shouted Lee Gonzales. It was 7:30 A.M., and Gonzales, a road grader, stood with his arms stretched sideways. He was attempting to block some two hundred Beatle fans from advancing through Stapleton Field's south gate, near where the Beatles' plane was scheduled to land. Patrolman Charles Coprich, who was among a contingent of policemen on three-wheeler motorbikes zooming through the heavy wheat stubble of the

The Beatles pose with the Bill Black Combo, Mal Evans, and tour managers Ira Sidelle (center front) and Bob Bonis, Toronto.

airport area flushing out fans, sped toward the gate, where another band of officers joined him in herding the crowd back far enough to close the gate. A force of fifty policemen was already on hand for the Beatles' anticipated 1 P.M. arrival, but the crowd was steadily growing. By noon, nearly ten thousand people blanketed two miles bordering the southwest corner of the airfield. Police were forced to close Montview Road and erect barricades to protect the Beatles' welcoming committee.

Huge crowds also descended upon the Brown Palace Hotel and Red Rocks Theater. Local law enforcement officials had planned and rehearsed their Beatle Invasion strategies for four weeks. All told, 250 Denver policemen, recruits, and auxiliary policemen, as well as Jeep patrolmen assigned concert detail, were briefed and rehearsed in how to handle Beatlemania and the expected crowd of nine thousand that would pour into the outdoor amphitheater. Weather predictions were calling for rain and emergency plans were being made to transfer the concert to the Denver Coliseum.

Red Rocks Theater is, acoustically speaking, one of America's finest music stages and has featured some of the world's best musicians. Earlier in the season it had hosted Igor

Stravinsky, considered to be the world's greatest living composer. The $6.60 general admission tickets for the Beatles' show, however, were nearly $3 more than tickets for Stravinsky's recent concert, which had bombed, according to the Denver *Post*. By 10 A.M., an estimated one thousand fans were encamped around the amphitheater, lounging on blankets, listening to transistor radios, reading Beatle magazines. One group rallied to shouts of "Draft Ringo for President!" The Beatles' appearance, unbeknownst to the four, was being used to test a new law banning alcoholic or other canned or bottled drinks in the park. Denver's entertainment scene had been repeatedly disrupted by a gang of rowdy youths who had, back in August 1962, hurled beer cans at Ray Charles. There were numerous such incidents, and following the most recent at a Peter, Paul, and Mary concert earlier this summer, the ordinance was passed. Would it work or would the Beatles be the next victims?

At 1:35 P.M., the Beatles' plane touched down at Stapleton Field and pandemonium ensued. Wild screaming fell to a breaths-held hush as the turboprop's doors opened. The screams returned as soon as John, George, Ringo, and Paul emerged. Screams and shouts and gasps melded into the normal decibel-shattering wail. After briefly posing for photographs on the steps, the boys were greeted by disc jockeys, newspaper reporters, Denver dignitaries, and the British counsul in Denver. "Sorry we're late, but there was quite a crowd when we took off," said Ringo. "Has the tour been tiring?" asked one disc jockey. "Not so far, we're still ready to go," said John. While local newsmen clung to them, the Beatles quickly walked to two waiting limousines. As they climbed in, a cameraman from a Hollywood-based newsreel supplier jumped into the front seat of the Beatles' limo and began filming. Bob Bonis asked him to get out. The Beatles and Brian didn't want any unauthorized filming going on for any reason because of the merchandising fiasco. It was strictly forbidden. They didn't buy the newsreel story and were convinced that the real point to the footage was to develop a commercial film. The cameraman ignored Bonis, who had his orders. Bonis reached in, grabbed the guy, and pulled. Standing at six feet tall and weighing 240 pounds, Bonis pulled harder than he intended. The cameraman and camera went sprawling by him onto the tarmac. A local camera crew filmed the entire incident. Meanwhile, the Beatles' limo pulled away, moving toward the southwest corner where the fans were waiting. But few saw much of anything. The limousines' windows remained rolled up and a cloud of dust blew across the fans. By the time the limousines headed for the exit, the procession had become a full-blown caravan, complete with a specially assigned police escort. As they headed out into traffic, frantic teenagers followed in their wake and cars jammed up in every direction. Throughout the area, cries of alarm were heard and police were momentarily helpless in unsnarling the traffic jams.

Back on the tarmac, Brian Epstein confronted Hull and Steck: "You have broken a federal law by stowing away on an airplane and crossing state lines, and you can get us all in a lot of trouble." "Uh-oh, we can't let that happen," said Hull, who had discovered they had only four dollars between them—

Toronto.

which wasn't much in this still cash-and-carry world. "No," said Brian in his controlled, calm voice. "We'll have to put your names on the manifest." Hull and Steck were then turned over to Derek, who took them to the hotel and got them tickets to the show. Following the show they would catch a flight back to L.A., at KRLA's expense.

While nearly five thousand people milled around outside the front entrance of the Brown Palace Hotel, the Beatles' limousines pulled up to a service entrance where only about two dozen lucky fans stood, caught off guard, as the boys were hustled inside. Police escorted them through the coffee shop and to a small freight elevator. Just as the elevator doors were about to close, a photographer from the *Rocky Mountain News*, Bob Talkin, slipped

inside. "Get that bastard photographer out of here!" yelled someone in the entourage, still burning from the "bad photograph" that had appeared in Los Angeles that morning, but it was too late; he'd already gained entrance and the overloaded elevator began groaning its way up. "Well, he could have at least brought lunch for us," grumbled one of the boys. Ringo asked the elevator operator to let them off on the seventh floor and they'd walk up one flight to their suites on the eighth floor. "We don't want any photographers around," he explained. For the Beatles, it was a matter of honesty, however brutal. For Talkin, it was humiliating. As luck would have it, the elevator, packed with some twenty people, got stuck between the sixth and seventh floors. A hotel engineer managed to release it after only a few minutes and the boys jumped off. A continuous supply of gifts, telegrams, and notes were accepted at the Beatles' suite. The press, however, was not. Tour strain had set in. The Beatles were homesick and more than a little tired.

The Brown Palace, one of Denver's elite hotels, had hosted presidents, kings, queens, and movie stars, but like others in its class it had never witnessed anything like Beatlemania. "Come down and watch me slash my wrists," hotel manager Carl Mehlman told a friend. The hotel had been under siege since 2 P.M. when the crowd of teenagers swelled to five thousand. Traffic had to be barred from Tremont Place between Seventeenth and Eighteenth streets. Transistor radios blared music; youngsters chattered and joked with each other and with policemen, and, at one point, quietly began singing "I Want to Hold Your Hand."

Suddenly a shriek from the entrance caused a stampede in motion. Two girls were knocked down and couldn't get up. Captain Walter Nelson, head of the Beatles detail, and reporters struggled to rescue them.

Inside the lobby, policemen carried sobbing and fainting girls to couches. All told, six teenage girls and one policeman, who had been bitten on the wrist, were taken to the Denver General Hospital for treatment. Among the afternoon's casualties: fractured ribs, abdominal injuries, hysteria, and a fractured right foot that had been rolled over by a car. Manager Mehlman set up a lost-and-found for younger brothers and sisters and then joined police in capturing infiltrators. "I'm weakening fast," he sighed.

Joan Baez, who would be appearing at **Toronto.**

Red Rocks two nights after the Beatles, wandered into the lobby, at first unnoticed. Four young girls recognized the folksinger, asked for her autograph, then begged her to deliver a note to the Beatles. Baez would spend a quiet afternoon playing guitar and singing and talking with the boys.

Despite all the police preparation at Red Rocks, some fans managed to sneak in and climb up on the huge boulder behind the stage, while others crawled up the sheer cliffs that frame the stage on the side, despite police strategies to prevent that. As radiomen Hull and Steck sat in the audience, waiting for the show, a young cub reporter approached. "'Dave, you've got to get me in,'" Hull remembers her saying to him. "She told me she was on the verge of getting fired and she had promised to deliver an interview with the Beatles. Could I help her? I told her I would see what I could do. She did get something of an interview, but when her story was published, the headline read: 'I Interviewed the Beatles in Their Underwear.' Her name, as it turns out, was Rona Barrett. I regretted that good deed."

Backstage, the Beatles watched the news on TV and chortled, then guffawed at the footage of Bob throwing the photographer out of the limousine. When they heard his recognizable footsteps approaching the dressing room, they dove under their cots, just as he entered. They huddled and shivered, feigning fear and holding their hands protectively in front of their faces. "Oh, please, Boboners," squealed John in a high-pitched voice, "don't throw me—I'll be good. Please, sir, don't kill us." They whimpered and rolled over laughing. They'd gotten the good-humored Bonis and he knew it. But the incident wasn't a laughing matter. In the end Brian worked his magic and all was forgiven.

At 9:30 P.M. the Beatles took the stage, and the audience jumped to its feet, screaming and pelting the stage—but not with beer cans. The now familiar jelly beans were the missiles of choice. However, the beauty of Red Rocks Theater aside, the altitude proved troublesome. Halfway through the first song, the Beatles were out of breath, and throughout the performance they would have to take frequent hits from canisters of oxygen. As the Beatles' performance came to an end, sheriff's deputies, patrolmen, and the Jeep Patrol rushed to the front of the stage to form a human wall of protection. Remarkably, and only by the grace of God, the wall held.

After the show, the Beatles retired to their suite at the Brown Palace, hung out with Baez for a while, and then got some much-needed sleep.

DENVER, COLORADO

THURSDAY, AUGUST 27, 1964:

The predicted rain finally arrived as the Beatles headed for the airport, but neither it nor the hail that began to pelt the Mile High City kept Beatle fans away from Stapleton Field. An estimated thirty-five hundred were waiting outside the fence, about six blocks from the plane. Once again, with a police motorcycle escort, the Beatles were driven around the field before being dropped off at the edge of the tarmac. The police had promised Denver youths that if they behaved well during the Beatles' stay, they would do what they could to allow them to bid the lads from Liverpool one last farewell.

As George, Ringo, Paul, and John got out of the limousine, they turned and stood at attention, then saluted photographer Bob Talkin and the other photographers. It was a gesture of redress for the grievance caused the day before when they had verbally abused Talkin in the elevator. At 12:07 P.M., the plane took off. Destination: Cincinnati. The beginning-of-the-tour partying had subsided, and reporters worked away on stories while members of the crew and opening acts either played cards, jammed, or slept. Photographer Curt Gunther had been concerned about investing his own money for the trip, since he was, in effect, freelancing. But he was a proven poker player and he had already earned enough to cover his expenses thus far.

CINCINNATI, OHIO

In the days preceding the Beatles' arrival, the Cincinnati local Musicians' Union had almost forced cancellation of the show by demanding that local groups be added to the bill. Once word of the dispute became public, picketers maintained a vigil at the union headquarters, and negotiators were deluged with hundreds of phone calls from teenagers protesting the threatened action. The dispute was quickly resolved. The show had been set and all the acts, except the Beatles, were American.

At the Vernon Manor Hotel, where the Beatles were scheduled to stay overnight, deejays from WSAI, the station promoting their Cincinnati Gardens appearance, had already arranged to purchase all the towels, soap, rugs, and furniture used by the group during their stay. For some Americans, the Beatles had come to represent a money-making opportunity.

The scale of advance preparation in Cincinnati, as in other cities on the Beatles' itinerary, equaled that normally reserved for presidential visits. But, because of the new improved tour strategy, not even the Cincinnati police were sure of the Beatles' plans for their stay in the Queen City, and their anxiety was mounting. At 3:45 P.M., police were forced to block off the streets around Lunken Airport where the Beatles' plane was scheduled to land. Almost on cue, the estimated eleven hundred spectators screamed when they first saw the plane appear in the west. The roar subsided until 5:05 P.M., when the Beatles' prop-jet finally touched down. As the door of the plane opened at the north end of the runway, Paul, Ringo, George, and John stepped out, looking rested and relaxed. "Yes, the flight was excellent," offered Ringo. "And no one got sick."

The opening acts filed, unnoticed, into a bus, as the Beatles were hustled into limousines. Following a quick pass at the crowd waiting some five hundred yards away, they headed down an approved alley passageway. About fifty fans managed to break through police lines and bolted for the cars, but police moved in, cleared the alley, and the Beatles were off to the Cincinnati Gardens.

At about 6 P.M. their entourage, complete with a police caravan—two patrol cars in front, two in back—arrived at the old boxing ring and sped to the back end of the arena. The caravan was slowed by howling, clutching girls, but the Beatles' limousine pushed on, depositing them at a door on the far side of the hall. "This way fellas, let's go!" someone shouted. Once inside, they were ushered to a locker room underneath the seats. There, by telephone, they talked with Elvis Presley for the first time. Among other things, Elvis told Paul about his new bass guitar and complained about the blisters it was causing. "Don't worry about it, man, they'll soon go," Paul assured him.

In a private room at the Gardens, the Beatles sparkled in a press conference, seemingly oblivious to the steamy evening heat. Another inflexible rule had been flexed and broken. Press conferences had become a vital part of the tour and were the only way to quench the thirst for Beatle quips from the overwhelming numbers of local and national reporters covering the Beatles' first American concert tour. The fact that Beatle press conferences had garnered kudos as entertaining shows on their own made them almost mandatory. Unlike press officers for other celebrities, Derek Taylor and Bess Coleman were responsible for keeping the press *at bay* until their needs could be conveniently satisfied.

Neither Derek nor Bess were prepared for what was confronting them in the States. "Nobody's ever satisfied in the end," George

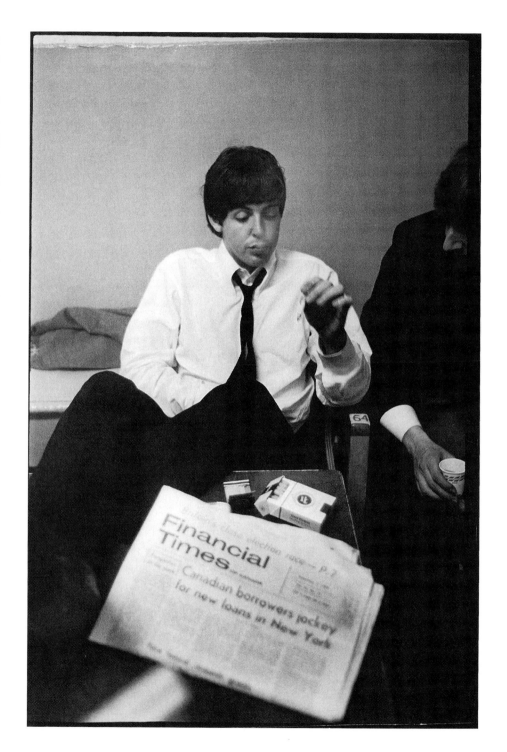

Montreal.

often said. And nobody knew that better than Derek and Bess. Nevertheless, both were skilled diplomats, friendly by nature, willing to help whenever they could, even in the most chaotic and impossible of situations. As a result the Beatles' image was elevated among the press. No exclusives were given, but usually at the end of a press conference Derek managed to move numerous reporters into corners to get at least a few one-of-a-kind quotes. "There was never any Beatleola," says Taylor. "Often it was the small people who got through, and the big guys normally didn't like that. But if they weren't going to be unpleasant or stupid, it didn't really matter whether they were from *Datebook* or *Time* magazine."

Lennon's quick wit and sarcastic, irreverent humor were often scathing. Sometimes, particularly for those newsmen lacking a sense of humor, it was offensive, though rarely was any comment directed *at* anyone. Always the rebel, John rarely offered the reporters a straight answer. Neither did George, who quickly became known as the quiet Beatle. He seldom responded to the rapid-fire questions and seemed content to let the others do most of the talking. While fully capable of quick, searing one-liners, Paul and Ringo served as the ballast. Since the same questions were asked over and over, the Beatles often traded their favorite one-line retorts, depending on their individual moods. They were so fast and usually so funny, it seemed as if they rehearsed. But, as John put it, "We just ad lib and take the rough with the smooth." The Beatles' style was in their Liverpudlian sense of humor and outlook on life; and whether the

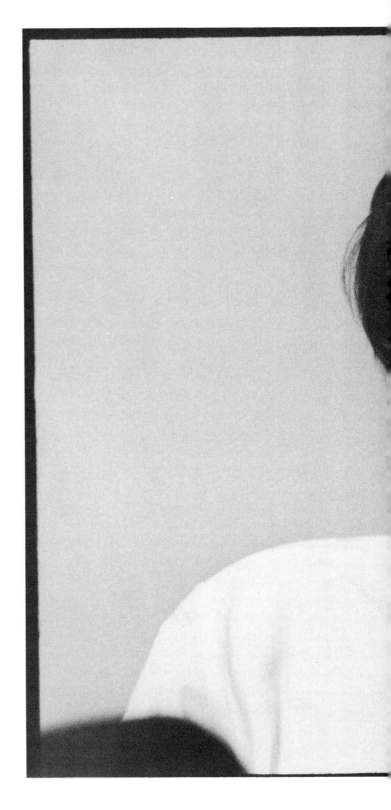

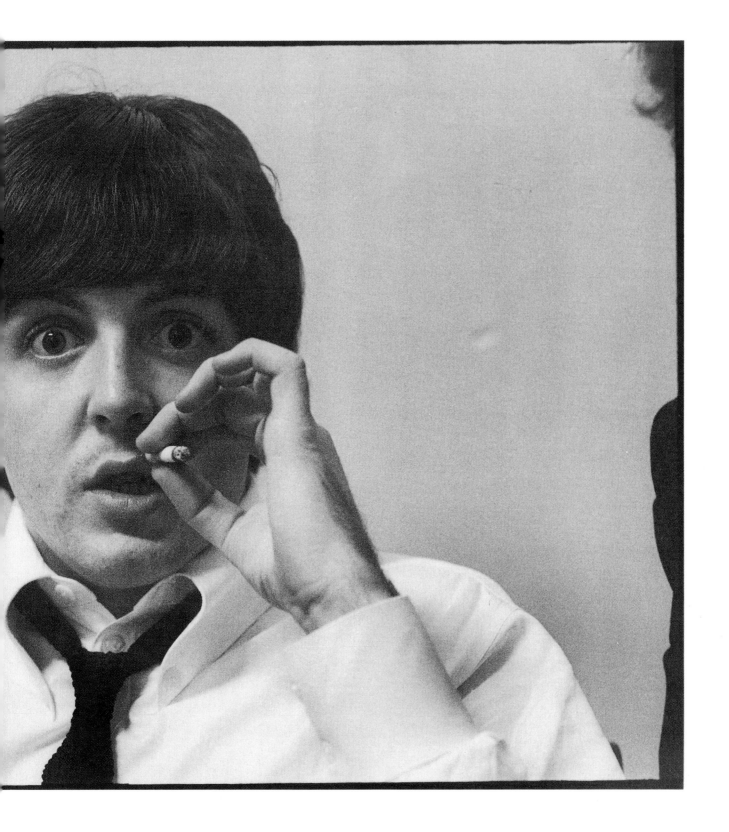

answers were funny or not, they were always honest.

"What will you do when the bubble bursts?" He was back. The same guy, Fred Paul. He would come to haunt the Beatles throughout the tour, showing up at nearly all their press conferences, asking the same question.

"Count the money," said John.

"What excuse do you have for your collar-length hair?"

"Well, it grows out of yer head," said Ringo.

"We don't need an excuse," snapped John. "You need an excuse."

"You ought to be able to handle a crowd of thirty thousand without police protection," said an overweight reporter from Dayton.

"Well, maybe you could," said John. "You're fatter than we are."

"Why do teenagers stand up and scream so piercingly?"

"We don't know, but I've heard that some teenagers pay to come to the show and scream," said Paul. "A lot of them don't even want to listen because they've got the records."

"What do you think of the psychiatrist who drew an analogy between the hysteria created by your beat and the speeches of Nazi dictator Adolf Hitler?"

"Tell him to shut up," said John. "He's off his head."

"What would you have done if you had not become the Beatles?"

"We would have just been bad entertainers," said George.

Meanwhile, it was closing night at the Democratic National Convention in Atlantic City, and in a cheering, weeping, emotional program, the party said good-bye to John F. Kennedy and the Kennedy era. The torch had been passed. To a new generation of Americans, one that would come to be known as the Love Generation. In Cincinnati and throughout America, a new Camelot was rising from the ashes of the old.

At 9:35 P.M., the Beatles ran onstage to the screams of fourteen thousand fans. Righteous Brother Bill Medley stood in the wings. Something had been bothering him. Every night as they left and the Beatles came on, the lights were turned up and he couldn't figure out why. Tonight he got his answer. "It wasn't the lights, it was the flashing of cameras," he says. "And it was almost exactly the same every night."

In the Gardens, you could feel the heat. Smell the sweat. The temperature, according to one reading, was 115 degrees Fahrenheit. "We would play the same show every night—thirty minutes, twenty-five minutes if we didn't like the audience, and every night we got the same reaction," recalls Ringo. "We must've looked like these figures just miming onstage. We quickly realized we could have farted and they would have applauded."

On the flight into New York City, the Beatles learned the results of the *Melody Maker* poll. The Rolling Stones had edged them out in the favorite national group category, but the Beatles took the top international honors.

NEW YORK CITY

FRIDAY, AUGUST 28, 1964:

"This is it! *This* is what it's all about!" Paul gazed out of the windows of the limousine. It was 3:30 in the morning. The lights of New York City sparkled. Skyscrapers reached for the heavens. People were out and about, moving to unknown destinations. The city felt alive, emitting a vibrant energy all its own. Inside the limousine, the Beatles' own energy was bouncing out of the radio.

They had flown into Kennedy International Airport at 2:55 A.M. and were greeted by the screams and wails of an estimated three thousand fans who had assembled on the observation deck thirty feet above the ground and about two hundred feet from where the chartered plane came to a stop. On the ride into Manhattan, the Beatles scanned the pop music stations up and down the AM dial— WABC, WINS, and WMCA all rocked with Beatle songs and announcements of their arrival. Their two performances at the Forest Hills Tennis Stadium in Queens had been sold out for months.

It was dazzling. The city. The nightlife. Hearing their voices command all the pop stations in America's Number One radio market. The Beatles drank in their success.

In this aura of excitement, they glided out of their limousine and into a mass of hysterical, crying, sobbing, pulling, grabbing young fans who were blocking the entrance to the Delmonico Hotel. They managed to hold their ground and push through. In the melee of their arrival, Ringo's St. Christopher's medal had been ripped right off his neck by a girl who vanished, squealing with delight, into the crowd. "That's the closest I've ever come to being got," said Ringo as the Beatles entered their sixth-floor suite. He looked at the shreds that were once a shirt and slumped, a torn man, into a chair. "Why don't we have all the dee-jays in, have a laugh and a talk?" Paul suggested in a rare spontaneous moment. Derek who would have to contend, one way or another, with the overflow of local newsmen in the lobby and corridor, was relieved.

Despite persistent predictions of doom, the Beatles still remained *the* story in American pop radio. So far, the tour was proving that, amidst the flood of new British bands, they were holding their own in the States, staying on top. They remained not only the titans but the darlings of pop radio, and stations everywhere aligned their call letters with the Beatles. In New York, for example, WABC created jingles proclaiming it to be "W-A-Beatle-C." But without radio, where would the Beatles have been?

For this visit, radio personnel from all of New York's pop stations infiltrated the hotel and the Beatles' floor.

It was, however, W-A-Beatle-C's Cousin Brucie, Scott Muni, Dan Ingram, and program director Rick Sklar who were the first into the Beatles' overflow suite. While John and Paul walked about the room, stretching their legs, George rested on one of the beds and Ringo—still a bit shaken—sat in a chair. Within seconds, Cousin Brucie was on the air, live via telephone hook-up, describing the scene, ad-libbing a tear-jerking appeal to that little villain in the night who had grabbed Ringo's medal. He turned the microphone to Ringo. "Hello, how are you?" Ringo started: "Good to be back in New York anyway. Cousin Brucie, somebody took my medallion. It means more to me than almost anything, a present from my auntie. I haven't had it off me neck since I was twenty-one. That was three years ago." Ringo was on a roll. In the background, John, Paul, George, and Derek were shaking with stifled laughter at the maudlin display of Ringo's emotion. "It's sort of a keepsake, just a gold St. Christopher's medal." Ringo, his voice now cracking, pleaded with his attacker, "If you just bring it back, I'll give you . . ." Everyone held their breath. Uh-oh, what would Ringo promise? Cousin Brucie took command of the microphone. "What greater reward could there be than a kiss of forgiveness?" Muni and Morrow went downstairs and into the crowd, to try and find the medal. "Anyone having the medal or knowing of its whereabouts should come directly to the WABC studios." The announcement was made every few minutes. Since every second person down below

had a transistor radio in hand, the news spread quicker than wildfire and WABC's phones began to ring. More than one hundred calls came in, all from girls claiming to have the medallion; but before long sixteen-year-old Angie McGowan arrived with the real gold St. Christopher's medal in hand.

In an effort to prolong the drama and increase the ratings, Sklar obtained Angie's parents' permission to keep her secured in the W-A-Beatle-C suite and the station continued to broadcast its appeals. Meanwhile, John, Paul, George, and Ringo talked with the disc jockeys until around 6 A.M., when the suite was cleared. Newspapermen who had been waiting outside for their turn were angry when Derek announced there would be no more interviews. By now both Derek and Bess realized that theirs was a no-win job. George was right, nobody *was* ever satisfied.

At dawn there were still an estimated three thousand fans holding vigil at Park Avenue and Fifty-ninth Street, standing eight deep behind police barriers, singing and swaying. Some carried signs attesting to endless love, others brandished tiny British flags. Since the

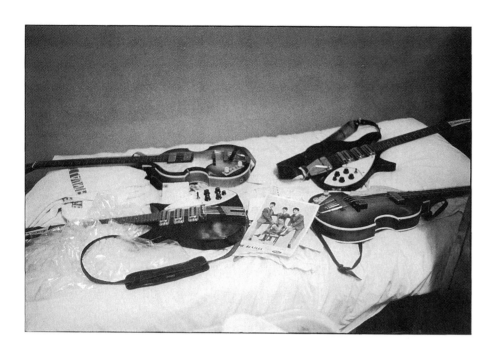

sonnel. For the fans, there was always a sense of urgency about getting to the Beatles if only for a moment. It was something none could describe, something that had to be felt.

Just before 1 P.M., some eighteen girls pushed a guard at the service entrance and flattened him against a door, but police came rushing to his aid immediately. At 1:10 P.M., about forty girls rushed the revolving doors below the Delmonico's leopard-skin marquee, but their mission was foiled by a mounted police officer who charged onto the sidewalk and scattered them in all directions. How was the staid old Delmonico holding up under the mania? "We used to be dowdy, but now we swing," said one hotel spokeswoman. "We welcome the Beatles."

The Beatles tried, but, with the din in the streets below, they didn't get much sleep and finally got up around 2 P.M. for a breakfast of corn flakes, soft-boiled eggs, orange juice, and tea. Ringo, still depressed, listened to the last pleading appeals for his lost medal. It was, in Pop Radio Land, the news story of the day. Finally, Angie, along with three girl-friends, appeared before the WABC microphones. She had, she said, accidentally pulled the medal from Ringo's neck when she tried to kiss him. At their meeting, a grateful Ringo soundly kissed Angie several times as she giggled with delight. Then Paul McCartney joined in, kissing all four girls. And Ringo, still tired, but happy, put the medal back around his neck.

At 5:30 the Beatles held a press conference in Delmonico's Crystal Ballroom. The working press, including the handful of those who'd waited for hours last night, were anxious for

Montreal. Beatles, everything British was appealing, especially those "foony" accents that every Beatleperson worth her weight in Beatle vinyl tried to duplicate. With binoculars and cameras, the fans scanned the hotel's louvered windows again and again. Every few minutes, other hotel guests or disc jockeys wearing Beatles wigs popped their heads out of their windows. It never failed to raise a howl of screams. But the real Beatles never did windows.

Nearly one hundred policemen—eighteen on horseback—and more than a dozen private guards prevented most of the fans from crossing the Delmonico threshold. All the tricks were attempted, but they all failed in the end. Some girls tried to bribe reporters for use of their press cards. Others, dressed in mature suits to disguise their true age, had made it through but were later ejected by hotel per-

some real time. As usual, the *Datebook* kids were also ready, press cards in hand. And since this was New York there was a host of teen-magazine editors and writers, along with numerous representatives of fan clubs, and, as always, the dee-jays, VIPs, and others with a good line all waiting to ask questions of the Beatles. The newspapermen were furious and they let Derek know it. But Derek had had no sleep, having spent the entire night taking one call after another. With a brandy bottle in hand, he was toughening up. They were, after all, trying to accommodate everybody. He still hadn't learned he could just say "no."

Meanwhile, Norman Weiss was upstairs waiting for an okay. There had been a great **Montreal.**

deal of concern about getting the Beatles from Manhattan into the tennis stadium in Queens, primarily because it meant they would have to drive through the Midtown Tunnel. "The thought of getting stuck in there was absolutely horrifying to everybody," says Weiss. "We would have been trapped—sitting ducks." The solution was simple—a helicopter. But the tennis stadium officials were horrified. Land a helicopter on the tennis courts? Risk the famed center court where Don Budge and Bill Tilden once bounded? Out of the question. Residents were already complaining about the noise it would make. The bureaucracy was thick. But the NYPD was experienced this time and they were on the Beatles' side. At 7:30 P.M. the Beatles and their entourage left Delmonico's, drove to the Wall Street helicopter pad, and lifted off for the Forest Hills Tennis Stadium. Everyone aboard marveled at this new perspective of Manhattan.

When Bob Bonis arrived at the stadium early to check things out, he discovered, to his chagrin, that promoter Sid Bernstein had set up a tent "backstage" as the Beatles' dressing room. "Where's the furniture?" Bonis asked. "Where's—anything?" The tent was empty. "This will never do, we're supposed to be in there," Bonis stressed, pointing to the tennis club. "They wouldn't allow that," Bernstein replied. "They're afraid the Beatles will wreck the place." This was insulting. Bonis had to do something fast. "We *can't* use this," Bonis reiterated, stretching his six-foot frame. "It's a little too late now, they're already on the helicopter," replied Bernstein. Bonis, in reality a gentle man, exhaled. "No. It's not too late." He pulled out a small

Montreal.

Key West, Florida.

machine from his back pocket, and stretched open the antennas. "I'll call them right now and tell them to go the hell back where they came from unless you get them proper dressing rooms." Bernstein, alarmed, took off and Bonis pushed the antennas down and put his portable AM/FM radio back in his pocket. Dressing rooms—inside the tennis club—were waiting when the Beatles' helicopter arrived at 8 P.M.

"The helicopter was so noisy on the inside," recalls Weiss. "The engines were really loud, and the sound of the propeller, but when we got down to about five hundred feet the screaming of the crowd overpowered the noise of the helicopter. Everybody must've had a flash camera, and as we're coming down, all the flashes are going off, the screaming, it was like gods or a UFO was descending. It was very surrealistic and other-worldly. And very touching."

On stage, the Righteous Brothers were struggling to get through their set, but gave up when the helicopter landed. "It seemed as if the Beatles were as amazed as anybody about what was going on," recalls Medley. "They seemed to be having a lot of fun with it. But for us, the opening acts, it was getting very, very difficult. It was like the bootcamp of rock 'n' roll." For Medley and Bobby Hatfield, it had become unbearable. "It was impossible to win," Medley says. "The tour wasn't great money for us—$750 a week, compared to $500 a night which we were getting at home in L.A., and it certainly wasn't doing anything for any of our careers. Nobody wanted to see us. Especially on the East Coast, the Righteous Brothers might as well have been a religious choir. It was that simple. We were just in the way." So that night, they asked Brian to be released from their contract and the show. "He was great," Medley remembers. "He just said, 'I don't blame you.' We weren't mad at anybody, certainly not the Beatles, but it just wasn't livable for us. The jellybeans, the screaming; everything that had happened when we played with them at the Washington, D.C., Coliseum in February was still going on, even though everybody really thought that was just a one-shot thing. Nobody expected it to go on and on and on." The Righteous Brothers agreed to stay on until a replacement was found. (When they went back to L.A., they recorded the song that took them to the top in December 1964, "You've Lost That Lovin' Feeling.")

Backstage, in the tennis club, Benny Goodman and his two college-age daughters were brought in to meet the Beatles. It was, as such meetings go, a difficult one, a compromising situation for the King of Swing, who in exchange for his coverage of the Beatles concert would get his own concert sponsored by and promoted by the radio station that had hired him. Epstein, who had been in New York and rejoined the tour on the Beatles' arrival, was, as usual, annoyed. He frequently cleared his throat, asked about the time, or brushed nonexistent lint from his trousers. Conversation between the two legends—Benny Goodman and the Beatles—didn't spark. "I have one of your 78's," Ringo tried. Goodman smiled. Only Derek had a real sense of appreciation for Goodman and when the agony was over the Beatles were relieved, Epstein was satisfied, and Derek was angry and de-pressed. "They could have tried," he said to Neil, scowling. "Don't be soft," Aspinall replied. "They're tired." Living amidst the mania was beginning to get to everybody.

An estimated crowd of seventeen thousand filled the tennis stadium to capacity and then some. Every seat was taken and even the aisles were overflowing. In the confusion of getting the Beatles to the show on time, nobody told the helicopter pilot to wait. When Weiss realized that there was no way out he headed for the phones. He wanted the helicopter back *before* they went onstage. From 9:15 to 9:45, the crowd stood and yelled, "We want the Beatles! We want the Beatles!" At 9:45 the chopper returned. At 9:50 New York got the Beatles. The once solemn citadel of tennis rocked and rolled. A young girl in a blue dress streaked down the aisle and scaled a fifteen-foot-high protective wire fence, heading straight for the Beatles and catching a squad of Burns Security Guards off guard. She made it up the fifteen feet to the stage and was only six feet away from *them* when two guards grabbed her by her heels and pulled her down, knocking production man Harry Hennessey right off the stage in the process. Dozens of the more than two hundred police officers on duty moved toward the stage. Four more boys and a girl hit the fence, but within seconds a contingent of at least twenty policemen captured them and hustled them out. The Beatles never missed a beat and it was one of their finest tour performances yet. Epstein and Taylor watched from the wings. Both had tears streaming from their eyes. These were the great moments that made everything else worthwhile. The Beatles bowed, then dashed for the red, white, and blue helicopter. In seconds, they were airborne for Manhattan. "It was extraordinary," remembers Geoffrey Ellis, Brian's friend from Liverpool who was then living in New York. "It really was like gods appeared from the sky and at the end of the performance, they went up again and—disappeared. It was very strange. And the effect lingered."

It was 10:45 P.M. when the Beatles arrived back at the Delmonico. As they walked down the corridor of the sixth floor, Ringo was in the lead. "Good evening, Mr. Starr," a tiny voice called out. Ringo looked down to see a perky five-year-old girl, all dressed in pink. "Hi—what a clean little girl. Would you like to come into our room for a while?" he asked. For Debbie Brandstatter, it was "like a dream." She had arrived and checked into the hotel with her eighteen-year-old Beatlemaniac sister, Penny, in hopes of seeing the Fab Four. Ringo took her by the hand and inside she met the others. They patted her on the head, but "treated me just like a grown-up," she said. She told them that Penny had painted pictures of them and saved $400 to go to London. Would they like to meet her? The Beatles were tired and wanted to relax. Little Debbie was escorted out, but she vowed never to take off her little pink dress.

The Beatles, Brian, Neil, and Mal retreated to one of the back bedrooms for dinner while Derek was down the hall in the hospitality room, tending to the press and other guests, including Peter Yarrow and Mary Travers of Peter, Paul, and Mary, and Murray the K. For the duration of the Beatles' visit, the hospitality room would be overflowing and

everybody wanted food and drinks. Despite their record earnings, the Beatles' expenses were mounting. Room service charges alone were staggering.

When Bob Dylan, road manager Victor Mamoudas, and *Saturday Evening Post* journalist Al Aronowitz arrived from Woodstock, they bypassed the hospitality suite and went directly to the Beatles' private suite, where the boys, Epstein, Mal, and Neil had just finished their dinners. Introductions made, Brian asked the American guests what they wanted to drink. "Cheap wine," Dylan responded. Middle-class American rebellion collided with upper-class British tradition. The only wines in the room were French, and expensive, so Mal was sent in search of a suitable vintage. In the meantime, pills were offered.

Uppers and downers had long been part of the music scene and this was a generation raised to believe that feeling good, or at least better, could be achieved through these little miracles of modern chemistry. Occasionally, pills served the purpose of flinging one to the edge of oblivion, where life was fast and euphoria beckoned. But for the most part, pills were simply a part of rock 'n' roll's survival kit, keeping one awake when the body and mind cried out for sleep. "I started on pills when I was seventeen, since I became a musician," Lennon said in later years. "Now that's drugs—bigger drugs than pot. The only way to survive in Hamburg, to play eight hours a night, was to take pills. I've always needed a drug to survive, the others too, but I always had more, more pills, more of everything because I'm more crazy probably."

John had brought an ample supply of chemical wonders along for the tour which he stashed in a pill box and kept in his leather bag. Among them were Drinamyls, tiny blue heart-shaped tablets known in England as "mother's little helpers," which featured a unique combination of stimulant and depressant; and Preludins, essentially a straight amphetamine.

Key West.

Getting through Customs was never a problem—in the U.K. and Canada the Beatles traveled without need of passports or checks, and in America nobody asked to look in their personal bags. John, and the others, were always extremely discreet and nobody outside the innermost circle knew anything about the pills. Around other musicians, however, it

was generally considered sociable to share.

The American visitors vigorously rejected the idea of pills. "How about something a little more organic?" Dylan suggested. "Something green . . . marijuana." The Beatles exchanged glances. It was a somewhat scary proposition. Shades of *Reefer Madness* still colored marijuana use—and it meant breaking the law in a foreign country and taking God knows what kinds of chances. "We've never really smoked marijuana before," Brian started. Actually, the Beatles had tried marijuana in Hamburg, and the effect had them all giggling. They had gotten stoned, but they hadn't really gotten high. It hadn't been a high-grade quality, "just the sticks," as Aspinall assessed later, and the experience had left them relatively unfazed. But, as the Beatles were about to find out, the quality of grass available in America was far more potent than that which was available in Europe.

"What about your song?" Dylan asked. "The one about getting high?"

Confused, John asked, "Which song would that be?"

"The one that goes, '. . . and when I touch you I get high, I get high . . .'"

"But those aren't the words," John said. "It's 'I can't hide, I can't hide'. . ." Misunderstanding aside, Dylan was anxious to turn them on and the Beatles were willing to give it a go. The procedure began. Doors were locked, most of the lights were turned off, candles and incense lit. Towels were stuffed along the bottom of the doorways, the shades pulled down, and the drapes drawn. Finally Dylan sat and began to roll thin little cigarettes, which, he explained, were called joints.

After lighting the first and issuing instructions on how to hold the smoke in the lungs, Dylan passed the joint to John, who passed it on to Ringo, "my official taster," he said. Ringo proceeded to smoke the whole thing. "What's it like?" John inquired, peering into Ringo's eyes and face for an answer since nothing was audibly forthcoming. Suddenly, Ringo burst out laughing. That did it. John, Paul, George, Mal, Neil, and Brian joined in and for the next several hours found new meaning in the words "I get high." Everything and everybody seemed funny, everything a laugh. A new door of perception opened that night, one that would not only come to profoundly influence the Beatles' creative genius but to have a strong impact upon the consciousness of a whole generation.

Meanwhile Derek, up to his eyeballs with guests wanting to meet the Beatles, called the suite. A voice answered. Who it belonged to, Derek was never sure. "Ay, doanbringennywon inere kozweerorl oussuvaredz." It was a Liverpool accent that could have belonged only to a Beatle, Mal, or Neil. Derek knew something was up, but what, he couldn't imagine. Nobody was going to have an audience with the Fab Four tonight. An hour later he picked up the ringing phone in the hospitality suite. It was Paul, instructing him to come "alone" to the suite. Bottle of Courvoisier in hand, Derek headed for the private rooms, where he found everyone "looking very happy." Brian, clutching a flower in his hand, welcomed him. "You must try it," Brian said. Paul gathered Derek up in a bear-hug and announced he'd been up there, pointing to the ceiling. The Beatles had gotten high.

"We've been turned on," said George, offering Derek a taste of "this wonderful stuff." Derek declined. "I'll stick to drink," he said. Somewhat alarmed by what he beheld, Derek felt it his duty to stay normal, "whatever that meant." For the next twenty minutes he listened to a host of new expressions before returning to the overflowing suite. "Get it down," Paul instructed Mal, convinced that words of brilliance were flowing from their mouths. Mal took notes throughout the evening. The Beatles spent the night "legless from laughing," as Harrison put it. Nothing would ever be quite the same again.

AUGUST 29, 1964:

"Is this a riot?" Cautiously, the tourist stuck his head out of his dusty station wagon. A tired policeman shook his head from side to side. "No," he sighed. "Just the Beatles." The Delmonico was still under siege. As the Beatles slept, the crowd chanted, "Show your faces!" Small groups of Beatlepeople continued mounting offenses, determined to infiltrate the hotel. Three girls scaled a building nearby, and in a series of over-the-roof ascents, climbed a water tower on an extension of the hotel, nearly reaching the fourth-floor level before being spotted. Several angry security guards pulled them down and led them back to the street. "Look," pleaded one girl to a policeman blocking the front entrance. "My name is Linda Beatle and I'm Ringo's sister, and I have to get inside to see my brother!" The policeman put his hands on his hips and laughed. "I happen to know that Ringo doesn't have a sister, young lady." The girl burst into tears. Foiled again. Two girls standing in ankle-deep rainwater along the curb looked dumbfounded when a reporter asked about the ill effects of standing in the water for so long. "What water?" said one of the girls.

Inside, four high school graduates, dressed in their Sunday best, made luncheon reservations and shelled out thirty dollars to get inside the hotel. As fate would have it, they found a reporter's press card in a telephone booth and made it all the way to the sixth floor—and into the waiting arms of security guards. Throughout the day, the hotel switchboard had been jammed with calls. According to switchboard supervisor Mrs. Lee Jacque, nearly 200,000 phone calls for the Beatles had been logged since their arrival on Friday. Everywhere, the air was rife with rumors. Was John really splitting from his wife, Cynthia? "Utterly ridiculous," Derek insisted. "They are the best-adjusted and healthiest married couple I know." Another rumor, however, was making the Beatles very nervous. The woman who had predicted Kennedy's assassination had just predicted that the Beatles' plane would crash the following week while en route from Philadelphia to Indianapolis. The Beatles tended to reject such rumors out of hand, but this one lingered in their minds, along with memories of Buddy Holly. Going down in a plane, in a burst of flames and twisted wreckage, was one of the Beatles' greatest fears. Who was this woman, they wondered, and had she really predicted Kennedy's assassination? "We've gotta find out," said Lennon.

Her name, they soon learned, was Jeane Dixon, and she claimed to be a psychic. Apparently, she *had* predicted Kennedy's assassination. That was good enough for John. "Let's call her and find out what's going on," Lennon said to Neil. They managed to reach Dixon at her Washington, D.C., office. "We hear you've been saying our plane will crash," Lennon began. "No, no, no, these are just rumors," Dixon responded. "It will not crash. Fly—fly—fly. Don't worry. Go ahead on your planned schedule, because nothing's going to happen, not by plane, train, or boat." Relieved, Lennon listened as Dixon explained that such rumors tended to pop up quite frequently, but that she had in fact made no such prediction regarding their airplane.

That evening, the Beatles were treated to hot dogs and salami sandwiches sent in from Nathan's Famous in Coney Island. With the last Beatle suit pressed and delivered by the hotel valet, they dressed, gave another press conference, and headed out. Two black limousines pulled up in front of the Delmonico and a group of the entourage climbed in and the cars sped away. The Beatles were still in the hotel, waiting at a side entrance on Fifty-ninth Street for two other limousines. With the blessing of the NYPD, the cars moved west on Fifty-ninth, normally an eastbound street. It was blocked to all traffic but the Beatles. As they turned down Madison Avenue and disappeared into the night, relieved police began dismantling the barricades on Park Avenue.

Key West.

The tennis stadium was packed to overflowing again tonight as the helicopter arrived. During the Beatles' performance, screaming, crying girls and boys tried to storm through the policemen and the barricades set up on the plywood floor that covered the tennis courts. Others closer to the front tested the wits and strength of some one hundred and fifty policemen and one hundred security guards who spread out around the stage. About fifty youngsters burst through but were carried away, screaming. This was a much more lively and determined crowd than Friday's. One girl made it up to the stage, ran to George and grabbed him in a hug, hanging onto his neck, as he struggled to keep up with the song. He hit the wrong note. She fainted and was carried off. "That was foony," Lennon said later, laughing. As the Beatles moved through their

137

set, nearly fifty girls who had passed out from hysteria or heat were carried, like wounded victims, from the field and delivered the the first-aid station set up in a tent. It got wild enough for the NYPD to call in members of the elite Tactical Police Force, used to handle such city emergencies as the Harlem riots, to strengthen the stage guard. One young man got one foot on the stage before being pulled off, but knocked out several footlights in the process. Someone hurled a tomato that hit Paul on the arm, spraying juice all over his jacket. This was getting to be a dirty job. The Beatles called it a night after twenty-five minutes onstage and bolted for the helicopter. A crowd of about fifty girls surged forward, broke through the police lines, and ran after them in hot pursuit. The Beatles won the race, ducking into the helicopter that would deposit them in Atlantic City.

ATLANTIC CITY, NEW JERSEY

SUNDAY, AUGUST 30, 1964:

It was midnight as the Beatles checked into the Lafayette Motor Inn, a boardwalk motel in the seaside resort. A cloak of secrecy had been dropped on their intended destination, and, for the first time on the tour, John, Paul, George, and Ringo managed to walk through the front doors like normal human beings. Brian had reserved the top floor for the entire cast and crew of the tour, and, for the first time since L.A., they could wander up and down the halls with ease. After room service dinners, the Beatles spent the evening playing cards and generally hanging out and talking with others in the entourage. "They missed out on a lot, being prisoners of devotion," Mal Evans recalled years later. "It was always difficult to know who really wanted to be their friends and who wanted to be close to them because they were the Beatles. They couldn't really sort out who was genuine and who wasn't."

By the time they awoke in midafternoon, the Beatles' hideaway had been discovered. They spent the afternoon reading and watching one of the few color TVs they'd seen in American hotel rooms before heading out by limousine to the Atlantic City Convention Hall at around 7:30 P.M., to perform on the same stage where Lyndon Johnson had accepted the Democratic presidential nomination three nights before. "The Beatles almost ate it that night," recalls Medley. "I remember looking out the window and seeing the kids, wall to wall in the street. You couldn't even see the street, and inside the hall it was packed. All of a sudden there comes two or three limousines and for some strange reason, the Beatles were in these limousines and for the life of me I don't know how they got in. Ringo almost bought it in the crush of the crowd. I saw one kid's leg get crushed between two of the limos and it was scary. There was nothing funny or cute about it."

As leftover blown-up posters of Lyndon Johnson smiled down on them, the Beatles performed before nineteen thousand fans, grossing $68,797.35, and sending eight hysterical young girls to Atlantic City Hospital. After the concert, the Beatles followed Neil's lead. He'd devised an escape plan. It was he who was directly responsible for the Beatles' well-being. They trusted him, felt lost without

Key West.

him. "I can never be at a loss for a plan or we'd still be stuck in some theater now," he told a local journalist. The Beatles took an elevator to the basement, and sprinted down a series of underground passages to a waiting medical van sequestered on a blocked-off street and headed back to the Lafayette, where they holed up for two days of rest.

MONDAY, AUGUST 31, 1964:

As the boys ate their breakfasts in midafternoon, Bob Bonis headed out to find some amusements for them. He figured since they were in Atlantic City that Monopoly might be an interesting game. As he inquired for help at the front desk, he overheard a mother instructing her daughter in the art of black mail. "Once you get up there, make sure John Lennon's in the room and then scream, 'Rape!'" the mother said. "We'll be rich." Horrified, Bonis went up to the security desk, relayed the overheard conversation, and issued strict orders: *No one gets in. Period.*

The Beatles spent a quiet, undisturbed afternoon and evening looking at the wares that local merchants brought to them, watching television, reading, and playing Monopoly with *real* money. Later, Ringo started a game of poker which ran into the early hours of the morning.

Still later, the Beatles put on an impromptu show of old-time vaudeville bits in their suite, complete with impersonations of comics, rah-rah musical numbers, and parody tunes. "They were great," recalls Bonis. "*Great.* it was the Beatles as Palladium, old show biz acts, and they were hysterical."

TUESDAY, SEPTEMBER 1, 1964:

The Beatles had been in virtual isolation since their Convention Hall concert and this particular day would be another devoted to sleeping late and hanging out. More Monopoly, Scrabble, poker, and blackjack, and, as always, listening to the radio and watching television. On the evening news they learned that Britain and France were negotiating on the joint development of a nuclear armed missle and that the "race riots" in Philadelphia, where the Beatles were headed next, seemed to be over.

The top floor of the Lafayette featured a lounge and on this night it was set up to show some movies. George Hamid, the promoter of the concert, owned the world-famous Steel Pier and also owned several movie theaters. He had instructed a projectionist to bring a couple of popular films to the hotel for screening between midnight and 4 A.M. The projectionist didn't know who the films were for, but as it happened one of the season's box office smashes was none other than *A Hard Day's Night*. As the Beatles sat and watched themselves on the silver screen, they laughed and gave a behind-the-scenes report on what the cameras didn't catch. Orders for the

soundtrack were now at two million and counting, and the film had made movie history as the most-sold-out-in-advance of any film.

Baltimore.

ATLANTIC CITY

Several hundred fans maintained their vigil outside the Lafayette, even though the Beatles had not emerged from the hotel since their concert on Sunday. Everybody in the crowd knew, however, that they would be leaving today. At 2:15 P.M., while the Beatles were being smuggled out through the kitchen and into a closed seafood delivery truck, the traveling press and other members of the crew ran out the front doors and jumped into the decoy limousines. The fans were foiled again and the Beatles were driven to a rendezvous point six miles west of the city, where they climbed aboard one of two chartered buses for the ride into Philadelphia.

PHILADELPHIA, PENNSYLVANIA

In the last week, the City of Brotherly Love had been anything but that. While tension in Philadelphia was easing, American blacks, still called Negroes, were anxious for the immediate implementation of their long-overdue civil rights. Philadelphia, nonetheless, held an allure for the Beatles. It was a rock 'n' roll city—home to the Philadelphia sound of Frankie Avalon and Fabian, as well as "American Bandstand."

Just before 4 P.M. the Beatles' buses, guided by a police escort, snuck unrecognized into the Convention Hall, using a lower-level entrance to avoid the crowd of thousands lined up behind white wooden barricades. Homemade signs—"City of Beatle Love," one read— bobbed up and down atop the crowd. A bedsheet crayoned with "Beatles 4 Ever" rippled in the hands of its holders. Nobody in the crowd realized the Beatles had just driven by. It was the smoothest, most subdued arrival they'd experienced in America.

As waves of screams ebbed and flowed outside, backstage, the Beatles ate, strummed their guitars, and played poker. Since the tour had suffered some serious backstage inva-

sions, it was decided, while in Atlantic City, to issue identifiable backstage passes—makeshift colored cardboard discs bearing the appropriate date. For the time, it was a novel idea. Those without passes simply would not be allowed backstage.

The tour had been suffering from huge expenses, and now Charles O. Finley had come back to Brian with an unbelievable offer of $150,000. It would help alleviate the expenses, and there was the consideration that no artist in the history of show business had ever been paid that amount of money for one concert. Would they mind giving up their rest day? "Whatever you say, Brian," replied John. Kansas City had snared the Beatles. After the show, Brian would fly to New York to sign the newly drawn contract.

143

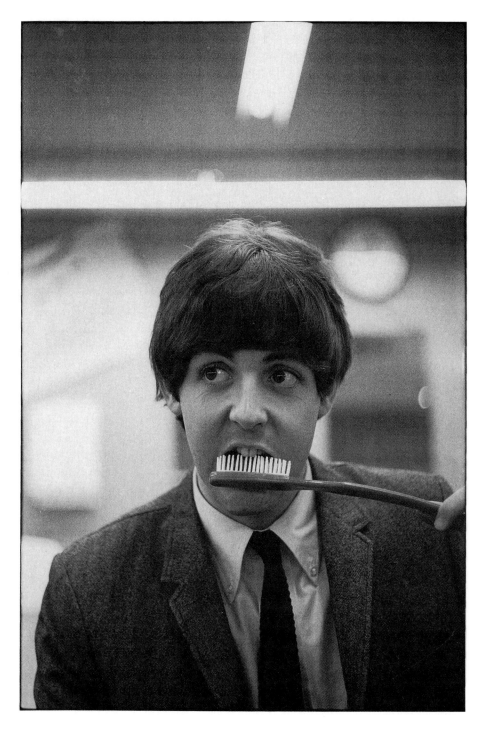

Baltimore.

Even though their cancellation at the Warwick Hotel had been announced to the press, a spokesman for all Philadelphia-area hotels said every hotel had been plagued with calls regarding the Beatles' reservation plans. And this afternoon the Warwick was surrounded. When a maid shook a mop out the window, it drew a roar of screams, and in the last twenty-four hours more than forty girls, who had infiltrated through back entrances and freight elevators, were ejected from rooms and broom closets.

At about 6 P.M. the Beatles held a press conference for twenty-five newsmen, twenty-five lucky teenagers, and fifty policemen, in a meeting room near the Convention Hall's main auditorium. Ringo, George, Paul, and John sat behind a table laden with fan mail and two cakes, one decorated with a Beatle wig and the other bearing the words "Beatles for President." As they sipped on soft drinks, they fielded some fifty questions adroitly and with obvious enjoyment. McCartney did most of the talking, though John, George, and Ringo were quick to jump in when the mood struck.

"Do the pushing, screaming fans ever get on your nerves?"

"We never have a bad time. It's just the police who get hurt," said Ringo.

"Do you think your popularity will last?"

"*No!*" they shouted in unison.

"What serious music do you like?"

"Rock 'n' roll," snapped John.

"But that's not what he means by serious music," said Paul. "All music is serious. It depends on who is listening."

"Oh, that's deep," quipped George.

"When you were here last February, you said you found American girls too forward. What do you think of them now?"

"Forward?" John asked. "No—*backward!*"

But the other three amended that one quickly: "Oh, they're great, we think they're great."

"Have you found American teenagers to be any different from teenagers in England or other countries you've visited?"

"No, they're all the same—except the accent," said Paul. "But they scream in the same tongue."

At 6:20 the Convention Hall doors were opened, and the thunderous rumble made by thousands of running, pounding little feet reverberated through the building. The 12,097 tickets available for tonight's performance had sold out ninety minutes after going on sale last May 4, and there were at least a thousand fans without tickets waiting outside, desperately hoping.

Clarence "Frogman" Henry had been brought on board as the opening act to replace the Righteous Brothers. Henry, whose style owed much to Fats Domino and Professor Longhair, combined elements of jazz and blues and fused them into rock. His first hit, "Ain't Got No Home," a Top 10 hit in 1956's R&B field, had given him the nickname "Frogman" because of the trick vocal effects he used on the track. Following the Bill Black Combo and Henry, were the Exciters, and then Jackie DeShannon.

Like the other audiences, this one just wanted the Beatles, and when they ran onstage

Baltimore.

145

around 9:30 P.M. the trademarks surfaced in force: Jellybeans, flashing cameras, screams of joy. "Take me back to Columbia Avenue," wailed one policeman who had just left the riot-torn North Philadelphia area. What had once been extraordinary had now become commonplace for the Beatles. Within the short space of thirty minutes it was all over and the Beatles were gone, their exit as smooth as their arrival.

At North Philadelphia Airport, they boarded the plane still a little jittery about the alleged and denied prediction of their plane crashing—tonight. By 10:45 P.M., they were airborne. There was no turning back now.

Baltimore.

INDIANAPOLIS

SEPTEMBER 3, 1964:

The flight ended up being a rather uneventful one, and, like a military troop staging an invasion under cover of darkness, the Beatles snuck into Indianapolis' Weir Cooke Airport shortly before 1 A.M., where Lennon made a humorous prediction of his own: "A big cop will grab me by the arm and take me to a waiting car." As Indianapolis *Star* reporter Frank Salzarulo later wrote, "It happened exactly that way." The Beatles were off, this time to the Speedway Motel.

Except for the two dozen police cars, the motel's parking lot was relatively isolated as the Beatles' entourage pulled up. Only a small crowd of about one hundred had risked restriction and appeared in the wee hours of the morning to greet them. Like so many roadside motels across America, the Speedway had an open layout with outdoor hallways leading to the rooms, something that made the Beatles' entourage feel vulnerable.

And, indeed, sleep was impossible that

Baltimore.

night because of people throwing pebbles at the windows. Later, John picked up the phone and paged Art Schreiber, news director of Cleveland's KYW radio and correspondent for its parent company Westinghouse Broadcasting System, who had picked up the tour in New York. Schreiber had covered all the major news events in America—Kennedy, Martin Luther King, civil rights, and the space program, and Lennon wanted to talk. "He had a genuine fondness for Kennedy and would always ask, 'Why was he killed?'" Schreiber recalls. Further, John was appalled at America's treatment of blacks. He'd been watching television news footage of police hosing them with water and chasing and beating them with sticks. And now he was seeing the police at their concerts start to resort to the same tactics

Baltimore.

with Beatles fans. "He couldn't understand why the police were being so heavy-handed at the concerts. He just couldn't understand what was going on in this country, and he couldn't understand the violence." It would be an ongoing conversation during the next month, with Schreiber and with Larry Kane, who was covering the tour for Miami's WFUN radio.

"They were really the first pop idols to say what they thought and they all had a real sense of moral consciousness," remembers Kane, who at twenty-one was a contemporary of the Beatles and beyond Schreiber the only other American newsman covering the tour. "They all had this sense, but Lennon had a rage and when it wasn't directed at people he didn't care about, it was directed at injustice. He used to lecture me about Vietnam, saying, 'You're full of shit over there and your country's making a terrible mistake.' I mean it's 1964—Vietnam had barely begun really, and I'm sitting there defending my country."

Later in the day, under heavy police protection, the Beatles headed out to the 500 racetrack, home to the world-famous Indianapolis 500, and took a spin around the track in their limousine. Inside the racetrack's office, the Beatles were shown a model of the track, complete with remote-control slot cars. It was state-of-the-art American toy-making and they were fascinated. Afterward, they headed to the miniature golf range on the grounds and proved to everyone that they were better musicians than golfers.

The Beatles were to perform two shows as part of the Indiana State Fair—one at 5 P.M. in the Coliseum, another at 9:30 outside in the grandstand. Remarkably there were still some four thousand seats, at three and four dollars apiece, available for the second show, but they were going fast. Just minutes before the Beatles arrived, police poured from the Coliseum doors and formed a human wall, making a path for the state police motorcade. The Beatles were whisked safely inside, but their limousines didn't fare as well: They were attacked and stripped for souvenirs. The windows were broken, the mirrors ripped from their mountings, the upholstery torn.

On the grounds, souvenir sellers were doing a furious business. One claimed his best-selling button was the one that read "I Hate the Beatles," which sold mostly to teenage boys. "Me, I like the Beatles," said the concessionaire. "They're making me rich."

The screaming began during the intermission causing one little boy to run in panic from the hall. A cordon of police surrounded the stage, nervously beholding the uncontrolled hysteria before them. "Ringo for President" signs waved in the fury. Then, at 6:21 P.M., the Beatles ran onto the Coliseum stage. Jellybeans. Flashbulbs. Screams. An estimated 12,513 voices let loose and some of the farmers wondered whether their prize stock would drop from fright. Nonetheless, there were actually some moments when the screaming died down and the Beatles could almost hear themselves sing.

As the Beatles sprinted from the stage, some four thousand young fans and a few oldsters packed the street between the Coliseum and the cattle barn in hopes of catching a glimpse of the Fab Four on their way to a

press conference in the Radio Building. Backstage, word circulated among the Beatles' immediate entourage that a bomb threat had been made. State Police Sergeant George Young and a six-man squad had already searched and secured the Radio Building, so they wanted the Beatles to go there immediately. The fair's entertainment manager, Robert Weedon, had received the telephone bomb threat from a man who said the Beatles "would be injured by either a gun or an explosion." The Beatles were slipped out through a special VIP emergency exit on the south side of the

Coliseum, taken around the hog barn, and delivered safely to the Communications Center inside the Radio Building. The bomb squad headed over to the grandstand to search for signs of explosives or gun-toting maniacs, but they only found a few thousand anxious girls.

At the press conference, the Beatles were introduced to Miss Indiana State Fair and were presented with an original cartoon from the Indianapolis *News*' Robbie Robinson. Then the questions came.

"It's been said that the girls scream because they are actually revolting against their

Baltimore.

parents. Do you take credit for that?"

"They've been revolting for years," said Paul.

"I've never noted them revolting," added John.

"How do you stand on the draft?"

"About five foot, eleven inches," said John.

"What would you do if the fans got past the police lines?"

"Die laughing," said Ringo.

"Where did you think of the hair-dos?"

"We've told so many lies about it, we've forgotten," said John.

"Actually we got the idea from a German photographer who had hair like ours," said Paul.

"Do you have any suggestions for possible American repayment to England for the Beatles?"

"Just let us off the income tax," snapped George.

They went on to play the second concert without incident—if you didn't count twenty-nine minor injuries—mostly faintings or cases of hysteria.

151

INDIANAPOLIS

FRIDAY, SEPTEMBER 4, 1964:

While America's largest scientific satellite, the orbiting geophysical observatory, rocketed toward an elliptical orbit to conduct the most exhaustive study yet of the dangers to manned space exploration, Ringo contemplated the dangers of exploring Indiana. "Can't sleep, chums, suppose we could go for a bit of a ride in the country?" It was 5 A.M. when Ringo approached two Indiana state troopers with his request. "Why not?" one of them said. Ringo climbed into the squad car and

Baltimore.

they drove off to tour Indianapolis. As they passed the governor's mansion, Ringo asked, "Is the wall to keep the governor in or the people out?" The troopers were charmed by his wit and politeness. When they had finished touring the city, they decided to drive out to one of the trooper's homes, a farm twenty-five miles north of Indianapolis. On the way they stopped for breakfast in a restaurant on U.S. 31 near Carmel. Two customers walked by their table. "Did you see that jerk with the Beatle wig on?" one snorted. The troopers looked at Ringo straight-faced; then all three laughed. As they finished eating, a woman, family in tow, walked up to the table. They had come from Kalamazoo, Michigan, hoping to see the Beatles, but had been unable to get tickets. Ringo shook her hand and the hands of her children and then gave each an autograph.

On their arrival at the farm, Ringo and the trooper went to wake his eleven-year-old daughter. "Am I dreaming?" she asked. She took Ringo around the farm, completely astonishing four neighborhood children who had dropped by to witness the unbelievable. As they headed back to the Speedway about 6:40 A.M., the troopers asked what it was like to be a Beatle. "They roll us out of bed, tell us to get dressed, shove us in a limousine, and then either take us to the airport, a hotel, or the theater where we're performing, and that's about it really," Ringo said. "Usually we don't even know where we are. When we landed here we thought we were in Canada, because of those hats you wear."

The Beatles, escorted by state troopers, left the Speedway Motel at 1 P.M. without the $86,950.96 they had earned for their two state fair performances. In a dispute over the motel bill, the check was being held at the request of the motel manager pending payment for five rooms used by security guards. According to tour manager Ira Sidelle, the State Fair Board, as promoter, was to pay for the security guards' lodgings, but they were saying the expense belonged to the Beatles. The motel thought it was "chintzy" of the Beatles' management to quibble over $500. But, as per the contracts, the expense did belong to the State Fair Board and money was becoming something of an issue.

There was already a major dispute brewing with the IRS. Rumors had been circulating through Washington that the Beatles' earnings from United States shows were being diverted to an offshore Bahamian corporation. It wasn't true, but the rumors—combined with everyone's awareness of how much money the Beatles were pulling in—was enough to bestir U.S. government accountants. There was a double-tax treaty between the United States and the United Kingdom so it seemed obvious that the Beatles should be exempt from U.S. taxation. Even *Variety* declared that the Bea-

Baltimore.

tles were exempt because of the treaty. But then there was the question of whether or not the four had a permanent American establishment, or agent. As far as the U.S. government is concerned, when in doubt, withhold first and resolve later. The IRS notified GAC and required that the agency withhold 30 percent of the Beatles' U.S. earnings pending determination of whether they were liable to pay tax to the United States.

Beyond that, the hotels where the Beatles stayed were making a fortune off them on room service charges alone, and most of the entourage were convinced the prices for them were higher than for other, less famous, guests. Since promoters supplied security only for the show, in most cities police had to be paid by the Beatles for their services.

Fair officials eventually indicated they would pick up the charges for the extra five rooms used by security guards, and Ira Sidelle was given a check, minus the $1,719.02 for Indiana state tax.

On the flight into Milwaukee, Paul swiped a "To Hell with the Beatles" button from Mal, who had gotten it from the flight engineer, Robert Miller, who had worn it onto the plane as a joke. One of the American Flyers Airline public relations women had made him take it off. With evident enjoyment Paul modeled the button for the cast and crew, clowning and garnering laughs from everyone.

Baltimore.

MILWAUKEE, WISCONSIN

"Beatles Go Home!" "Ringo's Sick" "Bugs—Leave!" Two teenage boys boldly carried these homemade signs into the corral of Beatle-people penned behind snowfences at General Mitchell Field awaiting the Beatles arrival in Milwaukee. A mob of girls turned on them and chased them out, grabbing the "Ringo's Sick" sign in the process. While numerous American religious leaders, psychologists, politicians, and parents continued to wage counterattacks on the Beatles in the press and on the homefront throughout the summer, it was mostly teenage boys who opposed them on the battlefields. The Beatles, as the girls saw it, were the epitome of cool; their hair was fab, their music gear, and American boys were nowhere with their butch-waxed crew cuts. It was more than some all-American boys could take, but it was a battle they never won.

The crowd that assembled to greet the Beatles had begun arriving during the night. By mid-morning, the fans took up the space of fifteen blocks, and sheriff's deputies were turning girls back at the airport terminal. Sixty-five Milwaukee policemen, thirty-two sheriff's deputies, and four airport police officers herded the nearly one thousand fans to an area just north of the terminal and put up snow fences around them, then reinforced those with barricades. Souvenir sellers hawked pennants and buttons while fire trucks were driven into position, their hoses readied, "to cool off the hysteria if the kids break through the fence," as Sheriff Michael Wolke explained.

At the last minute, fearing that the girls would stampede the barricades, escape onto the field, and be injured by the plane's propellers, police instructed airport officials to bring the Beatles' plane down far from the crowd. "We thought this would be the proper way to handle it," said Deputy Police Inspector W. Sheldon Jens, who added that the decision was made jointly by police, airport officials, and the Beatles' representatives. The American Flyers' Electra II touched down at 4:30 P.M., on the opposite side of the airport. By the time the crowd found out, the Beatles were long gone.

Milwaukee Police Captain Edward Kondracki moved to the fenced-off area with a loudspeaker: "The airplane has landed," he announced. "The Beatles are on their way to the hotel." The crowd was inconsolable; girls screamed and wailed. One girl tried futilely to control her tears as she told a reporter, "I waited a whole year to see them. They're only here once in a lifetime and we can't even see them then." Others were mad. "We've been here since 7:30 this morning, and they wouldn't even show their ugly faces," one bitter young

En route from Baltimore to Pittsburgh.

before 5 P.M., the real caravan darted into the blocked-off hotel gargage before the waiting teenagers knew what had happened. A few girls jumped over the barricades and into the street, but they were quickly snared and hustled back to the sidewalk. The hotel had been checked out the night before and again in the morning to ferret out any teenagers hidden in the woodwork. The last to go were four girls who had hidden overnight in a seventh-floor boiler room, subsisting on a banana, a pack of cigarettes, and a Coke.

The Beatles, minus John, whose throat was sore, headed downstairs almost immediately for a press conference. As local photographers snapped pictures of Ringo's rings, one of the newsmen commented on how pale they looked. "We're all ill, the lot of us," Derek Taylor said. Still, the Beatles were witty and won over even some of the toughest Midwestern skeptics.

"Do you think the pandemonium you cause is ridiculous?"

"Nothing's ridiculous when people enjoy themselves," said Paul. "We're not idols, you know. That's what the press makes us out to be, but it's all roobish. We're just chaps."

"Was there any need from a safety point to have avoided the fans at the airport?"

"We don't think so, no." answered Paul. McCartney was upset about the arrival. "The police told us we couldn't go past 'em. It's mean not to let 'em have a wave. It's a lousy deal . . . a dirty trick."

"But the police say it was your manager's decision to duck out," said a radio newsman.

"Ooh, it's a lie. Our manager wasn't even on the plane," said Paul.

girl stated. The Beatles, however, were at the mercy of local law enforcement and had little or no control over these matters. Belatedly realizing the anguish the girls had suffered, the sheriffs offered apologies.

Meanwhile, the Beatles' five-car motorcade raced through Milwaukee at speeds of up to sixty miles per hour, passing a factory where the workers leaned out of windows cheering them on, and a high school where the football team quickly lined up and yelled, "Hey, Beatles!"

Police had roped off and barricaded two city blocks around the Coach House Motor Inn, admitting only adults and teenagers who could prove they had reason to be at the hotel or nearby businesses. A funeral procession that happened upon the crowd was greeted with ear-piercing shrieks. Somebody's dearly departed got an unexpected send-off. Just

"Ooh, it was a dirty lying policeman who said that," said George.

"What deficiency in American youth are you supplying?" asked a priest.

Paul wrinkled his brow. "There's nothing like that. They're not deficient. They just like our records."

"What is your appeal?" the priest demanded.

"Our appeal," said Ringo, "is that we're normal lads."

"What are you rebelling against?"

"Ooh, we're not rebelling against anything," said Paul.

"Well, don't you hate your parents?"

"No," Paul said, looking startled.

"Well, don't you think all teenagers rebel against their parents?"

With the great Fats Domino, New Orleans.

"Well, it's the thing to do at a certain age. Didn't you when you were young?" answered Paul.

"You hate the press?"

Paul shook his head. "Not at all. They're chaps. They've got a job to do."

"Do you enjoy putting the press on?"

"We're not putting on the press. We're just being ourselves," said Ringo.

"How do the Beatles keep their psychic balance?"

"There's four of us so if one goes a little potty, it's all right," said George.

"Do you prefer to see girls in dresses?"

"Yes, yes, yes." They agreed unanimously. "Especially if they don't have the figure to take slacks, you know," added Paul, grinning.

SHORTLY after 8 P.M., the Beatles left for the Milwaukee Arena, where hundreds of letters had been stacked and bagged for delivery that night. Bundles of fan mail awaited them at every stop, along with homemade cookies, decorated cakes, and hordes of stuffed animals. Other gifts ranged from elaborate drawings to embroidered bras. The Beatles did keep those gifts that were compelling for their uniqueness or artistry. In some places, they didn't even get a chance to review the booty, but they always left instructions to have the gifts delivered to children's hospitals or a worthy charity.

At 6:30 P.M., a line of twelve thousand began moving into the Arena. Inside, a force of two hundred policemen, two hundred ush-

ers, and sixty doormen assumed their positions. Some of the cops grooved, chanting: "*Yeah, yeah, yeah*, use all the doors, please, *yeah, yeah, yeah.*"

Arena manager Elmer Krahn stepped to the microphone at about 8 P.M. "What a fine audience Milwaukee boys and girls are," he beamed. "I'm urging you to show the Beatles that we are the most well-behaved group in the entire United States." Being well behaved, however, was certainly against the grain of rock 'n' roll, and most certainly against the grain of Beatlemania.

Outside the Arena, eighteen-year-old Stanley Fronczak just about convinced police and a crowd of about seventy-five youngsters that he was Ringo's brother and had to get into the Arena. With his long hair, longer by a millimeter than even the Beatles, he looked the part, but when word arrived from backstage, it wasn't good. The little drummer had no brother. "Go on," one of the cops snarled. "Move on." Fronczak refused, and police took him into custody.

At 8:27, as the Exciters played onstage, the sound of the Beatles' motorcycle escort rumbled through the walls of the Arena. All heads turned in the direction of the engine sounds. The Exciters might as well have left. The Beatles had arrived and that was all that mattered to the audience.

Backstage, it was the usual scene. Police officers, photographers, and reporters milled about. The Beatles relaxed on their cots, sipped soft drinks, and checked out their gifts. Backstage I.D. passes had become part of the required routine, but it was an entirely new concept to most of the local folks, so at least one fan—a woman in her early twenties—snuck through "on courage" by telling people she was looking for her boyfriend. She made it as far as the dressing room door.

The Beatles slid through lines of police guarding the stage at 9:08 P.M. Their dark blue mohair suits glistened as flashbulbs popped. Parents and poker-faced policemen plugged their ears as the screams heightened in intensity. John made his characteristic funny faces at the audience to which the fans responded with jellybeans. Paul hammed it up: "Clap so we can hear you," he screamed.

"We may not have the Braves next summer," wrote Milwaukee *Journal* reporter Gerald Kloss, about the event, "but now our status as a cultural center can never be dimmed."

After the show, police recruits flanked out in a protective screen as the Beatle's car maneuvered its way slowly out of the Arena garage and sped back to the Coach House.

The Beatles arrived at the hotel without incident, despite the nearly one thousand fans crowded around it. John had a cold, as did several other members of the entourage, and after their usual late dinner the Beatles received antibiotic injections from the hotel doctor, conducted a few interviews, and called it an early night. Shortly after 11 P.M., police went around with loudspeakers announcing the 11 P.M. curfew for those under sixteen, and the crowd dwindled to only one hundred or so diehards.

Backstage trailer at the City Park Stadium, New Orleans.

"My problem is always the same—they don't get up early," Taylor told waiting newsmen. It was nearly 11:30 A.M. and the Beatles were still sleeping. Some one thousand fans gathered once again outside the Coach House to await their departure.

At 2:15, four black limousines and ten police motorcycles pulled up to the motel. While police revved their engines in the Coach House driveway, the captain in charge of security fumed outside the suite where Paul was making a phone call to fourteen-year-old Christine Cutler, who had bought a ticket to the Beatles show, but fell seriously ill two weeks before and had to be hospitalized. According to Christine's doctor her condition was aggravated by missing the Beatles. What was wrong with Christine? They didn't know. Tests, they hoped, would tell. The doctor's wife had called the Milwaukee *Journal* and the newspaper relayed the story to the Beatles. "Well, doctors are professionals. They don't make such requests unless they're serious," said Paul. Of course he would call. The *Journal* sent a reporter and made arrangements to connect a phone to the girl's room. With the hotel switchboard jammed with incoming phone calls to the Beatles, it took fifteen minutes to get through, but Paul finally made it. When the phone rang in Christine's room, nurses huddling just outside her room scurried in. "Listen, I heard you missed the show," Paul started. "Well, that's a bit of a drag for you. Well, I phoned to see how you were, so how are you?" "Fine," Christine feebly began. When it was over, Christine asked if she

New Orleans.

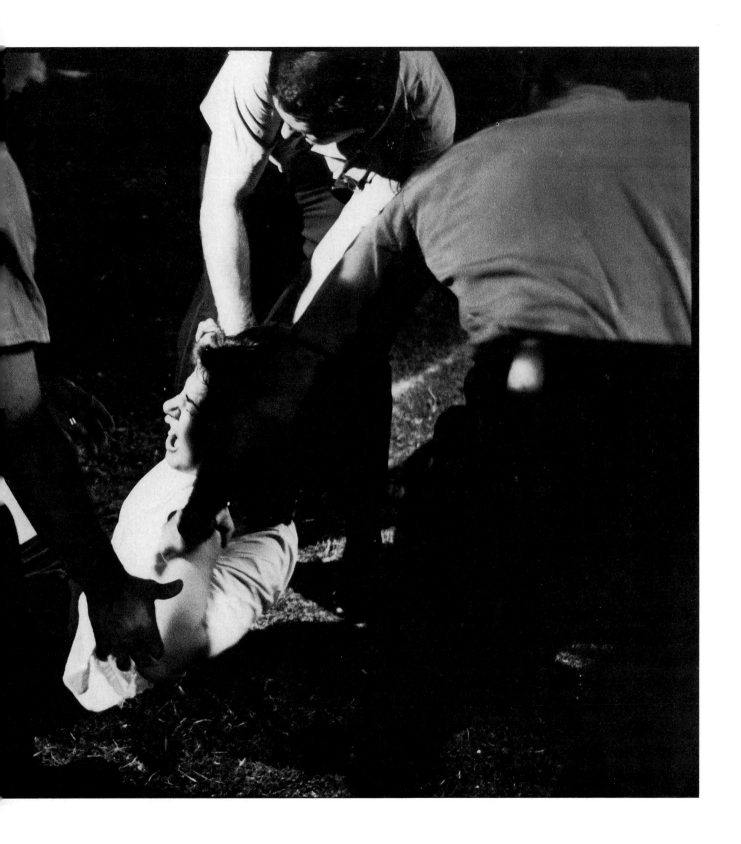

could take the phone home with her, and the nurses cried.

As George, Ringo, John, and Paul ducked into the limousines, hundreds of fans broke through police lines, momentarily stopping the cars. Meanwhile, fans invaded the Beatles' suite, snatching leftover eggs, toast, crackers, and ashtrays, before police ordered them out.

The boys waved to the several hundred screaming girls who had come to bid them farewell at the airport. "Sorry we haven't seen more of the fans," Ringo said to local reporters. "After all, that's why we're here."

Kansas City.

CHICAGO, ILLINOIS

"This is the cheapest publicity stunt in the history of the United States," bellowed Colonel Jack Reilly, the mayor's director of special events. Originally, the Beatles' Electra II had been scheduled to land at O'Hare International Airport, but at the last minute, officials had switched the landing to Midway Airport, and then decided the location should be kept secret. Local P.R. man Alan Edelson, however called the newspapers and radio stations. "I just wanted to save the fans the trouble of looking around," Edelson explained. But Reilly was steaming. Threatening to take all the police off detail, he yelled, "I hope they get torn apart and then I'm gonna charge you with

inciting a mob to riot." Edelson denied that he had tried to stage a publicity stunt and begged not to be put in the "clink" during Rosh Hashana. The recent race riots in Chicago had left the police tense. Eventually tempers cooled and a sixty-man police unit took up their assigned positions as an estimated five thousand fans converged on the airport.

"If you'll all try not to climb over the fence, maybe we'll let them either walk or ride by here so that you can all get a good look," was the announcement made by Captain Francis Dailey at five locations along a fence that separated the crowd from the tarmac. The

Beatles' plane touched down and taxied to a halt at the Butler Aviation terminal amidst screams of joy. Countless girls tried to scale the four-foot-high cyclone fence that bordered the field. All but three ended up in the arms of Chicago police. Each Beatle paused briefly at the door to wave at fans—McCartney, Harrison, Lennon, and then Starr. Grip, grab. Shake. Shake. Pull. Herd. Duck. The Beatles were in their limousines, headed for the Stockyards Inn.

After checking in they dined on steaks, got dressed, and headed downstairs to face yet another fusillade of questions from the press. Despite elaborate local precautions to insure that only newsmen would be admitted to the press conference, Derek, still unable to say no, acquiesced to several fan club members bearing gifts.

"Who do you support for President?"

"He's our political spokesman," Ringo said, pointing to Paul.

"Yeah, he is," John and George agreed.

"From what I've heard Goldwater say, I think Johnson should be President," said Paul. The crowd cheered.

"What do you do with your long hair in the shower?"

Kansas City.

"Get it wet. Dry it with a towel. Rub it," said Ringo.

"It does take a bit longer," John said.

"What would happen to you if the police didn't protect you?"

"I think they'd kill us," said Ringo, smiling.

"What would you like to see in Chicago?"

"The gangsters—with their broad hats and ties," said Paul.

"Do you consider yourselves entertainers or practical jokers?" asked one toughened copywriter.

"Entertainers," they chorused, deadpan. "To the core," added John.

After the press conference, the Beatles ducked out the back way, got into their limousines, and headed for the International Amphitheater. The fifteen thousand available tickets had sold out within hours of going on sale and outside four thousand ticketless fans wandered, watched, and waited. Numerous girls threatened suicide in a last-ditch effort to get inside. At the gate, ticket takers confiscated counterfeits.

At 9:20 P.M. the Beatles mounted a specially rigged stairway draped in gold cloth, and bounded up to the stage. When those outside heard the screams that quaked the Amphitheater, they mourned. Inside, some 320 policemen, firemen, private guards, and various functionaries labored to keep some fans from falling out of the balconies and to keep others away from the stage. "If the energy expended by the fans were directed properly, the United States could have a man on the moon tomorrow," reported the Chicago *Tribune*'s Leighton McLaughlin.

"Why don't you join in?" Paul yelled, hardly audible over the din. "Clap your hands, stomp your feet, maybe even *shout!*" Even when he was smacked in the face with a flashbulb, Paul carried on, hardly missing a beat. And someone obviously had a beef with Ringo, or wanted to give him one—a raw steak was pitched in his direction and landed near his drums. Casualties were minor; only six girls were delivered to Evangelical Hospital in various states of emotional disarray. For the Beatles, it was back to the limousines, out to the airport, and on to Detroit.

Kansas City.

DETROIT, MICHIGAN

The Beatles touched down at Metropolitan Airport at 12:30 A.M. Details of their arrival in the Motor City, home of the Motown sound they loved, had been a well-kept secret until two hours before they were due, when a suburban radio station was tipped off. The airport was besieged and an estimated crowd of three thousand cheered, screamed, and surged toward the Beatles when they deplaned. Sixty sheriff's deputies and forty state police kept the crowd from the limousines, which sped off, escorted by four carloads of police. But dozens of those with immediate access to automobiles ran to their cars and followed the caravan on the twenty-five-mile ride into the city. On the Edsel Ford Freeway, carloads of screaming teenagers hanging out of car windows darted in front of the Beatles' caravan and up alongside it. It was a wild race, but the Beatles survived unscratched. At the city limits, the limousine was met by a Detroit police motorcycle escort and whisked to the Whittier Hotel.

Despite the hour, thousands of fans, some with parents in tow, jammed the portico entrance to the hotel and completely blocked it. The contingent of police and private guards was increased so that a total of three hundred men were on duty. Even so, a group of girls made it up the back stairs and managed to catch a glimpse of the boys as a porter arrived at their suite with deliveries. For the Beatles, it was a quiet night: Dinner. Cards. TV. Radio. Two shows were scheduled at Olympia Stadium, and the day ahead was going to be a long one. George and Paul were sleeping as much and as long as possible these days, and Lennon, though usually a night owl, was still suffering from a sore throat. Ringo, however, loved American TV and spent hours watching old Western and science fiction favorites and shows he'd never seen. When they checked out, fourteen hours later, their bedsheets were put aside, uncleaned, to be cut up into one-inch squares as souvenirs.

About 3 P.M. the Beatles' limousine pulled out of the hotel garage, surrounded by motorcycle police escorts, and headed for the stadium. As the limousine pulled up to an intersection, a motorcycle cop would be waiting there, hands up to hold back traffic; and as the limo pulled through, another motorcycle would speed ahead and stop traffic at the next stoplight, and so on all the way to the stadium. In the display of pomp and circumstance, two policemen were thrown from their bikes and injured.

Detroit loved the Beatles and the mania was out in force. But for the boys, time was beginning to warp. Cities melted together. The flashbulbs, the jellybeans, the screaming. It was always the same. Dizzying and numbing at the same time. No matter where they went, no matter how they played. At Olympia Stadium, one guard near the stage stuck bullets in his ears. A girl was dragged screaming from the stadium. Others were hustled out for throwing jellybeans. But these things were happening everywhere.

Between shows, a long line of men in blue lined the hallway leading to the dressing room where the four were resting before appearing at a backstage press conference.

When the press was assembled, the Beatles were brought in and questions began, but not before Miss Michigan 1960 was allowed to present the Beatles with a scrapbook of various news articles about them, and Miss Armed Forces and Miss Vermont were allowed to extend welcomes. The beauty queens were thrilled. The Beatles were graciously irreverent. So many girls. So many beauty queens. They'd already stopped trying to keep everything straight, they just smiled and said what came to mind.

"How do you like Detroit?"

"It's all very flattering," said Paul. "We got a nice reception here, but how can I say I like Detroit? I haven't even *seen* it."

"Do you think girls should be thrown out of the show for throwing jellybeans?"

"No," answered Paul. "It has become a bit of a trademark with our shows, but we'd prefer they throw nothing at all."

"We've heard that you won't play in Jacksonville if they don't allow Negroes into the show, is that right?"

"Well, we understand that they let them sit in the balcony but not on the main floor, and that's part of our contract, that we will not appear unless they're allowed to sit anywhere," Paul said.

Following their second show, the Beatles sprinted to their limousines for the ride back to Metropolitan Airport. Twenty-three hours after their arrival in Detroit, they were bound for Toronto. During the flight, Paul played poker with Curt Gunther and other members of the traveling press. Ringo slept, his feet

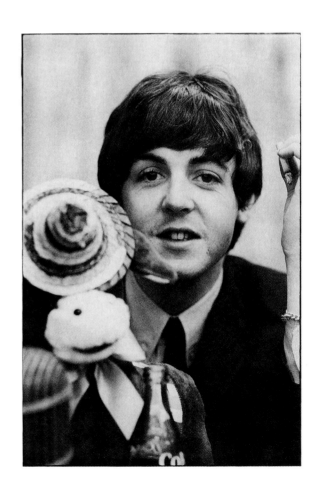

propped up on the seat in front of him. John, sporting sunglasses, withdrew to the back to be alone as George talked with Gerry Barker of the Toronto *Daily Star*. He was asked whether the tour had started to wear on them.

"To us this is a job. We're getting used to living in hotel rooms, you know. If we didn't like it, we would bag it right now and go home."

TORONTO, ONTARIO—CANADA

MONDAY, SEPTEMBER 7, 1964:

The Immigration officer boarded the plane and took a seat in the front. "This we can look at later," he said, taking the stack of passports and the manifest. "Let's have their autographs." It was 12:15 A.M., and the Beatles had just landed at the old Malton Airport at Toronto International. Outside, nearly ten thousand people were waiting behind the fence that bordered the tarmac, which they had dubbed the "Little Berlin Wall." Souvenir sellers offered the usual, as well as a Canadian Maple Leaf flag with the Beatles' pictures inserted around the edges of the leaf. A new version of "O Canada" was sung by at least one group of girls—"Oh Beatles, Our idols true and dear . . ."

The fans had begun arriving the night before and early that morning, fully equipped with stacks of Beatle records and portable record players as well as transistor radios and picnic-type lunches to pass the time. Throughout the day, girls who fainted with excitement or succumbed to the heat were hoisted over the chain-link fence to waiting policemen and St. John's ambulance workers. "Hysteria—resulting from shock, heat, or hunger," explained an overworked doctor. "It has the same effect as a punch in the stomach—leaves its victims writhing and trembling. No permanent damage." As evening turned to night, some three thousand fans, crammed into a seventy-five-foot-wide area, surged against a reinforced L-shaped chain-link fence which separated them from the landing area. Scores of policemen rushed across the tarmac to bolster the sagging structure. The sea of people stretched past the fence and into the darkness, thirty deep in most places. Those in front desperately clung to the fence to hold their place.

At 12:30 A.M. Paul emerged from the plane, followed by the others, and fifty more policemen ran to help their sixty fellow officers keep the steel fence upright. Fans climbed all over each other, screaming, crying, shouting. Nine motorcycle policeman roared along-

169

Kansas City.

side the limousines as they zoomed onto the airfield. It took the Fab Four two minutes and forty-two seconds to go from the plane to the cars. Sadly for the crowd, the cars then headed in the opposite direction.

At the King Edward Hotel, the Beatles made a run for the lobby, but this time they got swept up in the storm. Hundreds of kids had broken through the police lines, which were struggling desperately to hold back more than five thousand people. One girl swung her arms around Lennon's neck and held on. Lennon gritted his teeth and smiled, but struggled hard to break free. Several girls grabbed Paul's shirt and ripped it. Others latched onto Ringo's jacket.

As they entered their suite they found a fourteen-year-old girl in the linen closet, who, upon being discovered, stared at them catatonically and then ran from the room. Thirty Toronto policemen and hotel detectives crowded into the hallway behind them to protect the three-room suite.

"I thought I was in for it," said Paul, surveying the wreckage of his shirt. "But an immense copper lifted me up and shoved me into the elevator." Ringo looked at his torn jacket, and sighed. "We got separated from John and George coming in, but the police were very good." Cracked Lennon: "The best view of the country is over the blue shoulder of a policeman." Outside, the crowd chanted: *"We want the Beatles! We want the Beatles!"* "Oh, they're getting a little excited out there," said Paul. "Stick your head out and give 'em a wave, mate," suggested George. "Not me, son, I'm not for sticking my head out anywhere." None of them were. Instead, they relaxed, read papers from home, sipped soft drinks, and, for the moment, ignored a foot-high stack of fan mail and presents on the coffee table.

The hotel manager and his assistant came up later and asked if they needed anything. "How about breakfast, lads?" asked George. Cheese sandwiches, crisp bacon, and pots of tea appeared instantly. In the meantime, the hotel management brought up friends and friends of friends for handshakes. At one point, George offered up his foot instead. Cheeky. The man looked hurt. George was tired. The crowd, for the most part, dispersed, going home to sleep, and the boys did the same thing.

The Beatles were told that Richard Burton and Elizabeth Taylor had recently stayed in this very suite of rooms. Lennon, still battling a summer cold, modeled a red and black striped nightshirt, a gift from a fan, as he relaxed in the bed that Burton and Taylor had slept in. "I think it was lovely, putting us in her suite," he said with a grin. That afternoon the resident hotel doctor, Dr. Edward Foreman, was brought in to check on the boys and a couple of sick members of the entourage. "They've got bad colds but they're like race horses, raring to go," he said. This was the Beatles' toughest week yet. They had two shows that day at Maple Leaf Gardens in Toronto and were slated to perform two more tomorrow in Montreal.

The 3,500 fans waiting outside were getting anxious and had already twice broken through the police lines, trying to get to the hotel's main door. The girls who fainted or became hysterical were being carried into the hotel lobby, so many others feigned loss of control to gain entrance themselves. At 4 P.M., two decoy limousines drove up to the front of the hotel and were immediately surrounded. The Beatles had planned to risk it and leave by the front entrance, because thousands of kids had been waiting outside for a very long time, but Toronto Police Chief James Mackey had other plans for them: escape by freight elevator to a kitchen door, then outside and into a paddy wagon for the ride to the Gardens.

Maple Leaf Gardens opened its doors at 2:30 for those holding matinée tickets, and 16,761 people packed the arena, breaking the attendance record set in 1946 at a Toronto-Montreal hockey game. Thousands more waited outside for the Beatles to arrive. Inside, disc jockey Jungle Jay Nelson introduced the Bill Black Combo, reminding the audience, "Each of the supporting acts was hand-picked by the Beatles. . . . Any courtesy you extend to them will make the Beatles happy, so happy they will perform even better." The structure of the show had changed as the tour progressed. Following a couple of tunes by the Combo, the Exciters came on, followed by Clarence "Frogman" Henry. After a fifteen-minute intermission the Bill Black Combo returned, performed one song and backed Jackie De-Shannon through five tunes; and then the stage was rearranged for the stars of the evening.

Outside, the Beatles' paddy wagon pulled up to a back entrance. Whether the crowd knew the Beatles were inside or whether they just sensed it, didn't much matter. The vehicle was surrounded and John, Paul, George and Ringo, flanked by Toronto police officers,

171

shifted into automatic. Heads down, they moved to the openings and managed to slip through to safety.

It was 5:30 P.M. when the Beatles hit the stage. "It looked like hell," reported Ralph Hicklin of the Toronto *Globe & Mail*. "Picture if you can the fitful light of a million flashbulbs striking on an endless sea of adolescents, and each female particle of that sea rending her hair or garments, moaning and shrieking in every pitch the human voice is capable of. . . . I kept expecting any minute that Cecil B. de Mille or his successor would yell, 'Cut!' and we'd have to start shooting *The Revolt of Lucifer* all over again." For the fans, of course, it was really much more like *A Hard Day's Night*. On this afternoon, Paul teased the audience to clap more loudly. "So we can *hear* you!" he shouted. John mimicked him and the audience loved it. They didn't have to hear the songs. They could feel them. "If truth would out, it could be reported that there were no strings on their guitars, that there was no canvas on the drums. . . . It must've been a pantomime, the Beatles' version of Red Skelton's 'Silent Spot,' " assessed the Toronto *Daily Star*. But "It was all real," says McCartney. "We never lip-synched. As to what anybody ever heard, that was another matter, because in those days we used a kind of little speaker system, usually just the house system. At Maple Leaf Gardens, for example, there are just four or five little horns that come out and we used those, so no wonder nobody could hear us."

After the first show, the Beatles cooled off in a specially built dressing room and then were ushered, a half hour later, into a press conference. The Gardens' publicity director had actually issued 150 tickets for the meeting with the press to reporters and photographers, every concessionaire in the building, and the forty police and firemen who had flanked the stage. The Beatles reappeared on the stage and posed for photographs. One photographer kept snapping a movie clapper board in front of them until Derek told him it might be a good idea if he and his clapper board move away. The Beatles met the mayor, Canadian starlet Michele Finney, Miss Canada, and the president of a 54,000-member Beatles fan club. Capitol of Canada executives were also on hand to present the Beatles with a gold record plaque and they were also presented with a crate of letters— Ringo was still running as the three-to-one favorite.

As the Beatles settled in for the question-and-answer session, they lit cigarettes. Someone in the crowd suggested maybe they shouldn't.

"Why not?" asked George. "We're not here to set examples to people. We even drink."

"Does that excuse the performances that make kids keel over?"

"They don't get hurt," said John. "They collapse and get up again, and they enjoy themselves while collapsing."

"Is this trip wearing you down at all?"

"No, actually it's building us up," said Ringo.

"What do you think of the class struggle in Britain?"

"We didn't notice it," said Paul.

"What about all these stories in the papers about your appealing to the mother instinct in your largely female audience?"

"It's a dirty lie," laughed Lennon.

"Which do you prefer, American or English girls?"

"We like them all," said Paul. "We're all stuck on girls."

"What do the Beatles think of the Queen?"

"She's all right. She's doing a good job," Paul said.

"And what about Senator Barry Goldwater?"

"Not much fun, is he?" Ringo said.

"How long do you think you'll last?" It was a graying newsman who asked the obligatory question.

"Longer than you anyway," snapped Lennon.

Back in their dressing room, John, Paul, George, and Ringo watched an old war movie on TV and ate sandwiches. Later, McCartney wondered if there might be trouble in Montreal. The Quebec Libre movement—which supported the secession of Quebec from Canada—was gaining world attention, and momentum. A year earlier, a radical faction known as the FLQ (Quebec Liberation Front) began a series of bombings that were terrifying England. Numerous death threats had been lodged against the Queen, and the burning of British flags had become almost commonplace. McCartney was assured that Beatlemania was an international phenomenon without enemies. But in fact, Montreal police had received a death threat against Ringo which they were taking very seriously.

Kansas City.

The Beatles' second performance of the day was much the same, only louder. All together more than two hundred fans fell, afflicted by Beatlemania, and were treated on the scene by St. John's ambulance workers. What do you do with a quivering, sobbing, hysterical little girl? they were asked. "We wipe their faces with a cold cloth, be firm with them, give them no sympathy whatever, and they work themselves out of it in ten or fifteen minutes," said one of the nurses at the Gardens.

The Toronto *Daily Star* approached Dr. Norman Endler, a NYU psychologist special-

izing in social conformity, to comment on Beatlemania. "They'll drop down, but only to be replaced by some other fad," he said. "We're always seeking novelties. After all, you don't hear much about Elvis Presley these days."

At 10:30, the second show behind them, the Beatles headed out a back door and into the paddy wagon. On the way out, they were thrown towels and given bottles of pop to help them cool off. By 11 P.M. they were back in their rooms. While thousands of fans chanted in the streets below, they showered, played poker, and ate dinner.

TORONTO

TUESDAY, SEPTEMBER 8, 1964:

It was 1:30 A.M. when Toronto mayor Philip Givens, his wife, and others knocked on the door to the Beatles' suite. Paul and John were already asleep and George and Ringo were in the back bedroom talking to Louise. "They're not seeing anybody tonight," Bess Coleman, clad in her nightgown and bathrobe, told his honor. The mayor found the reception "rude." But Coleman and Taylor and Bonis found the mayor and his party rude. Recalls Coleman: "You couldn't do anything right. Most of the time we were now saying no. But there were certain people in every city who felt they had a God-given right, including the mayor of Toronto, as I recall."

At the Toronto International Airport the next day, several hundred fans who had gathered to see the Beatles off got a better look at them than anyone had had at any time during their stay in Toronto. Although George remained aloof, entering the aircraft and refusing to budge, John, Paul, and Ringo went over to the eight-foot fence that separated them from the fans and waved and shouted to them. They remained on the tarmac saying good-bye for almost fifteen minutes as Paul snapped pictures. Then they thanked the police officers and boarded the plane.

The mayor and his wife and children showed up at the last minute, wanting a signed photograph to hang in the mayoral quarters. Since landing in the States, the demand for autographs and signed photographs had been overwhelming. Nearly everybody in the Beatles' entourage was forging the four names to try and keep as many people happy as possible. Neil and Mal taught Derek, who taught Bess, who taught Bob Bonis and reporter Ivor Davies, and so on. "It was the only way to keep people at bay," says Coleman. "Every-

175

body wanted autographs and while they did seem to have good intentions, it just got ridiculous and there really was no choice. Besides, at this point, everybody was beginning to get frazzled beyond belief."

The aircraft took off and disappeared into the Canadian sky. Ten minutes after it had gone, crying girls were still clinging to the fence, hoping for a miracle.

On the flight into Montreal, reporter Ivor Davies supplied the crew with news—a hurricane named Dora had hit Jacksonville, Florida, the scheduled stop after Montreal. "While we were touring, the world was so busy, so many things were happening that we didn't and couldn't know what was going on everywhere," recalls Aspinall. One hundred miles of Florida coastline had been lashed and whether or not the Beatles' show was still on was open to question.

MONTREAL, QUEBEC—CANADA

It was raining and there was a chill in the summer air as the plane touched down at Montreal's Dorval Airport at 2:20 P.M., seventeen minutes late. Once again, their arrival plans were supposed to have been secret, but word got out and five thousand people crowded onto the second-story observation gallery, braving the rain to welcome the Beatles to Montreal. "I can assure you we are adequately prepared for anything," said riot specialist Chief Inspector Walter Boyle, who attributed the smaller than expected crowd to the opening of school. A detachment of 117 Royal Canadian Mounted Police, bolstered by a squad of officers from the Dorval Municipal Police Force, maintained control with seemingly little effort as the plane rolled to a stop.

Ringo, however, was headed into one of the worst storms of his life. Someone, somewhere out there, walking the lunatic fringe, was threatening to shoot him for being an English Jew. Like Elvis, the Beatles' international fame made John, Paul, George, and Ringo targets upon which jealous boyfriends could vent their frustrations, parents their fears, and weirdos their hostilities. Such notices of anger were for the most part run-of-the-mill hate mail, and few and far between in the avalanche of letters from adoring fans; but all death threats were taken seriously and turned over to the police immediately. In this case, the threat was made directly to the police. "We'll not be anybody's pawns," said Lennon. "We're here to play music." The world, however, was becoming a dangerous place. "We sometimes wondered after we stepped off the plane," Starr remembers, "if we'd walk to Customs or be carried . . . *Bang!*"

With the ongoing political turmoil, Canadian police weren't taking any chances and

176

two plainclothes detectives quickly climbed on board to brief the entourage on the planned routes. As the group emerged from the plane, the two detectives hovered protectively over the little drummer. The boys smiled and waved, but within seconds they were hustled into a limousine that pulled up on the runway. As the doors closed, the drizzle turned to a downpour and fans were soaked as they chased the limousine on foot.

The Beatles were taken quickly and directly to the Forum. As a rule, only Neil or Brian was allowed in the Beatles' car, but this time an armed officer accompanied them. When the chauffeur ran several red lights without a police escort, George, in no uncertain terms, told him to slow down. The Beatles had originally been scheduled to check into a hotel, but in light of the fact that nobody wanted to *stay* in Montreal, it was decided that they would go straight to the Forum, then fly out right after the second show—only no one knew where they would go. Since they had two rest days before their scheduled appearance in Jacksonville, they would fly to an intermediate location and wait to see if the Florida show was still on.

At the Montreal Forum, police stood guard at the back entrance along with several hundred fans. Just after 3 P.M., a taxi carrying several long-haired male passengers pulled up to the front of the Forum setting off screams that brought those waiting in the back running toward the main entrance. It was a lucky coincidence for the police, who immediately sealed off the back area. Ten minutes later, the Beatles' entourage drove in the back before fans realized what had happened.

Kansas City.

Once safely in their dressing room, the Beatles lounged on their beds, watched TV, and read the local papers. Their nerves were all somewhat jangled, but Ringo in particular was dreading today's two shows. Canceling them was never really considered. Such a move would disappoint the fans terribly, not to mention the money at stake. They knew the death threat was most likely an empty one and that the police were everywhere. Nevertheless, it was going to be a long, tense day.

At 5:20 P.M., John, Paul, George, and Ringo took the stage and the mania erupted, though this was a more subdued crowd than most others, earning notice as one of the best-behaved audiences on the tour. Still, it's doubtful that many noticed the detective hunkering down behind the drum riser next to Ringo. "God knows what he was going to do," recalls Starr. "I mean there's an assassin out there trying to get me and he's sitting next to me onstage as if someone in the back of a 12,000-seater is gonna go—*Bang!*—and he's gonna catch the bullet?" Ringo took his own precautions. Situating his cymbals straight up, he crouched behind them and "played low," as he puts it. "No one was seeing much of me that day. It was the worst gig of my life."

Following the first performance, the Beatles retired to their dressing room and learned they would fly into Key West for their two days of rest. They were relieved and delighted. Later, between shows, they reappeared on the stage to pose for photographs, and hold a press conference.

"Do the Beatles have any religious views?"
"We're all agnostics," replied Paul.

179

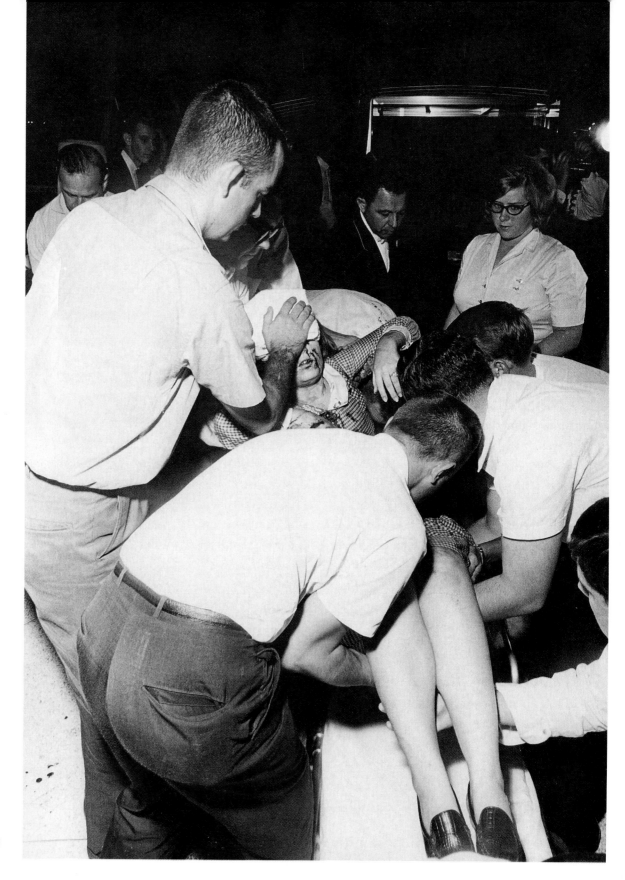

One of four fans who fell through plate glass window at Cabana Motor Hotel, Dallas.

"What about all the screaming?"

"We enjoy it. It adds to the atmosphere," said Paul.

"What do the Beatles do when they're cooped up in a hotel room between shows?"

"Ice skate," said George.

"Do any of you speak French?"

"*Nein*," said Ringo. "No."

"Who makes the decisions for the group? Who's the leader?"

"We have no real leader among us," said Paul. "It depends on who shouts the loudest."

THE ESTIMATED 11,500 who attended the second show seemed generally older, but their reaction was, as always, the same. As soon as they struck that last chord on "Long Tall Sally," the Beatles were on their way out of Montreal.

One Canadian in particular, media man Dr. H. Marshall McLuhan, director of the Centre for Culture and Technology, University of Toronto, was duly impressed with the Beatles. He stunned the Conservatives at the National Conference on Canadian Goals by announcing that the "electronic age" with its advanced television and computer technology had terminated the industrial age and that the Conservatives could learn much from the Beatles, whose operations "are perfectly attuned to the electronic age" which had created them.

At Dorval International, a force of seventy-five RCMP officers guided the Beatles cavalcade onto the tarmac to their waiting plane, cheered on by several hundred fans. "That detective," Starr remembers, "stayed with me from the minute I got off the plane until we got back on." Once safely inside the plane, Ringo heaved a sigh of relief and chuckled at the irony. "I am English. But I'm not Jewish," he says. "There were some ignorant oafs around everywhere we toured. But the point is, we never got hurt. None of us ever really got hurt in those days." At 11:46 P.M., nine hours after they had landed in Montreal, the Beatles took off, headed into another kind of turbulence.

KEY WEST, FLORIDA

WEDNESDAY, SEPTEMBER 9, 1964:

The plane rocked and bounced as it encountered stormy weather throughout the flight, but when it neared Florida in the early morning hours, the winds left in Hurricane Dora's wake seemed to lift and toss the aircraft like it was a cork in the ocean. It was pitch black outside, unsettling everyone and making them feel helpless. Hands gripped seats. Fear contorted faces. "The silence was deafening," recalls Coleman. "I think we all thought we were going to die that night." But nobody did. The Electra II landed safely at Key West International Airport about 3 A.M. and the Beatles, along with all their fellow passengers, cheered and applauded the pilot.

Now there were other problems. Local union members were threatening to throw up a picket line at the Gator Bowl in Jacksonville unless the Beatles agreed to join the American Guild of Variety Artists. Left with little choice, they agreed to pay the $1,200 for initiation fees and annual dues and join the union. At 4 A.M., after another delay, this time with Immigration processing, the Beatles finally emerged from the plane. They expected things to be relatively quiet since plans had been changed literally at the last minute. But nearly seven hundred people turned out in the pre-dawn hours to welcome them.

The entire entourage checked into the Key Wester Motel, with the Beatles taking up quarters in separate bungalows. That morning, Curt joined George and Paul for a walk out to the water's edge. The winds were still whipping around and an eerie, humid pall hung over the coastline. John, along with Derek and Neil, went out for a drive along the Keys, stopping for breakfast and a little shopping along the way. Wearing sunglasses, Lennon went unnoticed.

Word of the Beatles' whereabouts got out quickly and by late afternoon, motel officials had to rope off the accommodations. Fans stood beyond the rope waiting for a glimpse

of the group, but were generally quiet and never harassed them. It was, for the Beatles, an unexpectedly pleasant interlude and they came and went from the cottages with relative ease.

THURSDAY, SEPTEMBER 10, 1964:

When Tony Martinez, a local millionaire, offered the Beatles his pool, they accepted and spent the afternoon splashing around and lounging in the sun. Moments like these, completely away from the mania-stricken crowds, had become the one luxury that money couldn't buy. They later learned that the water from the pool had been bottled and packaged for sale as "Beatle Water" and the proceeds donated to charity. Whose charity they were never told. By now such sales and schemes were routine, but whether or not any bona fide charities ever gained from them is doubtful.

The Beatles spent part of the evening doing press interviews, and after the members of the Exciters cooked a full-course Southern meal, they had dinner, played cards, listened to music, and watched TV into the early hours of the morning.

JACKSONVILLE, FLORIDA

FRIDAY, SEPTEMBER 11, 1964:

Not even Hurricane Dora could stop the Beatles: The show at the Gator Bowl was on. For the Jacksonville police, it would be a full day: President Johnson had arrived to investigate the storm damage, *and* at the same time, final preparations for the Beatles' arrival and performance had to be made.

As the Beatles' plane approached Imeson Airport, it was instructed to circle the area until the President's plane took off; it was finally allowed to land at 5:30 P.M. As it taxied to a stop at a private hangar and the Beatles disembarked to their waiting limousines, hundreds of fans broke through police lines and came charging across the field. The President's police escort had remained at the airport to escort the Beatles, so amidst sirens, flashing lights, and a cavalcade of motorcycles and police cars, the Beatles escaped with ease and sped away to the George Washington Hotel.

There, they held a press conference before 150 people. As usual, the newsmen were outnumbered by teenage infiltrators. The Bea-

Dallas.

Derek organizes photo with Clarence "Frogman" Henry, Dallas.

[tle]s munched on turkey sandwiches, which they offered to the press, and sipped tea while fielding questions for the usual hour.

"Does your hair require any special care?"

"Inattention is the main thing," said John.

"Have y'all composed any new numbers over here?"

"Two."

"What are they?"

"We can't tell you that," said Paul.

"Do you ever go unnoticed?"

"When we take off our wigs," said Paul.

"If John doesn't like glasses, why doesn't he get contact lenses?"

"I've never taken time to go to an optometrist. Besides I wouldn't like glass in me head."

"How do y'all feel about you and the President coming to town on the same day?"

"Amazing," said John.

"What do you think you've contributed to the musical field?"

"Records," said John.

"And a laugh and a smile," added George.

"Why do you avoid the press?"

"We don't. We do what the police, the sheriffs—the posse—tell us," said Paul.

Following the press conference, at around 7 P.M., five hundred fans caused a near-riot as police were trying to get the boys from the hotel to their limousines, but nonetheless, at 7:15 the Beatles began a high-speed siren-heralded dash to their house trailer hideaway beneath the north stands at the Gator Bowl.

Once there, the Beatles had a roast beef and mashed potatoes dinner, served by a local cook. At 8:30 P.M., the opening acts started the show while forty m.p.h. winds ripped through the Bowl. Backstage, however, there was a problem. Cameramen from an L.A.-based newsreel-making company were out in force tonight, eight of them equipped with movie cameras and ready to roll. One or more had shown up almost every night of the tour, and every night they'd been thrown out. This time, however, they weren't moving, but neither were John, Paul, George, and Ringo.

While the crowd chanted feverishly, "We want the Beatles! We want the Beatles!" Derek was thrust out onto the stage by police and the boys to enlist the help of the crowd. Sleeves rolled up, and empowered by "brandy and the certainty of righteousness," he grabbed the microphone. "The Beatles are one hundred feet away." The audience roared. "They came

184

thousands of miles to be here and the only thing preventing their appearance are those nasty cine-cameramen." Derek pointed out the cameramen. The crowd booed and hissed, jeering the nasty cameramen. "Silence!" It was Derek's finest moment; he reveled in this newfound power. "Now if you want the Beatles to perform here tonight, tell the police to make the cameramen leave."

"Out," the crowd roared. *"Out! Out! Out!!"* Captain C. L. Raines and Captain I. L. Griffin led police to the offenders, and the moviemakers' lenses were clouded with the palms of policemen, who turned them

Dallas.

185

around and ushered them to the exit doors. As George Harrison recalls it, Derek was "like Hitler at the Nuremberg rally," and the speech would come to be known in the inner circle as the "Jacksonville Address."

For once, jellybeans were not a real problem. Winds, however, blasted the stage as the Beatles performed, whipping through their hair, rocking the microphones and the cymbals, at times threatening the instruments. Ringo's drums had been nailed down, but at one point Bob Bonis jumped onto the stage, crouched down, and held the drummer, convinced he was going to blow off. Following their show, the Beatles headed to the airport and took off for Boston just after midnight. For once the plane's location had successfully been kept a secret and there was no fanfare.

BOSTON, MASSACHUSETTS

SATURDAY, SEPTEMBER 12, 1964:

"Hurry up! Let's go! Come on—before you miss your escort." A man in a brown suit who introduced himself as Captain Teahan was standing inside the plane, urgently rushing the Beatles. They had arrived at Hanscom Field in Bedford at 3:15 A.M., changing earlier plans to land at Logan International, and no sooner had the plane stopped than police were on board issuing orders. John, Paul, George, Neil, and Mal were quickly shoved into cars for the fifteen-mile trip to the Hotel Madison. In the rush, Ringo and Derek were left behind. Plenty of local TV crews were on hand, however, and Derek ranted and raved about the rough, rude threatment they'd received from the Boston police.

With more than two dozen police escorts, the Beatles' cars raced into town. At the Hotel Madison, the boys were hustled onto a freight elevator and deposited on the eleventh floor at around 4 A.M. For all intents and purposes, the place was deserted. A mere seven very weary fans shrieked and sighed as they watched the Beatles get out of the car. "They must have thought that Boston is as populated as the Bikini Atoll before the A-bomb test," the Boston *Globe* later reported. The Beatles knew full well that wasn't the case, but they did actually wonder if the Boston police would allow them to perform. At this point, they were too tired to care.

The Beatles awoke at their usual mid-afternoon hours to find policemen waiting, autograph books in hand. It had been happening throughout the tour: All of the police—and there were hundreds—seemed to expect autographs and photographs. And some, in Boston, apparently expected other things. "It was like they were shopping at Woolworth's," says Derek. "It wasn't a frenzy, but, you know, they'd take something, and look at you and smile, nod, nod, wink, wink." Though conveniently located next to the Boston Gardens—home of the Celtics and Bruins—the Hotel Madison was dismal and depressing for the Beatles.

As word of the Beatles' presence spread, however, it became the town's main attraction. "He's the Beatles' butler on the way to the laundry!" The scream set the crowd charging. The poor unsuspecting man leaving the hotel with a bundle of soiled shirts was rammed, spun, and tossed into the air, shirts flying in every direction. In a matter of seconds, the shirts had been reduced to shreds and the man was left sitting disheveled on the ground, wondering what had hit him.

Every guest who peered through a window was greeted with cheers and screams that drowned out the whine of jets passing overhead. A bedsheet thrown out of a hotel window early in the afternoon was shredded before it reached the pavement. By early evening, the crowd had grown to about three thousand. Most of them were girls, all craning their necks for a view, trading time on binoculars for a glimpse of the eleventh-floor windows. Neighboring streets were completely blocked to traffic and the nearly two hundred police patrolling the area were ordered to remove their badges. Teenagers had been plucking

Dallas.

them from their rightful owners all day. Later, an eighteen-year-old boy sporting a Beatle cut was chased by dozens of screaming girls, who had mistaken him for one of *them*. When they caught him they screamed with ecstasy as they ripped the shirt from his back.

Whenever a shriek went up from the hotel, a flood of girls came running down the street. On realizing there was nobody to see, they would stream back to take up their positions outside the Gardens. But the Beatles would take a connecting hallway from the hotel into the old sports emporium and wouldn't be coming out of either building until the next day.

After brunch, the Beatles dressed and then headed down to the Madison Room for their Boston press conference.

"What do you think about all these psychiatrists?"

187

Dallas.

"We think they should see psychiatrists," said John.

"What is your reaction to the opinion of some psychologists who say you have a detrimental effect on the youngsters?"

"Rubbish," said John.

"There are rumors that you plan to break up?"

"Not true, not true," each of the Beatles responded.

"Do you ever get the melancholy thought that your days of song and money may be numbered, and that you may suddenly awake one day to discover you've gone the way of other fads, particularly miniature golf?"

"We'll get out before we fade," said Paul. "And anyway, we've made more money than anyone in miniature golf."

"How do you feel about the action of the state police upon your arrival?"

"Ridiculous."

OUTSIDE THE Gardens, the crowd was getting wild. Several scuffles and fistfights broke out and two glass doors leading into the arena were smashed. Some youths began yelling obscenities to the police, and as both sides of the crowd came together in the middle of the street, mounted policemen stampeded through the mob, scattering them in all directions. The turnout of police was of record proportions, and utilized a walkie-talkie system to speed officers to trouble spots. Still, they were completely outnumbered and the trouble spots were many.

The Beatles' show, like nearly all the

others, had sold out within hours, and even after those with tickets—13,909 of them—went inside to claim their revered seats, thousands without tickets roamed the grounds searching for a way in. An escapee from a reform school pulled a knife on another boy and stole his ticket. The victim remembered the seat number, and police seized the offender and turned him back over to juvenile authorities. Numerous boys were sporting long hair like the Beatles' and police were forever rescuing them from mobs of frantic girls.

Vendors were doing a landslide business, selling balloons for twenty-five cents, posters for eighty, and signs to order for thirty-five. Ringo still led the others in sales.

Meanwhile, across town in the Boston Arena, another English rock group, the Minets, had managed to garner nearly five hundred fans all their own, including a few who had sold Beatles tickets for the experience. The hype was that they possessed musical talent superior to that of the Beatles. Only time would tell.

The Beatles checked out of the hotel and walked over to the Gardens. As they sprinted onto the stage, jellybeans fell like hail. The arena lit up with popping flashbulbs and the screams seemed almost primal. But it was the same thing all over again. Nobody heard them. Didn't the audience ever want to listen? Did it really matter what the group played? Frustration was running rampant. "I used to play 'Love Me Do' as a quick step and a rumba and we'd play to keep ourselves alive, 'cause we knew that no matter what we did, it would come down to the same screaming situation," recalls Starr. When the Beatles bowed at the show's end, a barrier of twenty-five policemen, hands clasped to form a chain, created a human wall of protection. As they dashed from the stage, John turned to Ed Leffler and asked, "How'd we sound tonight?" Leffler just laughed. Out front, police had set up the decoy—a black limousine and six motorcycle police lined up as if making preparations to escort the Beatles through the waiting crowd. Meanwhile, the boys jumped into a freight elevator, which deposited them on the ground floor at the rear of the Gardens, where another limousine was waiting.

The Beatles arrived at Hanscom Field at 10:15 P.M., and after the hour's wait for their instruments and the remaining cast and crew

Dallas.

Backstage at the Memorial Coliseum, Dallas.

members, they took off for Maryland. On the plane, Derek lashed out at the Boston police again. The unremitting hustle and bustle, while they were constantly being told what to do, was no kind of life at all, and everyone was beginning to rebel. Still, the Beatles' image was important above all, and Brian Epstein disowned Taylor's complaints and issued an apology. Later, the Boston Police Department earned kudos from the Massachusetts State Chamber of Commerce for a job well done in handling "the potentially dangerous appearance of the Beatles at the

Dallas.

Boston Garden. The important factor," read the Chamber's press release, "is that there is this dangerous and widespread phenomenon involving today's youth that finds expression in senseless demonstrations of varying degrees of seriousness."

BALTIMORE, MARYLAND

SUNDAY, SEPTEMBER 13, 1964:

The Beatles' plane landed at Friendship Airport at 1:15 A.M. and taxied to Pier B, where a stretch limousine and twenty-two state, airport, and Anne Arundel County police cars had just arrived. One hundred yards away, five hundred Beatlemaniacs, who were trapped behind terminal windows, clawed and screamed and witnessed the moment. As in the other less populated cities, only the number of fans was smaller—the enthusiasm was just as urgent. A security force of about two hundred police officers had been mobilized to keep the fans from breaking through to the field.

Dressed in casual suede and woolen jackets, Paul, George, John, and Ringo walked down the landing steps and then quickly and easily through the contingent of local press, flashbulbs spotlighting them as they crowded into the back of their limousine. As their car lurched into the blackness of night, police cars fell into line. Teenagers with their own cars gave chase to the caravan, tailgating and

Dallas.

hitting speeds of up to eighty miles per hour on the highway and roads leading into Baltimore.

At the city limits, the Baltimore police took over and the caravan careened the wrong way up several blocked-off one-way streets and sped into the underground garage of the downtown Holiday Inn. The four famed visitors were handed over to yet another security force, which led them up a service elevator and to their rooms on the heavily guarded tenth floor.

One local photographer, who had managed against the odds to stay with Paul and George until they were esconced in Room 1013, turned to leave when he was asked to do so. Amidst much cheeky humor about the photographer's being kicked out, George exuberantly gave him a swift one. He turned and glared. "Who did that?" He demanded to know. Accused of the assault, George lifted his bad-schoolboy face, grinning. It was a joke, a cheeky, harmless incident, and it relieved tension. But it has also left the photographer embarrassed and humiliated. Realizing this, Paul left the room minutes later and offered the photographer a conciliatory picture-taking session of the group. George, however, refused to take part. Paul excused him by saying, "'E's not feeling very well."

Beatlepeople gathered early and stayed around the clock. Numerous groups of girls managed to gain entrance and clustered together on the three elevators, riding up and down in hopes of getting out on the tenth floor. In the lobby, one girl, her eyes glazed, wandered aimlessly. "I saw Paul," she kept repeating. "I saw Paul."

Dallas.

The Beatles, however, were tired and aching for some peace and quiet. They were content to follow the rules, stay out of sight, and avoid public appearances other than those for which they were getting paid. John and Paul worked on new songs. As John strummed his Gibson Sunburst, he sang "I'm a loo-ser, I'm a loo-ser, and I'm not what I appear to be . . ."

In their two performances at the Baltimore Civic Center, the Beatles played to audiences that numbered more than thirteen thousand

Alton, Missouri.

about my homosexuality!" Brian said icily.

"Absolute rubbish. I refuse to even argue about it. Some of my best friends are Jewish and others are homosexual and some are both," Derek responded. Brian didn't say anything. "Why don't you ask the boys, then? They'll tell you if it's true." With that, the case was closed. The matter was never again discussed.

Back at Beatle Central, a war was brewing. Radio station WHK was promoting the concert at the Public Auditorium, but as usual there was the rival station, KYW, that also needed information. KYW had been represented on the tour by news director Art Schreiber and disc jockey Jim Stagg. Still, WHK was sponsoring the press conference this afternoon at the Sheraton and the personnel from that station didn't want the KYW people involved—it was a crack in WHK's exclusivity.

"The dee-jays from the competing station were usually in a state of high tension by the time we arrived," says Taylor. "They would have a list of proposals and needs. In some cities, they'd even bring along a number of handicapped children or contest winners who were to meet the Beatles, but the promoting station would say, 'There's no room in the press conference, because it's our press conference,' and here are all these handicapped children. It was my job to be tactful, personable, and helpful. But you knew when they brought in handicapped children it was just another ploy. If we didn't do something with them, it could be turned around, 'Beatles Reject Handicapped Children.' " Often, jobs were on the line and numerous otherwise strong men were reduced to tears if it appeared that things weren't going to work out. If appealing to people's sense of honor didn't work, then Derek was left to try and make other arrangements for meetings in the dressing rooms. Everybody, everywhere wanted the Beatles.

"I don't know *what* to do," said Brian, washing his hands of the whole affair in Cleveland, disappearing like a magician as he was so often prone to do. "He was at that time probably the busiest man in the world," says Taylor. Derek mustered together all the logical reasons he could to try and get the two stations to come to sensible terms. In the end, the fact that KYW's Schreiber and Stagg had already established a relationship with the boys made it almost impossible for WHK to exclude them. Meanwhile there was the usual host of autograph hunters, fan club officers, teenage reporters, and other local VIPs who wanted in to the press conference.

Finally, Derek came up with an acceptable solution. The main press conference would be opened to the rival radio station and all the others who had a legitimate reason to be there. Then, the Beatles would hold a special second mini-conference for the WHK contest winners.

Before the main press conference began, representatives from the city of Cincinnati, where the Beatles had played three weeks before, welcomed them back to Ohio and presented them with a gold key to their city. Then the questions flew.

"WHAT DO YOU THINK of adult attempts to psychoanalyze the kids who like you?"

"They have nothing better to do," said John.

"Are the answers they come up with right?"

"No, wrong," John sighed.

"How do you personally explain Beatlemania?

"We don't even try," John answered.

"Is it true that you don't trust American barbers, Ringo?"

"That true, but we don't trust British barbers either."

"What is your educational background?" asked a woman.

"Lousy," said John.

"Do you plan on going to Mexico?"

"We never plan anything. It's planned for us," Paul said.

Throughout the press conference George drew pictures. "He always does that," Lennon said. "He makes cartoons of you journalists."

LATER, THE BEATLES appeared before the winners of WHK's Beatles contest. Warned that the first person who screamed would be put out of the room, these people knew when to stay quiet. John, Paul, George, and Ringo shook hands with everyone, then sat down and answered five minutes' worth of questions.

Outside the Cleveland Public Auditorium, scalpers were getting $30 for $5.50 tickets. The seating capacity was said to be 10,000, but some estimates maintained that 11,000 fans were crowded into the hall. A police officer took the stage and microphone, warning the crowd: "I'm not running this show, but I am responsible for your safety. If you get out

of hand at any point, the show will be stopped immediately. You can make as much noise as you want as long as you behave." The crowd cheered and applauded him.

A police cordon guarded the stage throughout the performances of the opening acts, and, following intermission, their force was strengthened with additional officers. When the Beatles hit the stage, the crowd went wild. Screams. Jellybeans. Flashing cameras enveloped the Fab Four. Suddenly, ten minutes into the set, the crowd spontaneously charged the stage, rushing down the center aisle toward the barricades. Some forty policemen tried to hold them back, but the crowd pushed through. A brass railing that was bolted to the floor

about ten feet out from the stage was ripped out, and five or six girls were trampled on their way to the barricades. Officers from all over the hall came running to pull back the crowd. Deputy Carl C. Bare, a large burly man, strode to center stage and grabbed the microphone from Lennon. "This show is over!" he hollered. The crowd howled and booed and the Beatles continued playing. Bare walked up to stand face-to-face with Lennon, who did a little dance and made a face at him, causing the audience to boo the officer. Bare wheeled around and glared at the audience. Standing at his side was Inspector Michael (Iron Mike) J. Blackwell, who was in charge of the detail of five hundred police used for Beatle duty.

204

and the limousine pulled into its position in the motorcade, back on track to the hotel.

Hundreds of people lined the streets of the motorcade's route, and hundreds more were on hand at the Congress Inn. The Beatles ran into the lobby and were led down a hallway to their three-room suite—Room 100. Councilman Daniel Kelly arrived some minutes later and stood outside the door waiting to present them with the mayor's proclamation making that Wednesday "Beatles Day," but he was never invited to make the presentation.

By 4 A.M. most of the crowd had disappeared. Kelly was leaving and police were still entrenched in front of the Beatles' suite. Windows in the room had been boarded up to prevent fans from breaking in. Paul and George were already sleeping. John and Ringo were looking for something to eat.

The Beatles slept well into the afternoon and then held a press conference at the hotel. For the first time on the tour, Brian consented to having the L.A. newsreel cameramen in to film the Beatles' interview. It was an unprecedented move on Epstein's part and wouldn't happen again. They certainly would not be allowed to film a performance. Before the questions began, Mayor Schiro presented each of the Beatles with a key to the city and a certificate of honorary citizenship, and then asked each for an autograph. Countless local politicians throughout America had realized the publicity potential of the Beatles, and many orchestrated advantageous meetings.

the tatt[...]
would h[...]
charged[...]

Afte[...]
stormed[...]
turned l[...]
ning's tu[...]
accused[...]
the crov[...]
police r[...]

Together they stared the crowd down and as they did the curtain dropped. Bare had to drag George off the stage. "The police here are stupid!" Ringo announced as they were led offstage.

It was the first time a Beatles concert had been stopped in America. The Beatles were furious. John grabbed Art Schreiber as they sprinted back to their dressing rooms. Derek ran up to Bare. Slightly built by comparison and ashen-faced, he made his appeal. "I know I could probably control the crowd if I could just talk to them." Bare had trouble with that

one. "You?" he asked. "Control *them?*" Bare went out to the microphone himself and bellowed at the crowd. The crowd snarled back.

"They locked themselves in the dressing room," recalls Schreiber, who immediately picked up the phone and started interviewing them live on KYW while the concert sponsored by WHK was stopped. "The guys from WHK were downstairs, helpless to do anything. We owned the story in Cleveland, absolutely *owned* it, and that was one of the greatest things that ever happened to me in my life."

The Beatles were already getting changed

The Beat[...]
3 A.M., [...]
that rese[...]
been a si[...]
to land a[...]
then be [...]
Inn. A la[...]
on hand [...]
helicopte[...]
limousine[...]
were sen[...]
national [...]
last minu[...]
Orleans I[...]
announce[...]
Beatles w[...]
official ga[...]

each, but were, according to the *Baltimore Sun*, "not quite as many as appeared last year for Peter, Paul and Mary." The seventy-one uniformed city and private police who ringed the stage watched with puzzlement. "I can't even hear the goddamn music," one police lieutenant shouted. While the flashbulbs continued to light the darkened arena and screams blocked out the music, there was only one reported instance of jellybean throwing.

Between shows, the Beatles held what was now the mandatory press conference.

En route to the Ozarks. Brian turns thirty and tries out antique telephone gift from the Beatles.

"DO YOU EVER get dandruff with all that hair?"

"We have dandruff occasionally," said John. "Like normal people."

"Do you have any plans for a haircut?"

"We don't make plans like that. Our manager does," snapped George.

"What do you think of American television?"

"It's great—you get eighteen stations, but you can't get a good picture on any of them," said Ringo.

"What do you think of all the Beatle imitators and people who wear Beatle wigs?"

"They aren't imitating *us*—we don't wear Beatle wigs, you know," said Paul.

"And the other British competitors coming to the United States?"

"Why not? There's enough money over here for every group in England," said John.

"What will you do when the bubble bursts?" He was back. And this time, John fielded the question.

"Then basketball."

"How do you feel about putting the whole country on?"

"We enjoy it," said Ringo.

Added Paul: "We're not really putting you on."

"Well, just a bit," corrected George.

AFTER the Beatles' last performance in Maryland, most of the crowd journeyed around the corner to the Holiday Inn. Police massed together and began dispersing the hordes with the aid of dogs. Inside, an all-night private party was held for the entire Beatles' cast and crew in the La Ronde, the hotel's top-of-the-building revolving restaurant. Dinner consisted of prime rib, with plenty of cognac and brandy, as well as Scotch and Coke and desserts. The boys were dressed casually in Levi's and English boots. John, decked out in sunglasses and a black-and-white polka-dotted shirt, was described by one local reporter as looking like "a blind Dalma-tian." The members of the Exciters began an impromptu sing-along with members of the other opening acts. The Beatles watched, then retired to their rooms for the night.

MONDAY, SEPTEMBER 14, 1964:

The Beatles were awakened by Derek, who greeted them with glasses of orange juice, pens, some gold leaf, and a guitar. Tony Saks, a man in his fifties who was making a name for himself as the world's oldest Beatle fan, had persuaded Derek to ask them to sign their names in gold leaf on his guitar "for charity." It was an unusual and outrageous task, and one that Derek took upon himself to see through. Bleary-eyed from sleep, they signed without much resistance and Saks got his signed-in-gold-leaf Beatle guitar, which is still in the possession of the Saks family.

The Beatles ate, showered, dressed, and pulled away in a chauffeured limousine in the early afternoon, proceeding to Friendship Airport with the same tight security that had accompanied them in. Looking fresh and rested, they hopped from their car to the airplane. A half hour later, Baltimore was history.

PITTSBURGH, PENNSYLVANIA

"I hope they don't scream. I don't think it's fair. You come to hear them, you know. What's the sense of coming here if you're going to cover your face and cry?" Tina Wenskovitch, fifteen, of New Kensington said as she stood outside the Pittsburgh Civic Arena. Police had spent a long night shooing fans away, but offered no resistance in the morning as schoolgirls ladened with bag lunches arrived in droves for the day-long wait.

Meanwhile, at the Greater Pittsburgh Airport, more than four thousand Beatlepeople crunched against the airport's specially erected snow fences. They came from as far away as Canada and New York, Kentucky and West Virginia. Many carried signs reading "We Luv You Beatles!" "United We Stand, United We Fall for John, Ringo, George and Paul."

When the plane landed at 4:40 P.M., the screaming canceled out the noise of the jet

each, but were, according to the *Baltimore Sun*, "not quite as many as appeared last year for Peter, Paul and Mary." The seventy-one uniformed city and private police who ringed the stage watched with puzzlement. "I can't even hear the goddamn music," one police lieutenant shouted. While the flashbulbs continued to light the darkened arena and screams blocked out the music, there was only one reported instance of jellybean throwing.

Between shows, the Beatles held what was now the mandatory press conference.

"DO YOU EVER get dandruff with all that hair?"

"We have dandruff occasionally," said John. "Like normal people."

"Do you have any plans for a haircut?"

"We don't make plans like that. Our manager does," snapped George.

"What do you think of American television?"

"It's great—you get eighteen stations, but you can't get a good picture on any of them," said Ringo.

"What do you think of all the Beatle imitators and people who wear Beatle wigs?"

"They aren't imitating *us*—we don't wear Beatle wigs, you know," said Paul.

"And the other British competitors coming to the United States?"

"Why not? There's enough money over here for every group in England," said John.

"What will you do when the bubble bursts?" He was back. And this time, John fielded the question.

"Then basketball."

"How do you feel about putting the whole country on?"

"We enjoy it," said Ringo.

Added Paul: "We're not really putting you on."

"Well, just a bit," corrected George.

AFTER the Beatles' last performance in Maryland, most of the crowd journeyed around the corner to the Holiday Inn. Police massed together and began dispersing the hordes with the aid of dogs. Inside, an all-night private party was held for the entire Beatles' cast and crew in the La Ronde, the hotel's top-of-the-building revolving restaurant. Dinner consisted of prime rib, with plenty of cognac and brandy, as well as Scotch and Coke and

195

desserts. The boys were dressed casually in Levi's and English boots. John, decked out in sunglasses and a black-and-white polka-dotted shirt, was described by one local reporter as looking like "a blind Dalmatian." The members of the Exciters began an impromptu sing-along with members of the other opening acts. The Beatles watched, then retired to their rooms for the night.

MONDAY, SEPTEMBER 14, 1964:

The Beatles were awakened by Derek, who greeted them with glasses of orange juice, pens, some gold leaf, and a guitar. Tony Saks, a man in his fifties who was making a name for himself as the world's oldest Beatle fan, had persuaded Derek to ask them to sign their names in gold leaf on his guitar "for charity." It was an unusual and outrageous task, and one that Derek took upon himself to see through. Bleary-eyed from sleep, they signed without much resistance and Saks got his signed-in-gold-leaf Beatle guitar, which is still in the possession of the Saks family.

The Beatles ate, showered, dressed, and pulled away in a chauffeured limousine in the early afternoon, proceeding to Friendship Airport with the same tight security that had accompanied them in. Looking fresh and rested, they hopped from their car to the airplane. A half hour later, Baltimore was history.

PITTSBURGH, PENNSYLVANIA

"I hope they don't scream. I don't think it's fair. You come to hear them, you know. What's the sense of coming here if you're going to cover your face and cry?" Tina Wenskovitch, fifteen, of New Kensington said as she stood outside the Pittsburgh Civic Arena. Police had spent a long night shooing fans away, but offered no resistance in the morning as schoolgirls ladened with bag lunches arrived in droves for the day-long wait.

Meanwhile, at the Greater Pittsburgh Airport, more than four thousand Beatlepeople crunched against the airport's specially erected snow fences. They came from as far away as Canada and New York, Kentucky and West Virginia. Many carried signs reading "We Luv You Beatles!" "United We Stand, United We Fall for John, Ringo, George and Paul."

When the plane landed at 4:40 P.M., the screaming canceled out the noise of the jet engines. The plane came to a halt near Gate 16 and wild shouting arose from the crowd. Private detectives were first on the plane. A crew of bored-looking lawmen, including county deputy sheriffs, and an assortment of other uniformed men stood on guard in the immediate area where the plane landed. For the first time Allegheny County Mounted Police—fifteen in number—stood guard between the Beatles and their admirers. No president or **Dallas.**

Alton, Missouri.

as the word spread that the Beatles were on their way. An estimated five thousand people had now gathered to await their arrival there. The pressure of the crowd against the Arena's huge plate glass windows was so great that barricades were erected to prevent their breaking. *"We want the Beatles! We want the Beatles!"* The crowd screamed as the Beatles' limousine darted in through a back entrance and the boys vanished from view.

At 6 P.M. in Conference Room A in the basement of the Arena, the Beatles held a press conference.

presidential candidate had been accorded that police accolade. A total of 120 county policemen and deputy sheriffs were detailed to the airport—patrolling on horseback, foot, and motorcycles. In addition to the county police, twenty Allied Detective Agency men put a personal bodyguard around the Beatles. Surrounded by all these policemen and private detectives, the Beatles were hustled into a big black limousine. The crowd got its glimpse, but not much more than that.

The motorcade sped off, with police escorts leading the way down the Penn-Lincoln Parkway West to the Civic Arena. Thousands cheered along the route, much like the crowds that line the route for presidential motorcades.

A contingent of one hundred city policemen assumed their positions at the Civic Arena

"YOU HAVE HAD trouble with your tonsils, will you have an operation in America?"

"No," said Ringo.

"Any plans to get your hair cut while you're here?"

"No, we'd have trouble trusting an American barber. It'll have to wait until the end of the tour. But I could stand a bit off now," said Ringo.

While the Beatles dined on a catered dinner, an estimated 12,603 fans jammed into the Pittsburgh Civic Arena. Policemen wore earmuffs, and parents stuck fingers and tissues in their ears, and the crowd screamed on. Then the Beatles ran offstage and into their dressing room. A police car had been waiting out back, but the driveway was blocked by fans who had never gotten inside. The boys were quickly led through an underground passage to another exit driveway and into a limousine, bound for the airport.

CLEVELAND, OHIO

TUESDAY, SEPTEMBER 15, 1964:

"It is statistically probable, based on eight previous appearances of the Beatles in the United States and Canada, that twenty girls will faint from hysteria during the evening," Jan Mellow predicted in an article announcing the impending arrival of the Beatles in the Cleveland *Plain Dealer*. Cleveland, however, was ready for the invasion.

Police prepared as never before. Not even a visiting king or president had ever commanded as much attention or concern as the Beatles did in Cleveland. Leaves were canceled and officers were assigned twelve-hour shifts, along with firemen and Civil Defense Auxiliaries. Some five hundred uniformed men were dispatched to downtown in the afternoon and evening. It would cost the taxpayers $17,000 in police overtime pay to kept Cleveland intact during the Beatles' visit.

The Beatles' arrival at Cleveland's Hopkins Airport was shrouded in secrecy. As the Electra II landed at 12:32 A.M., it was directed to the southwest corner of the airport near the Cleveland Ordnance District plant. Grip. Grab. Shake. Shake. "Good flight? Let's go." Pull. Herd. Duck. Plop. The Beatles were in their limousine and on their way to the Hotel Sheraton. A welcoming crowd of about twenty-five hundred people waiting at the other side of the airport never even knew they had landed. About fifteen minutes after the three limousines and their police escort left for downtown, a delayed announcement of the Beatles' departure came over the public address system. It was greeted by boos and hissing. *"We want the Beatles! We want the Beatles!"* But the Beatles were gone.

Alton, Missouri.

For the final run to the hotel, the caravan was beefed up by seventeen extra prowl cars at West 150 Street and Bellaire Road S.W. Hundreds of fans were awaiting the Beatles' arrival at the Sheraton, but the motorcade slipped in the back way. They had been scheduled to stay in the Presidential Suite, but at the last minute Police Chief Richard R. Wagner decided that too many people knew where they were going to be and asked that they be moved. The Beatles were then directed to a suite on the parlor floor.

Allen J. Lowe, managing director of the Sheraton, had ordered that everything movable or breakable be taken out of the lobby for fear of souvenir hunters. They even debated removing the carpeting from the floor of the lobby, but hotel officials decided to rely on the ultimate good sense of northern Ohio's teenage girls.

It was a relatively quiet night; John and Paul stayed up working on some new songs, while Ringo watched television. By dawn they were all sleeping. In the early hours of the morning, only a few girls tried to gain entrance to their suite, but all were caught by guards and told to leave. With daylight, however, the masses returned to hold their vigil outside and every trick in the book was enlisted to penetrate the inner sanctum. One girl said an uncle of hers was staying at the hotel. "What's his name?" asked the policeman. "I—I—I don't remember," the girl sighed, defeated. Another girl fainted on the sidewalk outside of the hotel, and was carried off to the side. She came to moments later, confessing she had thought there was a first-aid room inside the lobby. A boy with fuzzy cheeks insisted

Reed Pigman's horse ranch in Alton, Missouri.

that he had reservations for cocktails at the Kon Tiki restaurant inside the hotel. Another girl of eleven offered to sell a stolen key to a thirty-five-dollar-a-day suite, and a very determined boy tried to hide in a packing crate that was being trucked in.

As the day wore on, the girls took up the old football cheer: *"We like the Beatles and couldn't be prouder! And if you can't hear us, we'll yell a little louder."* And they did, raising grins on nearby policemen. As always, the Beatles were the talk of the town. Cleveland *Plain Dealer* columnist George E. Condon proved to be one of the rare few who saw something of the bigger picture, and wrote an article encouraging non-Beatlemaniacs to keep an open mind about the four English lads. "International peace begins between individuals, a fundamental principle which is recognized in the government's Person-to-Person program, as well as in the Peace Corps," he wrote. "People from different countries meet face to face, talk with each other, examine each other's viewpoints. . . . I fully expect that the music will sound strange to most of us at first, but we should strive to be as patient and appreciative as we can until the harmonics begin to make sense or take on an attractive form." That same day, Russian Premier Nikita Khrushchev announced that the Soviet Union had developed a "monstrous new weapon."

As the Beatles slept, Derek left the hotel in a limousine to meet Brian, who was arriving from New York to rejoin the tour. As the two approached one another, Derek knew something was wrong. "Trouble?" he asked.

"I hear that you have been making anti-Semitic statements and laughing with John

"WHAT DO YOU think of topless bathing suits?"

"We like them. We've been wearing them for years," said George.

"What do you expect to see when you visit Dallas?"

"Oil wells." Paul.

"You've experienced both—what's the big difference between poverty and riches?"

"Money." John.

"Dave Brubeck told the Dallas *News* that America is reaping the harvest from the musical garbage it exported to England years ago. Comment?"

"Quite true," said John.

"What is your chief gripe against the United States?"

"The quality of your tea," Paul said.

"Will the draft break up your group?"

"There is no draft in England anymore. We'll let you Yanks do the fighting," John snickered.

"Don't you think it's morally wrong to be influencing your fans with your atheist views?"

"We're not atheists," Paul declared. "We're agnostics. The story which said we're anti-Christ is not true. We simply don't know enough about it."

Following the press conference, Brian and Derek headed for dinner at Antoine's, and backstage the Beatles met another Antoine— Fats Domino. The New Orleans–born singer/ songwriter/pianist had been an early influence on the Beatles and one of their rock heroes. They had grown up on his music, imported from America via the Liverpool docks. It was music they genuinely loved. His "Ain't That a Shame" and "Blueberry Hill" were rock

Alton, Missouri.

209

Alton, Missouri.

As Derek and Brian finished their desserts, the Beatles were fighting a new Battle of New Orleans. Despite the heat and humidity, an estimated twelve thousand fans were creating unprecedented noise and commotion. At about 9:40 P.M., fifteen minutes into the Beatles' set, some seven hundred teenagers jumped from the stands onto the field. The Beatles were, at first, unconcerned and kept on playing. For the duration of their performance, 225 New Orleans policemen and special patrol guards hit the field, and mounted policemen charged up to the stage area. They chased teenagers with nightsticks, and though none were actually hit, police physically tackled some of the youths, mostly girls, who were attempting to crash through barricades separating them from the Beatles. "It was like watching the police play stickball with the kids," said Ringo. A couple of times the Beatles' microphones went dead, but they played on. Brian and Derek arrived at the stadium during the final half of the Beatles' performance, and watched as the boys shared the spotlight with what Paul later called "the football game."

The police finally succeeded in bringing the crowd under control, but Police Superintendent Joseph I. Giarrusso called the episode one that "was both amusing and tragic at the same time." He said he could not recall a similar incident in the city involving teenagers. Police administered spirits of ammonia to more than two hundred people during the performance. One teenage girl suffered a broken arm, but refused to be taken to a hospital; her arm was bandaged and she returned to the stands.

classics and set a high standard for popular composers and musicians. Domino and the Beatles had much in common. All were keenly interested in the fusion of various styles and techniques into the grander scheme of rock music. They were all self-taught, and they all wrote music. For the boys, it was one of the finer and more memorable moments of their first American tour. They couldn't help but remark on the wristwatch Fats wore. It was one of the most amazing watches they had ever seen—a star-shaped timepiece made of gold and silver and ivory, and set with diamonds, rubies, emeralds, and pearls.

Following their performance, the Beatles headed back to the airport. "Whew, that was the closest we've come on the tour to getting worried," said Paul. "When I saw them coming for the stage, I wondered, would they stay at the barricades or rush the stage and we'd be massacred." When the Beatles excitedly told Derek of their meeting with Fats Domino, he was greatly disappointed at not having gotten the chance to meet "the great man." "Serves you right," said George. "You can't have dinner with Brian Epstein *and* meet Fats Domino."

KANSAS CITY, MISSOURI

THURSDAY, SEPTEMBER 17, 1964:

A box marked "Caution" covered the space where a fountain once stood. Officials at the Hotel Muehlebach had stripped the lobby bare. "We just don't want to take any chances," said Earl Reynolds, vice-president of the hotel and manager of operations. "Other hotels have had some trouble." The lobby had been cleared on only two other occasions—once for the Junior Chamber of Commerce national convention several years ago, and again when President Kennedy came through on the campaign trail in 1960. "Now that I think about it, the Kennedy visit didn't require us to take out all of the furniture, just part of it," said Reynolds, who added that neither the floor the Beatles would be staying on nor their room numbers would be disclosed. A force of about fifteen police officers was to be stationed throughout the building—on back stairs, at the loading dock, near elevators, and at every other strategic place infiltrators might be. Two rooms were reserved for security headquarters.

More than 40 percent of the entire Kansas City police force was to be on hand for the show. Officials said that only the flood of 1951

Alton, Missouri.

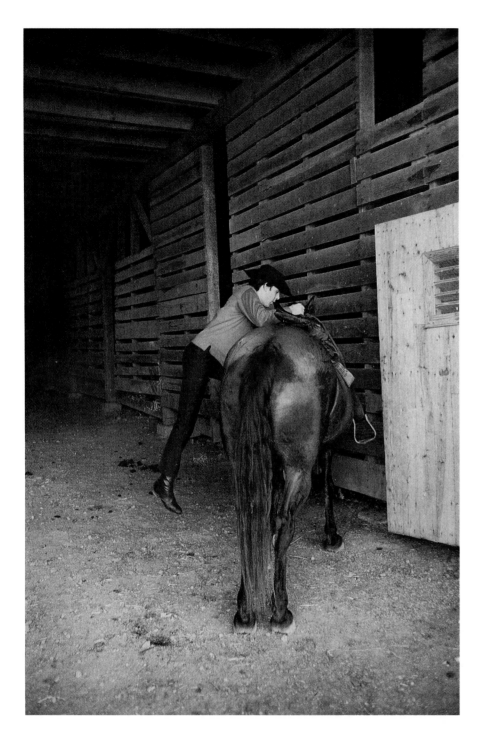

and the Ruskin Heights tornado disaster in 1957 had ever required such a concentration of police officers.

The Beatles arrived in Kansas City at around 1:45 A.M. and launched into yet another poker game. Derek and Curt headed out to the Kansas City *Star* and watched as the Beatles headlines and the rest of the newspaper went into production. In national news, President Johnson announced that the United States had achieved major break-throughs in defense—one being radar that can "see" beyond the horizon, meaning that the United States could now spot missiles beyond the curvature of Earth and destroy bomb-carrying satellites in space. Johnson was quick to point out, however, that "we have no reason to believe any nation now plans to put nuclear warheads in space."

Downstairs, the bare lobby was jammed with hundreds of teenagers who hoped one of the Beatles would come down and pass through. They never did.

That evening, the Beatles gave Kansas City a press conference and then appeared at the Kansas City Municipal Stadium for their $150,000 performance, which was sponsored by Charles O. Finley. As they took the stage, the 20,280 fans screamed. Flashbulbs lit the night sky and jellybeans rained on the stage. Would it ever, the Beatles wondered, be different? A long line of policemen separated the crowd from the bandstand and a total of 350 were on duty in the stadium. Backstage, Finley had pleaded for them to play two extra songs "for Kansas City." "We never do more than eleven, Chuck," John said. "You never should have paid all that money, Chuck." But for Brian, garnering that kind of money for one performance was a box-office coup—it was the largest take for a single show in the history of show business. Besides, they'd even gotten two cartons of green Athletics baseball bats, along with the check. The Beatles did give Chuck, and Kansas City, one more song. While the crowd did not fill the forty-one thousand seats arranged for the event, the Kansas City audience remained one of the four- or five-largest on the '64 tour.

At the end of their performance, the Beatles were hustled from the field as a crowd of several hundred rushed the line of policemen to yell good-bye and wave. Once safely in the limo, one of the Beatles turned around as their car sped away and raised a hand in farewell. Finley lost money, but his manager Pat Friday gave a check for $25,000 to the Children's Mercy Hospital anyway, despite the fact that no profit was made. An Athletics official said sales of 28,000 tickets had been needed to break even. The gate was estimated at about $100,000. But Finley said he was delighted with the performance and that he considered the behavior of Kansas City teenagers commendable.

At 11:13 P.M. the Beatles' plane took off from the Municipal Air Terminal, headed for Dallas, dreaded Dallas. For the Beatles, just as for all Americans, Dallas now brought to mind one thing—Kennedy's assassination. It had been less than a year since the President was gunned down there, and the city had been cursed as one of the most violent spots in America. To say that the Beatles were concerned would be an understatement. They wondered if *they'd* make it out alive.

Alton, Missouri.

DALLAS, TEXAS

FRIDAY, SEPTEMBER 18, 1964:

Several Dallas nightclub owners had wired the Beatles in New Orleans, inviting them to spend an evening on the town. Nobody, however, wanted to stay in Dallas. Following the concert, "we will go directly to the airport and take off for New York and a day of rest," Epstein told reporters and others. That had been the initial plan. But another invitation had come up and Epstein accepted for all of them. Reed Pigman, owner/pilot of American Flyers, had a horse ranch in the Ozarks of southern Missouri, and he invited them there to get away from it all before heading into New York and their final charity performance at the Paramount Theater. Besides, the next day was Brian's thirtieth birthday and he wanted all of the boys with him.

On the ride in from Dallas' Love Field, the Beatles' motorcade followed part of the same route as the Kennedy motorcade and as they drove through the infamous underpass, they found it chilling. "Are we safe?" John asked. They all looked around. The ride, however, turned out to be relatively uneventful, with just the normal masses of fans along the way.

The entourage checked into the Cabana Motor Hotel, a ghastly Roman-type motel according to their recollection, amidst much mania. Despite all the police, they seemed to have been guided right into the eye of the storm. The Beatles, along with their opening acts and crew, took the entire ninth floor; aside from them, the place was filled with American Legion conventioneers. Just minutes after they arrived, one group of fans crushed up against a plate glass window at the motel and broke it, four of them getting cut up by the falling glass. Three were hospitalized. Dallas police, rifles loaded and at the ready, staked out every corner and stood guard at every lamppost, security precautions that the boys found even more unsettling than the crowds.

A legion of Beatle fans stormed the Cabana Motor Hotel by land, sea, and even air-conditioning vents. When policemen finally managed to extract a boot-clad girl from one air-conditioning vent, she explained, apologetically, "All I wanted to do was just tap on the pipes and see if they would hear me." The Beatle Olympics between "the girls, the police, and Cabana management was just about an even match," reported the Dallas *Morning News'* Carlos Conde. Around 4 A.M., Cabana executive director Michael Rosenstein, bleary-eyed, hair a mess, sank wearily into a lounge sofa. "Operation Beatle has been an interesting affair. There has been no confusion. . . ." he said wryly. Three girls did get to meet the Beatles—Stephanie Pinter, Yolanda Hernandez, and Marie Leggett of the Dallas Beatle Fan Club. The girls were brought up by Mal and they spent several hours talking with the group. It would be the last time the Beatles would have a chance to talk to their American fans, for a while anyway.

Later in the day, Neil and Derek went to Neiman Marcus on a shopping spree for the Beatles. Marcus' assistant showed them the vast extravagance of the store. They purchased cowboy hats, shirts, and boots for the boys and Brian; silk scarves, purses, perfumes, and other items for the girlfriends and wives back home. An antique telephone was purchased for Brian as a birthday gift.

Just before the doors of the Dallas Memorial Coliseum were opened, someone called and reported that a bomb had been planted inside. The opening of the auditorium was delayed while police searched the hall. Instead of a bomb, police found Beatlepeople, and flushed two of them out from under the bandstand and four more from a washroom, where they had hidden for five hours.

As the Beatles left the Cabana and headed out to the Coliseum, the police escort once again delivered them to a back door that was

215

Alton, Missouri.

surrounded by fans. No matter what the Dallas police escort seemed to do, it always seemed to wind up in the center of huge crowds. The Dallas press conference was scheduled for 7 P.M., backstage at the Coliseum. It "just may have been the zaniest press conference in modern times," reported the Dallas *Morning News*' Larry Grove. Most of the seats at the conference were filled with thirteen-year-olds representing radio stations "with call letters unknown on this sphere." But, hey, it was the end of tour, obviously the youngsters had each come up with a good enough line, and Derek was too tired to say no. The old-timers, who knew very little about the Beatles, didn't seem to mind that the younger set asked all the questions.

"Are you an anarchist, Paul?"

"I don't know what the word means."

"Are you scared when crowds scream at you, John?"

"More so here [in Dallas] than other places, perhaps."

"John, where do you write your songs?"

"In hotel rooms."

It was the Beatles' last press conference in the United States and they were relieved. Earlier, a hospitalized ten-year-old victim of a hit-and-run driver, Cheryl Howard, who was recovering at Methodist Hospital, received a call from Paul as did those who had fallen through the Cabana window. Backstage, Ringo relaxed on a chair, feet resting on the back of another one. "I could do another week," he said. The others, all homesick beyond words, just stared at him, deadpan.

The Dallas show, promoted by Super Shows, Inc., of Washington, D.C., had sold out in less than twenty-four hours, and as in most other cities, the police took extraordinary precautions. Two hundred policemen lined the auditorium and two hundred more were on stand-by call. Police Chief Jesse Curry was on hand, his daughter and two grandchildren in tow. Even the stage was three times higher than during normal auditorium performances, perching Ringo at least fifteen feet off the floor.

When the doors opened, every ticket holder stormed the entrance, creating a pedestrian jam that had some policemen calling for help, but within a half hour or so all ten thousand ticket holders were inside and in their seats. As Ringo, Paul, George, and John ran onstage, the Beatle trademarks were all there: screams, jellybeans, and flashbulbs. Still, the audience set a record for polite behavior. The Beatles played for a full thirty minutes, pleased that they could actually, at some points, hear themselves. It was, in Derek's words, "a sensational concert." While they were onstage, thousands of ticketless fans stood outside, listening for the music and hearing only the screams.

The Beatles and five others snuck out of the auditorium through a tunnel and headed back to the airport. The rest of the entourage stayed behind in Dallas for the next couple of nights. The Beatles group boarded their Electra II and lifted off from the Love Field runway at 11:08 P.M., well ahead of most of the hundreds of fans who converged to wave good-bye. They were headed for what would be a real rest, away from all the crowds, the cities, everyone. It would be only the boys, Brian, Neil, Mal, and Derek, and also Curt—

217

who'd managed in his inimitable way to gain an invitation. "He'd become the favored member of the traveling press," says Taylor. "A refugee from Nazi Germany, he was so much more worldly than the rest of us. There wasn't much Curt didn't know about life, and more importantly, he was good company and that's what life is all about." Even Brian welcomed him aboard the plane. Curt, however, wanted more than a good rest. He wanted that special picture that no other photographer would get of the Beatles in America. And this was his last chance.

SATURDAY, SEPTEMBER 19, 1964:

At midnight, Brian turned thirty and during the flight the boys gave him his birthday presents—the classic antique telephone, along with other nonsense gifts. Then they toasted his third decade with a bottle of Rémy Martin, as the Drinamyls further elevated their moods. Turning thirty was, despite his fame and fortune, a bit unnerving for Brian, and the boys reassured him that he was still young and well loved. The Beatles were seldom sentimental about such occasions, but on this particular night, they were. Eveyone on the aircraft visited with Brian in the lounge at the back of the plane and Derek was pleased to finally have an over-thirty companion in the crew.

They flew into Walnut Ridge, Arkansas, where Reed Pigman met them. Curt, Derek, and Mal went to rent a car, and the others got into Pigman's own small plane for the short hop to the ranch in southern Missouri. As they took off in the dark, George, in

particular, was concerned. It felt like a little motorcycle in the sky and reminded him so much of what had happened to Buddy Holly. At one point Pigman, a map on his knee, a small light on overhead, lost track of their location. He rubbed the windshield to remove the condensation, and George thought it was all over. But Pigman, an experienced flyer, had it under control, and finally set the plane down in a field. Tin cans filled with burning candles guided them in.

ALTON, MISSOURI

It was around 3:30 A.M. when the Beatles finally fell into the sofa and chairs of the Pigman living room. It was supposed to be a day of complete rest, but who could sleep now? Everyone was still on edge from the visit to Dallas, and coming down from the general excitement and hysteria that had come to be part of the tour took time. Besides, everyone but Curt had fortified themselves with pills, and so poker won out over sleep. About 5 A.M., Curt began to tire and suggested sleep. John pulled out a bottle from his carrying bag and handed him two Drinamyls. "Here, take these," he offered. "And you won't be sleepy at all." Curt had never taken drugs without a specific need or doctor's prescription, but on this particular night he cast his fate with rock 'n' roll and swallowed the pills, too bleary-eyed to argue.

At 6 A.M., Curt went to look for a special location in which he could photograph the Beatles. He would know it when he found it. The boys had been pestered and followed and hounded by the media throughout the tour,

only to be asked the same questions over and over, and to pose for the same pictures again and again. Curt had learned early on not to harass them for photographs, and they appreciated that. Still, the tour was almost over and he'd yet to get something really different, something unique. If it were to be found, it would be here. He spent an hour surveying the grounds before returning to the house to get Derek. With the gleaming enthusiasm of a child, Curt led him to an old barn, and, specifically, to the door of the barn. "Here it is!" he proclaimed as if showing him a secret buried treasure. "If I can photograph them here, I'll die a happy man." One by one, the boys came together for Curt's camera and stood there in the sun-dried, aged timber doorway. Fatigue lined their faces. It had been a hard day's night in America. This picture, Curt knew, said it all.

Curt's mission accomplished, the Beatles and Brian, Neil, Mal, and Derek decided horseback riding was in order. Mrs. Pigman chose a horse for each and they rode off over

Alton, Missouri.

the mountain trails and into the light of the rising sun. As they came upon a gate, three young boys took notice of them; one jumped down to open the gate and slowly it dawned on them just who these cowboys were. The Beatles trotted through the gate, kicking up dust and heading into the changing colors of early autumn, as the young boys' faces froze with wonder. The Beatles? Here? In the middle of nowhere? Couldn't be.

After riding, they all took turns on Reed Pigman, Jr.'s, go-cart and the Beatles reveled in the freedom to walk around without being hounded for something. As they toured the ranch, later in the day, they did run into some local fans, and cheerfully offered their autographs.

When they awoke later in the evening, they celebrated Brian's birthday with a cake Mrs. Pigman had made and decorated with thirty candles. Their retreat, however, had been discovered by local dee-jays. By midnight, all roads to the ranch were packed, with carloads of teenagers driving in from as far away as St. Louis. They never got past the ranch's gate, but they were there.

Alton, Missouri.

SUNDAY, SEPTEMBER 20, 1964:

The Beatles stayed up most of the night playing cards and went fishing in the morning. Later they loaded into vans and headed back to Walnut Ridge Airport. Meanwhile, in Dallas, the entourage's equipment and luggage were being loaded into the Electra, just before 9 A.M., when a call came in to the Southwest Airmotive terminal at Love Field. "This is a bomb threat," said a man's voice in a deep Southern drawl. Then there was a dial tone. At 9:03 A.M., the phone rang again. "A Beatle bomb threat," the same voice specified. And then there was another dial tone. Police at the terminal began searching all the luggage aboard the chartered Electra. They left no container unopened, including Ringo's drums, but they found nothing. After a half-hour delay, the plane took off for Walnut Ridge to pick up the Beatles and the others for the trip to New York and the Paramount Theater charity performance.

As soon as the Electra touched down at Walnut Ridge, the boys climbed aboard the plane. The mayor and other locals, all of whom had allowed them their privacy, now wanted autographs and photographs. The boys were tired and not at all anxious to oblige. "Tell them we want to go out there, but you won't let us because we're too tired," suggested Paul. Derek knew it wasn't much to ask, but he felt bad for the friendly folks in Arkansas. Still, the Beatles had given their all on this tour and they deserved some private moments. Had it not been the end of the tour, Derek knew he probably could have made things happen. Instead, within minutes, the plane was taxiing down the runway.

During the flight to New York, the Beatles

presented gifts to all the members of the entourage. The men received gold-plated money clips, and Bess, Jackie, and the girls in the Exciters received gold-plated I.D. bracelets that were engraved "American Tour 1964" on the front and "With Love and Thanks, the Beatles" on the back. "It was most probably Brian's idea," says Bess Coleman. "But it was such a nice touch at the end of the tour when everybody was so exasperated and tearing their hair out. It was so special for all of us."

NEW YORK CITY, NEW YORK

The Beatles' chartered plane landed around 5 P.M. at a remote cargo area at Kennedy International Airport, avoiding the several thousand fans on hand for their arrival. Upon disembarking from the plane, the Beatles, Brian, Neil, Mal, and Derek were guided to the helicopter pad, and at 5:30 P.M. they lifted off for Manhattan. The ride, the sights of New York at night, the lights, the Brooklyn Bridge were all beautiful; those were among the most enjoyable moments the Beatles had spent in the American air. At the pier, Norman Weiss was waiting with limousines for the ride to the Paramount, where stars like Frank Sinatra and the Glenn Miller Orchestra had performed.

The Beatles weren't exactly thrilled to have one more performance, but as Norman explained, this was for charity, and, with all they'd earned from the American tour, it would be a nice gesture. Brian certainly agreed. The money would go to the Retarded Infants Service and Cerebral Palsy of New York. It was, after all, for children, many of whom were no doubt Beatle fans. What bothered the Beatles was that such performances always brought out the diamond-studded matrons and tuxedoed misters, who were not really their fans. Tickets for this show, however, ranged in price from five to one hundred dollars and proved to bring out an audience as mixed as the bill, which also included Steve Lawrence and Edie Gorme, Leslie Uggams, the Tokens, Bobbie Goldsboro, the Shangri-Las, the Brothers Four, Jackie DeShannon, and Nancy Ames. It was, of course, sold out.

Teenage girls began lining Seventh Avenue between Forty-third and Forty-fourth streets around midafternoon, causing traffic jams and confusion in the Times Square area. While 240 cops maintained order, hundreds and hundreds of girls—some carrying banners reading "Ringo for President," "If You Can't Marry Me, George, Please Just *Look* at Me," and "Beatles Please Stay Here Forever"— paraded in the streets. By early evening, the crowd had grown to an estimated four thousand.

At 6:10 P.M., the Beatles' chauffeur, Louis Savarese, slyly maneuvered the rented Cadillac limousine through West Forty-fourth Street, driving up on the sidewalk just past Sardi's. A few dozen fans, as usual, spotted the car and those famous haircuts. They hit the street running and howling, but forty policemen moved in and formed a protective ring around the singers. As John, Paul, George, and Ringo darted inside the theater, the crowd hit the car, but the most they could do was touch it and rock it back and forth. The Beatles had, once again, put their heads down, gone for the openings, and slipped safely away.

By 8 P.M. the theater was filled, with 3,862 seats occupied. Inside, many of New York's elite, dressed to the formal hilt, sat amid bouncing teenagers. At 8:30 P.M., when

Alton, Missouri.

225

the theater finally darkened, the girls released shrieks and cheers. Although the Beatles were not scheduled to appear until 10:45 P.M., when the announcer merely mentioned their name in the line-up, the entire theater rumbled from the thundering cheering, screaming, stomping, and thumping. "The kids were making these people with diamonds very nervous," recalls Bonis. "They even started climbing all over them during the show and these older people were simply outraged, but helpless to do anything. They didn't *know* what to do. It was funny, but also kind of sad." Bonis went back upstairs to the dressing room and grabbed the boys and directed them to his viewing place in the wings. They laughed as the girls yelled at the other acts, "Get off the stage! We want the Beatles!" Nobody mattered but the Beatles. It got to the point where other performers were asked to cut the length of their sets, and, on this night, they may have been insulted but they agreed. Back in the dressing room the Beatles were visited by Ed Sullivan and Bob Dylan, among others.

Shortly after ten, well ahead of schedule, the Beatles ran onstage to the same thunderous reception that had greeted them throughout the tour. The bejeweled were bewildered. Tired-looking policemen stood elbow to elbow in front of the high stage. Jellybeans were thrown. Stuffed animals. Powder puffs. Lipstick. Toilet-paper rolls. Girls jumped onto the arms of their seats. Others flung themselves against balcony railings. The bejeweled were appalled. The kids were in luv. The bejeweled were not amused. In the wings, Gloria Steinem, seeking an interview with Lennon for *Cosmopolitan* magazine, asked, "What are

227

those bursts of light, part of the lighting effects?" No, Derek explained, it was from the flashing of cameras. And from the orchestra to the far reaches of the balconies, flashbulbs lit up the hall and everybody in it. As usual, throughout it all, the Beatles never missed a beat—even when a stuffed rabbit fell onto Ringo's drum. While a crowd of ten thousand waited outside, they ripped through ten songs in twenty-five minutes. Most of the adults had absolutely no idea what was happening, or what the Beatles sang. "Anyone over twenty-one years of age felt ready for Social Security," Gay Talese reported in the New York *Times*. After "Long Tall Sally," the Beatles ran off the stage and left the building at 10:45 P.M., slipping out and driving with their police escort down several one-way blocked-off streets before the crowd could get to them. Those holding the fifty- and one-hundred-dollar tickets had no interest in chasing the Beatles, for they had a champagne party awaiting them downstairs in the lobby.

In a motorcade of seven limousines, the Beatles and fourteen members of their entourage—not including Brian—sped to the Riviera Idlewild Motel for their last night in America. Tomorrow they would return to London and home. Derek had rounded up Steinem of *Cosmpolitan* and several other New York journalists, bringing them along for a few last quotes and interviews—if, that is, the boys would go for it.

When the Beatles arrived at the motel, only two people were in the lobby and they weren't Beatlepeople. They nonchalantly looked up from their newspapers as the entourage arrived, and when the Beatles disappeared into an elevator they returned to reading the day's news. It seemed strange that on their last night in America the Beatles would be able to walk into a motel like normal human beings. Several Manhattan hotels had turned them down, and so they decided on staying there because it was close to the airport; Brian had booked the entire floor for this last night in America. Though the boys and the members of the entourage had invited numerous guests, including VIPs and some young ladies—among them an heiress or two—to their farewell party, when the guests arrived Paul had already gone to his room to sleep and would not reappear until morning. George too was nowhere to be found. John and Ringo were behind closed doors with Bob Dylan and his manager, Albert Grossman. Only Neil, Mal, and Derek said a proper good-bye to the madness.

MONDAY, SEPTEMBER 21, 1964:

It was well after midnight when Brian arrived at the motel, "looking like Bela Lugosi," according to Derek. He began screaming in a manner more hostile than Derek had ever heard from him before: "You took my limousine!" Derek denied it. "You took it," he yelled. The argument became worse. Finally Derek screamed, "I resign!" "Accepted!" Brian retorted. "Great!" Derek answered. "Fine!" Brian shouted. Brian went to his room. Derek dashed off a letter of resignation and slipped it under the door.

In the hospitality room, huge trays of sandwiches and Scotch and Coke and other drinks were getting attention. Steinem was still waiting for time with John, but John was stalling, hardly into an interview just then. The Beatles had been through enough at that point, and they'd come to distrust most journalists. Several other journalists were also waiting, along with some girls. Derek finally escorted Steinem in to see John. It was touch-and-go for a while, but then photographer Robert Freeman, who had photographed the group for their first American album cover, said she was a friend of friends. John opened up and Steinem got her quotes. It was dawn when she left. Soon thereafter, John left with Dylan and Grossman to get breakfast.

The Beatles left for England from Kennedy International Airport in relative quiet aboard a commercial airliner. One hundred and fifty fans were on hand.

At the airport, Epstein told reporters that the group had grossed more than a million dollars with thirty performances on their tour of twenty-four U.S. and Canadian cities. "Of course, there are many expenses that come out of that, such as the $75,000 to charter the plane for the trip," he said. The gross figures Epstein was talking about were the Beatles' share, following the deduction of the promoters' shares.

Neil, Mal, and Derek headed for seats in the tourist-class section, while Brian and the boys went to first class. Paul came back through the dividing curtains and asked, "What're you doing back here then?" Neil explained that this was how Brian had booked the flight. "I'll see about that," said Paul. A few minutes later, Brian came back through the curtains. "The boys told me they wanted you to join us and I'd be happy to take you through. Everything has been taken care of."

In first class, Derek sat next to Brian, at Brian's request. He handed Derek a note that said maybe they both had been a little hasty and if it could be forgiven and forgotten he would be happy to take back Derek's resignation. Then he started to cry. It was an agonizing situation, but Derek had already committed to his decision. "It's all for the best," Derek said. "It wasn't really your fault." Brian was a good man; Derek knew that. He'd held up well, considering the pressures, and he wanted only the best for the Beatles. But Derek knew, too, that he had to stick with his decision. He had to get away from all this hysteria and live a normal life again.

For John, Paul, George, and Ringo—and for Brian—nothing would ever be normal again. The Beatles' first American tour had been the most phenomenal and profitable tour in show business history, establishing not only another record for the group, but solidifying their place in rock history. It had catapulted them past the point of no return. The Beatles had become living legends. Where they went now was up to them. It was no longer a question of *could* they tour again, but *would* they tour again. As the Beatles, exhausted and more than a little homesick, settled in for the long flight home, they seemed—as always—unaffected by it all. From now on it would be upward and onward. There were, musically speaking, many more horizons to conquer. Deep down inside, however, they all felt the glow that comes from remarkable achievement. "The intensity of what had gone on was just incredible," assesses Weiss. "There was just no way to have foreseen it, or to have guessed that it was going to happen like it did, because nothing like that had ever happened before. Not even with Elvis, who was still playing small halls. Sure, the audiences went nuts for Elvis, but they would never gather by the thousands outside the hotel when he spent the night on the road."

All told, the Beatles earned more than a million dollars—$992,716.97 in America, and an additional $194,906.84 in Canada. From that, expenses had to be deducted, and the U.S. government did get its $297,815.09, or 30 percent withholding tax.

The Beatles returned for shorter tours of America in 1965 and 1966 and, since the matter of tax liability had still been undetermined, the U.S. government again withheld 30 percent of their earnings. It wasn't until fall of 1967 that Epstein's New York attorney, Walter Hofer, contacted J. Blake Lowe, an expert in international taxation at Peat, Marwick, Mitchell, & Co., for assistance in straightening out the matter. On only one occasion—Kansas City, September 17, 1964—did NEMS agree to and sign a contract in America, and that one time is not habitual, Lowe asserted, and therefore not to be deemed by the U.S. government as constituting a permanent establishment in America. Lowe and Hofer submitted the brief to the Office of International Operations. The U.S. government folded its claim. The Beatles finally did receive the 30 percent withheld on their first,

and subsequent, American tours—plus 6 percent interest—in 1968.

Beyond the money, the Beatles' concert tour set up the rock touring industry—taking concerts out of the small halls and theaters and putting them into baseball fields and huge coliseums and arenas. Technically, it spurred the advent of more sophisticated sound systems, so that bands could be heard. In 1965, the Beatles returned to America with a specially designed Beatle amplifier made by Vox, one of the precursors of today's amplifier systems. In terms of logistics, the tour had instituted the use of chartered aircraft for major continental tours, something that has become commonplace today. "We didn't even realize this was all new," says Aspinall. "We just thought that's how everbody in America toured." Out of necessity, it established detailed performance contracts with specific riders regarding the needs (four cots, TV, ice cooler) of the artists, something done on a grand scale these days—often out of ego, not necessity. Not only did the Beatles prove that rock 'n' roll could be taken on the road on a grand scale successfully, but that it could be done with class and control. Moreover, the $5.50 ceiling on tickets had limited the profits, but ensured that people would not be ripped off.

Only one other event was accorded more space than the Beatles in the world press in 1964, and that was the Kennedy assassination. Journalists, psychologists, psychiatrists, world leaders, politicians, religious leaders, and parents spent countless column inches trying to analyze Beatlemania, define it, pin it down, and figure out what it all meant. Some were

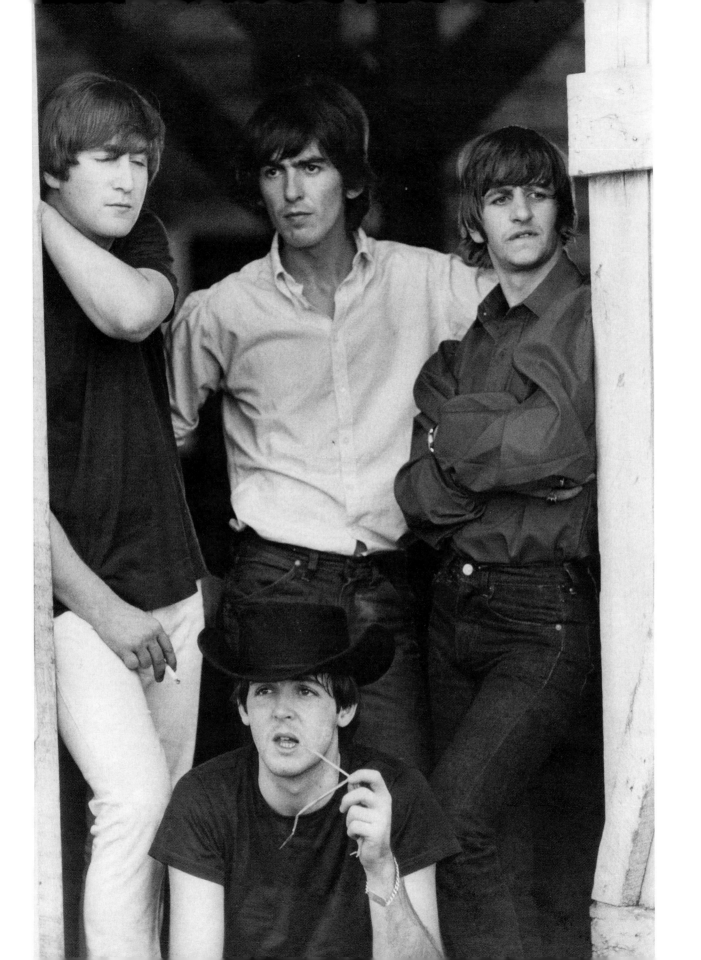

convinced it was Hitler's Nazi youth movement revisited. Most found it part of the natural rebellion that comes with the adolescent-to-adult growth process. All the "experts," however, agreed that the appeal of the Beatles was largely a passing fad.

What did make the Beatles happen the way they did? As Lennon said in the Beatles' first American press conference in 1964: "We've no idea. If we did, we'd get four long-haired boys, put them together, and become their managers."

"At the beginning, we were four guys that gave all our energy to this entity called the Beatles, and we fought, John and Paul fought for our songs, and we put all of our energy into it," recalls Starr. "And there was nothing else to get in the way. There was nothing going on at the time, musically. We were fresh. We were new. We had a certain style of dress and attitude on our songs, and we had an image. It always used to surprise me when we were together, the likes of de Gaulle, Khrushchev, the British Army and a lot of people in America all got on our case and we were just a rock 'n' roll band and there's all these world leaders shouting at these little guys playing music. It used to blow me away and I'd wonder, 'Why aren't you guys running your country instead of worrying about what we're playing?' That always did freak me out. We were just fighting to make something of ourselves. The touring, the screaming got to be a media situation. I loved the shouting and screaming, 'cause they were having a good time and so did we a lot of nights. That was the groove then. And in the end, we were playing the finest music any band at the time was playing."

"It wasn't as much fun for us as it was for all of you," Harrison remembers. "What was happening was that we were four relatively sane people going around the world and everybody else was going crackers. They were using us as an excuse to go mad. 'Here come the Beatles!' Crash! Rip up limousines! 'Let's have fun and go mad!' And we were in the middle of it, getting blamed. It was, I must admit, a privilege to have had that experience, of being one of the Fab Four, because there were only four of us who had that experience. It was fun. It was, however, that time. That period of history, and it will always be there."

"We always had some kind of faith in ourselves," says McCartney. "We commented on the world as we saw it. We were honest and our approach was honest. We were straight and said what we thought and that shocked a lot of Americans. But it takes forever, and will take forever, to get used to the whole trip. I mean, you start in a little group and you think, 'What do we call ourselves?' Every band in the world knows that one. Well, the Beatles. And then you go and get very famous."

No one has ever been able to say why it happened the way it happened. The feelings, emotions, the hope the Beatles stirred transcended words or even comprehension. That was the magic of Beatlemania. In one of his last interviews, with *Playboy* magazine, Lennon said: "If the Beatles, or the sixties, had a message, it was to learn to swim. Period. And once you learn to swim, swim." For

232

American youth, the Beatles represented new hope, and through their music and their personalities they offered up a new way of looking at the world and at their generation's place in it. In 1964, a generation lost its innocence, but learned to swim.

With the first American tour now part of show business history, the Beatles garnered newfound respect from the establishment; but it would take several years before the older generations realized what the Beatlepeople heard all along. The Beatles had a talent that was greater than the sum of its parts. For the Beatles, the monumental success of their first American tour did not destroy their artistic integrity. In fact, the mania may have served the ultimate purpose of driving the Beatles further inward, personally and professionally, enabling them to find expression and release with a sense of artistic freedom that few musicians ever achieve. In addition, the Beatles never lost sight of something else. As Ringo put it back in 1964: "It's the fans who make you. Without them, you're nothing. We love the fans as much as they love us." That love came through loud and clear and set the tone for the rest of the decade.

When the bubble did burst, it was the Beatles themselves who did it—about five years later, true, ironically, to Lennon's prediction. And though John, Paul, George, and Ringo went their separate ways, the Beatles lived on, still giving us a smile, timeless in their music.

ACKNOWLEDGEMENTS

The authors would like to thank Derek Taylor and Norman Weiss, whose anecdotes, assistance, and willingness were absolutely indispensable to this book. We are deeply grateful for their belief in and support of this project.

We would also like to thank the following people for their time, contributions, and/or assistance: Muhammad Ali; Neil Aspinall; Ken Barnes; Shirley Temple Black; Bob Bonis; Pat Boone; Shirley Burns; Vince Calandra; Robert Carp; Bess Coleman; Ray Coleman; Ivor Davis; Dave Dexter, Jr.; Jeanne Dixon; Robert Downing; Lloyd Dunn; Geoffrey Ellis; Clive Epstein; Bob Eubanks; Roy Gerber; Cynthia Gilbert; Laura Gross, especially for so kindly offering hours of her recorded interviews with the late Mal Evans; Wendy Hanson; Dave Hull; Larry Kane; Mark Lapidos; Jay Lasker; Ed Leffler; Alan Livingston and Nancy Olson; J. Blake Lowe, Jr.; Paul Marshall; George Martin; Bill Medley; Brown Meggs; Gordon Millings; Janey Milstead; Tom Morgan; Scott Muni; Michael Ochs; Hilary Oxlade; Colonel Tom Parker; Bob Precht; Art Schreiber; Don Short; Rick Sklar; Alistair Taylor; Art Unger; and all the dedicated folks at the Library of Congress, who helped locate the three-hundred-plus newspaper and magazine clippings that were included in the research process.

We thank our editor, Shaye Areheart, who hung in there—calmly—through thick and thin; our agent, Sarah Lazin, who believed when others didn't; our design director, Marysarah Quinn, whose exquisite eye never failed us; and Holly Holden for her role in the genesis of this project.

A. J. S. Rayl, Curt Gunther

I would like to personally thank my father-in-law, Siegbert Altmann, for his support and his friendship; my wife, Lisett, without whose patience, love and understanding I would not have been able to do this book; and my children, Steven, Diana, Susan, Ann, Josie, and Paul, for their ceaseless vitality and their enthusiasm for the Beatles and this project.

Curt Gunther

My heartfelt thanks go to Roger C. Helms, who has supported me in every way throughout this endeavor and who indulged me in traveling back in time with the music to the memories and events of 1964— over and over and over again; to my grandmother, Pearl Rayl, whose own love of old family photographs taught me early on the importance of stopping to see and remember, or learn from moments frozen in time; to my father, Dr. Donald F. Rayl, for his musical medicine for melancholy, for always knowing, and for buying me *Meet the Beatles*; to my mother, Marian F. Rayl, for her guidance, tolerance, and for sharing her spirit; to my brother, Don, for always being there with poetic words in times of turmoil; to my sister, Susie, for her constant belief; to Holly Gillette, Miriam Owens, Cindy Filippone, Linda Barley, and Leslie Kopman—I'll never forget the times that went with the music; to Wayne Sumstine, who understood in a way others didn't, and for sharing the sixties with me and helping us both survive the experience; to Bob Jeffers for all those rock 'n' roll days and rock 'n' roll nights; to Anne E. Hart for mental and mobile support; to Brian Murphy for his day-tripping enthusiasm; to Margo Warren and H. Darr Beiser for their warmth, years of friendship, and support; to Kevin McKinney for his advice, encouragement, shoulder, and Manhattan apartment; and to Jacques, who taught me something about life and who stayed by my side through it all.

A. J. S. Rayl